Sidrah Sparks

Talking Torah at the Table with Your Family

Rabbi Dov Peretz Elkins

AuthorHouse™
1663 Liberty Drive
Bloomington, IN 47403
www.authorhouse.com
Phone: 1-800-839-8640

First published by AuthorHouse 3/11/2010

ISBN: 978-1-4490-9200-9 (e)
ISBN: 978-1-4490-9201-6 (sc)
ISBN: 978-1-4490-9202-3 (hc)

Library of Congress Control Number: 2010902483

Printed in the United States of America
Bloomington, Indiana

This book is printed on acid-free paper.

Dedication

For our children's spouses:
Dany Adatto
Rachel Levin
Rachel Gutman
Abigail Silverman
Vivian Lehrer
With love from Saba

Books by Dov Peretz Elkins

Jewish Stories From Heaven and Earth

Chicken Soup for the Jewish Soul

The Wisdom of Judaism: An Introduction to the Values of the Talmud

Rosh Hashanah Readings

Yom Kippur Readings

The Bible's Top 50 Ideas

Hasidic Wisdom

A Shabbat Reader

Moments of Transcendence

Jewish Guided Imagery

Forty Days of Transformation

Meditations for the Days of Awe

Shepherd of Jerusalem

Moments of the Spirit: Quotations to Inspire, Inform & Involve

Enveloped in Light: A Tallit Sourcebook

A Treasury of Israel and Zionism

The Eulogy Book

Prescription for a Long and Happy Life

My Seventy-Two Friends: Encounters with Refuseniks in the USSR

God's Warriors: Dramatic Adventures of Rabbis in Uniform

Clarifying Jewish Values

Jewish Consciousness Raising

Experiential Programs for Jewish Groups

Teaching People to Love Themselves

Glad To Be Me: Building Self-Esteem in Yourself and Others

Twelve Pathways to Feeling Better About Yourself

Books for Teens

(both books with Azriel Eisenberg)

Worlds Lost and Found: Discoveries in Biblical Archeology

Treasures From the Dust: Biblical Archeology

Children's Book

Seven Delightful Stories for Every Day (ages 3 to 6)

Contents

INTRODUCTION

SIDRAH SPARKS

How To Use Sidrah Sparks

From time immemorial Jews have been studying the assigned Sidrah (Torah lesson) every week of the year. Jews study the Sidrah beginning Shabbat afternoon, when the Sidrah for the following week is read in the synagogue. A favorite time to study has always been at the Friday night Shabbat dinner table. As soon as all the prayers and rituals are chanted and performed, the delicious Shabbat meal has been consumed, and Birkat HaMazon (Grace After Meals) has been chanted – and perhaps several zemirot (Shabbat hymns) have been sung with gusto – a traditional family will turn to the "parshah," as it is familiarly known. If they are more advanced they may open a Humash. Or they may have before them some single sheets distributed by their synagogue, religious school, or other educational organization.

The purpose of the discussion triggers in this book, *Sidrah Sparks*, is for just such an occasion. It can be for the family to munch over after Shabbat dinner, or used in any way you see fit. There are five volumes of *Sidrah Sparks* in the book, so that enough material is available for a five-year cycle. Some may like to begin using the "sparks" again in the sixth year, because new people may be at the table, new ideas may emerge from the same questions that follow each Sidrah Spark, and different approaches may be found to use the material.

Serious discussion is a lost art at the family dinner table, and Torah study is surely not common among most families today. Using *Sidrah Sparks* is a wonderful way to revive the inspiring and enlightening Jewish custom of turning our attention to serious discussion, and to opportunities for Jewish educational enrichment.

Whether there are two friends sharing a meal (Friday night or any other time during the week), or an entire extended family – or substitute family, including neighbors, friends, schoolmates and others – there should naturally be time for serious discussion of current events, cultural and educational topics of the day, new books, and other words of intellectual and spiritual enrichment. Surely among these topics there should be time, as always in a Jewish home, for discussion of matters of Torah. *Pirke Avot* (*Ethics of the Sages*) admonishes us to make discussion of Torah matters a part of every meal – and this certainly applies most aptly to Shabbat meals.

Psychologists have a technical term for groups that use things like the television, or newspapers, or other distractions that pull away from warm intimacy: triangulate. That is, we bring in a third party (a person or a machine) to distract us from relating one to one on an emotional and authentic basis. Using traditional Torah texts to share our ideas, our philosophies, our values and our feelings is a wonderful way to enrich our minds and spirits, and also our closest relationships.

Sidrah Sparks and the "Four Questions" that follow each D'var Torah, are designed to provoke healthy and meaningful dialog around historical, theological and moral subjects that emerge from each week's Torah lesson. The questions are arranged in a specific order. The first one or two questions open the discussion with factual matters, to review what was read and studied. The third question then moves to a conceptual level, discussing ideas on a broader and higher level. The final question is always geared to the individual values of each responder, so that the deepest feelings and attitudes of the participants can be reached. When reaching the fourth question, we begin the level of discussion that has the potential for creating the deepest levels of intimacy and sharing.

The discussion can be geared, of course, to the age and maturity level of participants. With younger children, one may find that they are at first interested only in listening to the thoughts and ideas of their "elders," perhaps thinking that they have nothing significant to contribute. After a while, with patience and warm inviting encouragement, this will change, and all will learn that the discussion is for everyone. This cannot be "forced," any more than one can pull up a flower from the soil to make it grow. It needs gentle nurturing, feeding, and readiness; when the time is ripe, the flower will blossom. In facilitating a discussion, with a class or a family, I have always found it useful to share my own personal thoughts and feelings first. Others then are encouraged to follow without feeling pushed or threatened. This is preferable to intimidating or aggressive attempts to pull ideas out of children (which they will inevitably resent).

Children will eventually want to emulate the actions of their parents and other adults if they watch and listen to them. Thus, it is often better to keep the discussion among adults first, and let the children join when they are ready. If the questions are "thrown" at the children, it will feel like school, which for many has a connotation that implies the kind of structure and accountability that we do not want to foster at home, especially on Shabbat. If young people experience their parents in serious discussion, the message will come through loud and clear that Torah study is an adult thing, not for grades, degrees or attaining marketable skills, - but just because that is what a Jew does. Eventually they will want to be part of the discussion.

Discussions on the Sidrah can take many turns, and one need not be afraid of tangents or diversions. They are all part of what the talmudic rabbis like to call in Aramaic "shakla ve-taryah" – "discussion and dialog," the use of sacred texts as pegs on which to hang all kinds of interesting and useful debate and conversation. Through such dialog families will get to know their tradition better, their families better, and even themselves and their own ideas and attitudes more intimately.

The discussion that grows organically out of these "Sidrah Sparks" can fan into glowing flames of sharing, caring and learning. Above all it should be an experience that is filled with joy, mutual respect, and satisfaction for having achieved something real, meaningful and enriching.

Dov Peretz Elkins

BOOK ONE

D'var Torah - Bereshit

"When God began ["Bereshit"] to create heaven and earth...." Genesis 1:1

Many Jewish scholars have spent much time and energy figuring out why the Tanakh (the Hebrew Bible) begins with the Hebrew letter **bet**, the second letter of the Hebrew alphabet, instead of **alef**, the first letter.

Rabbi Levi Yitzhak of Berditchev (Poland, 1740-1810) in his commentary *Kedushat Levi*, thinks it is because each tractate (**masekhet**) of the Talmud begins with "page two" instead of "page one" (or, in Hebrew, page **bet**). Why do both the Torah and the Talmud begin with **bet**, the second letter of the alef-bet instead of the first letter, **alef**?

Answer: To help us understand this message: only when you realize that you have not yet, and never will, reach the beginning of knowledge, or the totality of knowledge, (i.e., you haven't even reached **alef**, the very beginning) will you be aware of how little you really know. In other words, the ultimate goal of learning is to know that you will never know everything. The purpose of learning is to learn **more**, not **everything**, (which you never will). This thought is humbling and challenging.

Four Questions

1) Do you think Rabbi Levi Yitzhak's teaching is designed to encourage you to stop studying, or to study more? Explain.

2) Why is learning so important in Judaism? How can one measure a learned person, according to Rabbi Levi Yitzhak's explanation?

3) If you cannot know everything, why continue learning? What is its goal?

4) What effect does this comment have on your own involvement in Jewish education? How can you find time to devote more time to Jewish study?

D'var Torah - Noah

"Make a window in the Ark...." Genesis 6:16

This is the only place in entire Tanakh, where Hebrew word translated "window", **tzohar**, appears. This is extremely unusual, and makes it difficult to give an accurate translation. The general idea is clear: some source of light should be provided. Rashi (llth century, France) tells of the legend that **tzohar** refers to a precious stone that lit up Noah's Ark.

A contemporary writer, Rabbi A. L. Scheinbaum, suggests that the window was placed in the Ark so that Noah would be aware of the destruction of the rest of the world, and not be able to sit inside protected and safe, and not be concerned about what was going on outside. To rejoice in his own salvation and ignore the tragedy of the havoc wrought by the flood outside, would be insensitive of Noah, so he needed to see what was happening.

Four Questions

1) Why would the Ark need a window? Would it not be safer, in a flood, without windows? (For one answer, consult chapter 8, verse 6).

2) What would be Noah's natural feeling being inside the Ark, and why does the commentary mentioned suggest a different one?

3) Where else in Jewish tradition do we find rules or suggestions about responsibility to the community and the world?

4) Have there been times when you concentrated your thoughts on your own sense of relief, and tried

to put out of your mind the welfare of others? Please explain with an example.

D'var Torah - Lekh Lekha

"And you shall no longer be called Avram, but your name shall be Avraham [father of a multitude], for I am making you the father of a multitude of nations." Genesis 17:5

A modern Israeli rabbi and popular commentator, Rabbi Ben Zion Firer, explains the custom of granting a child a Hebrew name at his **Brit Milah** by pointing to this section of Bereshit, dealing with Avraham. Avraham is the first to be circumcised as a sign of the Eternal Covenant between God and the Jewish People. At the time of Avraham's circumcision, he is given a new name, Avraham (no longer Avram). So it is with all Jewish boys since then. Their Hebrew names are bestowed at the moment of their circumcisions. Both of these acts, explains Rabbi Firer, preserve the child's identity. The **Brit Milah**, the circumcision, is a permanent mark in the Jew's flesh, and the bestowing of a Hebrew name is a permanent mark in the Jew's soul.

Four Questions

1) How does Rabbi Firer tie together the two customs of **Brit Milah** and getting a Hebrew name?

2) In what ways do these two acts, circumcision and receiving a Hebrew name, have impact on a person's Jewish identity?

3) Are these two customs still observed, and considered important, today? Why is each of them significant?

4) Do you feel strongly about preserving these customs for your children and grandchildren? Explain.

D'var Torah - Vayera

"Avraham said to God: Will You destroy the innocent along with the guilty [in Sodom]?" Genesis 18:23

Avraham argues with God, hoping to save the evil cities of Sodom and Gomorra from complete destruction. A pious teacher and founder of the famous Yeshiva of Slobodka, Rabbi Natan Tzvi Finkel, known as the Alter of Slobodka (b. Lithuania 1849; settled in Hevron in 1925, opening another famous Yeshiva, and d. 1927) asks an interesting question on this verse. Would we not expect Avraham, the saint, to want two evil cities to be destroyed? Why does he then argue with God to save them?

The Alter of Slobodka refers to a Talmudic interpretation of Psalm 104:35, "May sinners disappear from the earth, and the wicked be no more," implying that when wicked people stop sinning, there will be no more sinners (cf. Talmud, Berakhot 10a). Avraham wanted the sins to be destroyed, not the sinners.

Four Questions

1) Why does the Alter of Slobodka find it difficult to understand why Avraham would not want to destroy the wicked cities of Sodom and Gomorra?

2) What is the difference between destroying sinners and destroying sin?

3) Why would God want to destroy the wicked cities - is not God as compassionate as Avraham?

4) How is it possible to persuade a bad person to change, and be good? Have you ever succeeded in doing so? Can you give an example?

D'var Torah - Hayay Sarah

"...these were the years of Sarah's life." Genesis 23:1

The Hebrew original and most translations render the first verse of this chapter literally: Sarah's lifespan was one hundred years and twenty years and seven years; these were the years of Sarah's life." The commentators are puzzled why the term "years" is repeated, instead of merely saying "Sarah lived one hundred and twenty-seven years."

The classic explanation is given by Rashi (**R**abbi **Sh**lomo **I**tzhaki, 1040-1105, Troyes, France), who said that each of these three separate numbers (100, 20 and 7) is given separately to teach us that all of Sarah's years, all 127, were "equally good." In other words, the Torah compares each section of her life to each other section, longer or shorter; they are described in different quantities to show that no one year was better than any other year.

The collection of commentaries called *Itturay Torah* asks how is it possible to understand Rashi's comment, since Sarah's first 90 years were barren, and she had other misfortunes as well? He answers by saying that "a person must thank God for the bad as well as for the good;" that is, in Sarah's mind, all of her life was good. She accepted whatever came, good and bad.

Four Questions

1) What is the textual problem that the commentators are trying to solve?

2) What is Rashi's answer, and is it reasonable?

3) Do you think that Sarah truly accepted everything that happened to her with serenity and calm?

4) Do you try to accept things in that way, with equanimity? Have you succeeded? When, and when not?

D'var Torah - Toldot

"This is the story of Yitzhak son of Avraham. Avraham was father to Yitzhak." Genesis 25:19

When a Jewish child is born, it is given a Hebrew name - its own and that of its parents - for example: Yitzhak ben Avraham ve-Sarah. Before modern times, children were known only by their father's name, and so our verse names Yitzhak: "Yitzhak son of Avraham." The connection between parent and child throughout Jewish history has been more than biological. The Jewish parent bestows upon the child his/her values, and hence the parent and the child reflect glory upon one another.

There is a famous saying in the Talmud, that starts with a question: "Who is wise? The one who sees what is born" (Tractate **Tamid** 32a). The meaning is that one who sees what is coming who can look a bit into the future, is wise. Rabbi Simcha Bunam of Pshis'cha (1767-1827) gives the Talmudic sentence a slightly different, homiletic, translation in teaching it. His translation comes out with an important message about parents and children. It is thus: "Who is the wise person? By seeing who is born of him." In other words, you can tell a wise person by the behavior of his (her) offspring. Look at the child, and you will know who is a wise (parent)!" This is what is implied in our verse, says Reb Simcha, "Avraham was a father to Yitzhak." Namely, that Avraham was a wise parent, because he raised a child like Yitzhak.

Four Questions

1) What idea does Rabbi Simcha Bunam read into our verse?

2) Do good parents always produce good children?

3) Is it always possible to judge parents by the actions of their child?

4) Relating Rabbi Simcha Bunam's message to yourself, how have you benefited from being raised by your parent(s)?

D'var Torah - Vayetze

"Yaakov left Beersheva, and traveled toward Haran." Genesis 28:10

Rabbi Menahem Hakohen, a leading contemporary Israeli teacher, suggests in *Torat Am* (Tel Aviv, Modan, 1994), that Yaakov's constant traveling is reminiscent of Jews throughout history, starting with the patriarchs. He relates the word "Hebrew," "Ivri" with **ovayr**, "one who is passing, traveling." In other words, the Hebrew nation, beginning with Avraham, was always traveling.

Examples: Avraham went from place to place, and in Genesis is called "Avraham Ha-Ivri." Yosef traveled from Eretz Yisrael to Egypt, and is referred to as "a Hebrew lad." Even Moshe is called by the Egyptians "one of the Hebrew children." The Prophet Jonah describes himself to the sailors: "Ivri Anokhi," "I am a Hebrew."

A Hebrew, a Jew, explains Rabbi Hakohen, is not a person who can be penned up in one place; he must be constantly on the move. But "on the move," or "passing" (**Ivri, ovayr**), refers not merely to the frequent moves from place to place of the Jewish people, but to their capacity to change and grow. Jews, he says, are a people who cannot be limited in time, space, or ideas. They are people who have continually moved with innovation, from one discovery to the next, one moral level to the next higher one. The Jews are a very progressive people.

Four Questions

1) What are the various interpretations and meanings of the Hebrew word "Ivri?"

2) How does Rabbi Hakohen explain the term "Ivri", and connect it to Yaakov?

3) Has it been good or bad for the Jewish People to be wanderers and movers?

4) Do you identify with this quality of the Hebrew People? How have you gained from it?

D'var Torah - Vayishlah

"I am unworthy of all the kindness that You have so faithfully shown Your servant." Genesis 32:11

Yaakov returns from 20 years of exile, having lived with Lavan in Haran, and is now frightened that Esav may still harbor resentment against his twin brother. Yaakov prays to God for help, and begins with this humble entreaty, thanking God for the kind treatment he has received until now. It seems that Yaakov has mellowed, and now feels a sense of vulnerability that he was incapable of before, during his narcissistic youth.

Rabbi Yaakov Yitzhak Halevi Horowitz, the Seer of Lublin (Poland, 1745-1815), a famous Hasidic master, turns the verse on its head, and interprets it this way: The most important kindness You have shown me, God, is that I now "am unworthy." I have not fallen into the pit of arrogance. That, to the Seer of Lublin, is the best gift God can bestow upon anyone - to avoid the hubris (overbearing pride) that life can easily bring us, and to feel, at times, unworthy of our many blessings. Yaakov escaped such arrogance, or left it behind, and for that he thanks God.

Four Questions

1) What did Yaakov mean, and what does the "Seer of Lublin" imply that Yaakov means when he says "I am unworthy"?

2) What kindnesses did Yaakov receive from God, and why does he mention them now? Is he truly humble, or is he simply afraid?

3) In what way is humility a prerequisite for a spiritual personality?

4) A hard question: Do you think of yourself as humble or arrogant - or both? Explain. Can a humble person talk of his humility? Though difficult, and maybe impossible, give it a try. It's worth it!

D'var Torah - Vayeshev

"And Yosef's brothers took him and threw him into the pit.... Then they sat and ate a meal." Genesis 37:24-25

Rabbi Ovadiah Sforno (Italy, 1475-1550) is struck by the close positioning of these two verses. Yosef's brothers threw their youngest brother into a pit, and then sat nearby and enjoyed a meal. They could hear the agony and the cries of their brother, and yet they could sit calmly and satisfy their appetites, enjoying a pleasant meal. This is the height of cruelty and insensitivity. It is the opposite of what Jewish tradition demands.

Four Questions

1) If Yosef's brothers were cruel enough to throw him into a pit, and then report to their father that he had been killed by a wild beast, why should Rabbi Sforno be surprised at their subsequent conduct?

2) Which sin was worse - throwing him into the pit, or then ignoring his cries and pain?

3) Can you think of any comparable behavior by individuals or nations in modern times?

4) What is the responsibility of a Jew when someone is crying out in pain? What if it is someone with whom you are angry? Has this ever happened to you? What would you, or did you, do?

D'var Torah - Miketz

[Said the Chief Cupbearer to Pharaoh]: "A Hebrew youth was there with us [in jail, with me and the Chief Baker], a servant of the Chief Steward (Potiphar); and when we told him our dreams, he interpreted them for us...."

Genesis 41:12

Yosef was in an extremely difficult situation in Egypt. He was in a foreign land, in a country in which slavery flourished, inside the walls of a jail, living together with all kinds of unsavory creatures, - murderers, thieves, violent thugs. Yet, he had no hesitation in telling them that he was a Hebrew. (The Chief Cupbearer knew that Yosef was a Hebrew, because in the previous chapter, Genesis 40:15, Yosef had said to those with him in jail: "I was kidnapped from the Land of the Hebrews"). (*Torat Am*, ed. Rabbi Menachem Hakohen; Tel Aviv: Modan Publishers, 1994).

Four Questions

1) Why does the commentator take special notice of Yosef's admission to being Jewish (a Hebrew, in biblical terms)?

2) Did being an Israelite (Hebrew, Jew) in the days of the patriarchs and matriarchs have negative minority status as it did in later history? Would that affect the commentator's point? To whom is the commentary addressed?

3) What Jews in recent times whom you know, or have heard of or read about, have been alternatively

proud or ashamed of admitting their Jewish background and Jewish heritage?

4) Have you ever been in a position when you denied your Jewishness; thought of denying it, or wanted to hide it? When, why, etc.? What is good or bad about denying who we are? Is there ever a time when it is proper to "pass," i.e., to pretend one is not Jewish?

D'var Torah - Vayigash

"Yosef kissed all his brothers and wept upon them." Genesis 45:15

An observant commentator (*Oznayim La-Torah*) notices that Yosef often cries, and counts 8 different occasions when he did. He notes that "one who has suffered much in difficult times cries more readily even in better times." Because Yosef was accustomed to crying, especially for others, he was worthy of achieving his exalted rank.

The Torah freely describes Yosef as expressing his emotions, and holds him in high esteem for doing so. Crying is not seen as weakness, but rather strength, and deserving of reward. In modern society, several leaders have been criticized for showing their emotions in public. Their viewpoint is different from the one expressed in this verse.

Four Questions

1) How does the commentator view Yosef kissing his brothers and weeping on their shoulders? Explain what value or harm that crying may have on a human soul?

2) Is public affection something that one should try to restrain or exhibit freely?

3) Can you think of other examples of biblical characters, or biblical passages, in which deep emotions are displayed?

4) How do you react to Yosef's emotional behavior? Do you think it proper for public figures to display their emotions in front of the community? Would you feel free to do so were you in a position of public prominence?

D'var Torah - Vayehi

"And Yaakov blessed Yosef, saying: 'The God in whose ways my fathers Avraham and Yitzhak walked... bless these lads (Ephraim & Menasheh, Yosef's sons). In them may my name be recalled, and the names of my fathers, Avraham and Yitzhak, and may they be great multitudes upon the earth." Genesis 48:15-16

There seems to be some confusion here. Is Yaakov blessing his son, Yosef, or his grandsons ("these lads"), Ephraim and Menasheh? Rabbi Isaiah Horowitz, known as the **Sh'lah**, an acronym for his famous book, *Shnai Luhot HaBrit** explains that there is no greater blessing for a parent than the aspiration that his children will follow in his footsteps and those of his ancestors. Thus, when Yaakov blesses his grandchildren with the blessing that they will follow in the footsteps of his father and grandparents, his is blessing both them and their father, Yosef, at the same time.

Four Questions

1) Why is there confusion as to whom Yaakov is blessing? How does Rabbi Horowitz resolve the problem?

2) What is the essence of Yaakov's blessing?

3) Why is it important for someone to have her children follow in her ways?

4) What are some of the hopes you have for your children and grandchildren? In what ways do you want them to be like you, think like you, behave like you? In what ways would you like them to be different, or have them improve upon your behavior?

*(*The Two Tablets of the Covenant*) [1560-1630, Prague, Poland, Frankfurt & Jerusalem]

D'var Torah - Shemot

"But the Israelites were fertile, and expanded so that the land was filled with them." Exodus 1:7

In his commentary called *Moreshet Moshe*, a well-known modern British Rabbi, Moshe Swift (1907-1983), writes that the phrase "the land was filled with them" means that the Israelites could be found everywhere, placing no limitations on their comings and goings. He suggests that this may have been the beginning of their decline into an assimilated and enslaved society. The fact that the "land was filled with them" implies to him that they did not restrict themselves to places where they could maintain their Jewish values. When Jews begin to frequent nightclubs and seasonal parties and fill their lives with fun, pleasure and sybaritic self-indulgence, this is one of the first steps to assimilation, and the decline of our unique, individual identity.

Four Questions

1) Explain the difference between the literal meaning

(the **peshat**) and the homiletic interpretation (**drash**) of the text.

2) Is there anything wrong with enjoying one's life? Why does the commentary condemn that lifestyle?

3) How can one "inoculate" one's children from the assimilationist environment? Is it desirable and possible to do so?

4) What things do you do in your life that help maintain your Jewish identity? How do you prevent

your value system from becoming affected by the hedonism of today's world?

D'var Torah - Va-era

"I will bring you into the Land which I promised to give to Avraham, Yitzhak and Yaakov, and I will give it to you for a heritage...." Exodus 6:8

In a modern commentary (*Wellsprings of Torah*) the author notes that the Hebrew word for heritage (**Morashah**) appears only twice in the Torah - here, in connection with the Land of Israel, and in Deuteronomy 33:4 in connection with the Torah ("The Torah which Moshe commanded us is a **morashah** [heritage] for the community of Yaakov"). [This is the popular song which children often learn: "Torah tzeeva lanu Moshe, Morashah kehilat Yaakov"]. He draws the conclusion, which traditional Jewish commentaries do in comparing the use of certain words in different contexts, that there must be a connection between these two passages.

The connection made is that we have a right to the Land of Israel only when we keep the statues of the Torah. Further proof is offered from the verses in Psalms 105:44-45: "God will give them the lands...so that they may keep God's statutes."

Four Questions

1) What assumption about the nature of the Torah does a commentator make when comparing identical words that appear in different places?

2) What other connections could one make between the Land of Israel and the Torah of Israel?

3) Do you agree that the Torah must be kept in the Land of Israel? To what degree? Explain. Why in Israel more than anywhere else?

4) If you could declare the Torah the Law of the Land in the State of Israel, would you do so? What problems and what benefits do you see accruing from this declaration?

D'var Torah - Bo

"...Pharaoh said to Moshe and Aharon: 'Go, worship Adonai your God. Who shall go?' Moshe replied: 'All of us, our young and our old....'" Exodus 10:8-9

When Moshe and Aharon ask Pharaoh to let the Israelite People go out of Egypt, they put the children first, and then mention the elders. In the very next verse, when Pharaoh continues his answer, he says: "I will send you out and your children," placing the adults first, the children second. Commenting on this Rabbi Hillel Silverman explains: "Only when we place emphasis upon educating the new generation can we march toward the Promised Land of Jewish self-fulfillment and creativity."

In past generations, education for the adult community was a normal, standard and accepted phenomenon. By studying and practicing Judaism, the parent community thus taught the children. In many Jewish communities today, it is the children, learning about Judaism at Religious School, who come home and teach their parents. Ultimately, we know that unless both parents and children learn Torah, it will in the long run be forgotten.

Four Questions

1) Why might Moshe and Aharon mention the children first, and Pharaoh mention them second?

2) Does it really matter who learns first, as long as both generations study, learn and grow?

3) Which way was more effective for the long term, in the Jewish community, for parents to teach children or children to teach parents?

4) If you are an adult, how and when do you teach young people (including your children if you have any) about being Jewish? If you are living with your parents, is there any thing or way you can or do teach them?

D'var Torah - Beshalah

"Then Miriam the Prophet...took a timbrel, and all the women joined her in dance and timbrels. And Miriam chanted to them: Sing to Adonai...." Exodus 15:20-21

Both the Torah Reading for this Shabbat, and the Haftarah (Judges, chapter 5) include songs of thanksgiving to God for redemption from the enemy. Moshe and Miriam sing **Shirat Ha-Yam** - the Song of the Sea - in the Sidrah. Devorah and Barak sing in the Haftarah for delivery from the Amorites. This Shabbat is called **Shabbat Shira** - the Shabbat of Song, because of the two biblical songs prescribed for this week's Scriptural lessons.

Rabbi Macy Gordon, an American-born Orthodox rabbi now living in Jerusalem and serving as Director of the Council of Young Israel Rabbis, makes this comment on the fact that both the Sidrah and Haftarah contain songs by women who participated in their people's redemption: "...to suggest that in biblical times the roles of men and of women were identical and interchangeable would be to impose a contemporary bias on Jewish history. But to say that the Jewish woman was merely a passive member of male society, object and never subject, follower and never leader, is to be untrue to the clear and irrevocable text of the Torah." (*Wavelengths*, 1994, p. 68)

Four Questions

1) What point is Rabbi Gordon trying to make in his comment? Is he being unnecessarily defensive?

2) What is the difference between the role of women today and in biblical times?

3) Some have said that the equal role women play in Jewish life today is a unique contribution of American Judaism? Do you agree?

4) What further steps should society take to make men and women fully equal? What things can you change in your life to help make women and men more equal?

D'var Torah - Yitro

"And Adonai spoke all these words...." Exodus 20:1

In the rabbinic tradition of commentary, the word "all" is included in a biblical verse to make it more inclusive, to add something that one would not ordinarily expect. Thus, the Talmud (Tractate Hagigah 3b) comments: The word **all** in this case comes to teach us that the **words** which Adonai spoke include the explanations which were offered by later rabbis - some who argued one way and others who argued the opposite way; some who said something was kosher and others who said it was non-kosher; some who permitted a certain deed and others who forbade it. All these words - even though some of the words directly contradict the others - they were **all** given by Adonai at Mt. Sinai, as it says in the Torah: "And Adonai spoke **all** these words...."

Four Questions

1) Explain the principle of interpretation by which the Talmud arrives at its conclusion.

2) Why did the ancient rabbis find it necessary to include opposing points of view under the divine umbrella?

3) Can two opposing points of view both be consider hypothetically correct? Can both be considered divine?

4) Construct a cogent argument in response to quesetion # 3 for each side, and defend them vigorously.

D'var Torah - Mishpatim

"When you buy a Hebrew slave, six years he shall serve; in the seventh year he will be freed.... But if he says: 'I love my master, and my family, and do not wish to go free'... he shall be brought to the door, or the doorpost, and his master shall bore a hole in his ear, and he shall remain his slave for life." Exodus 21:2, 5

The Torah does not look favorably upon a person who gives up freedom and voluntarily chooses slavery. The rabbis of the Talmud explain in further detail:

"Rabban Yohanan ben Zakkai comments: Why was the **ear** chosen of all the parts of the body? When the Blessed Holy One learns of a person denying one's own freedom, God says: 'The ear that heard Me proclaim on Mt. Sinai, "The Israelites are **My** servants" (Leviticus 25:55), and not servants **to other servants** [all humans are God's servants, including a slave owner] - such a person who voluntarily buys into the slavery system - his ear shall be pierced." (Tractate **Kiddushin** 22b)

Four Questions

1) Why did the Torah and the Talmud discourage voluntary slavery?

2) What is the reason which Rabban Yohanan adds to the Torah's reason?

3) In what way does slavery violate Divine Law, as well as being inhumane?

4) In democratic countries today, slavery is no more. In what ways do we still enslave ourselves? How do you enslave yourself? Are you thus violating

God's Law? How does God punish you for enslaving yourself?

D'var Torah - Terumah

"The Keruvim shall spread their wings on high... and their faces toward each other." Exodus 25:20

The Hebrew word **Keruvim** has come into the English language as *cherubim*, a type of angel. In the ancient Mishkan and the Temples, they sat above the Holy Ark. In the Middle Ages, they were thought to be angels in the form of little children, but biblical scholarship has shown that a cherub was a winged sphinx (a sphinx is a lion with a human head). In the Bible they appear, as here, made of wood overlaid with gold, sitting at the two ends of God's throne above the Holy Ark. They were also embroidered on the curtains of the Mishkan, and on the veil separating levels of holiness. In Solomon's Temple, they were carved on several walls and doors.

Many commentators have pointed out that in this verse the **Keruvim** have their wings facing Heaven and their faces turning toward earth - an apt combination for servants of God.

Four Questions

1) What function might carved or embroidered figures have in biblical ritual?

2) Does this violate the second of the 10 Commandments, not to have any images or pictures of anything in heaven or earth?

3) How have the commentaries used the depiction of the **Keruvim** to relate to daily life of humans?

4) In your spiritual life, how do you balance "facing" God and "facing" other humans? What part

do religion, prayer and ritual play in your life, and how do they compare with mundane concerns of daily life?

D'var Torah - Tezaveh

"You shall command the Israelites to bring clear olive oil to have the lamps burn continually...from evening to morning... before Adonai...." Exodus 27:20-21

The Menorah (not the *Magen David*) is the central symbol of Judaism, since it gives light - the magical representation of the mysterious, the elusive: awe, transcendence; as well as the concrete: knowledge, truth and justice. It has been the focus of comments, elaborations, and moral lessons since its first description in the Torah.

Rabbi Ovadiah Sforno, commentator, philosopher and physician (Bologna, Italy, 1475-1550) gives his interpretation of the 7 branches of the Menorah (cf. on Numbers 8:2) by explaining that the three lights on the right and the three on the left all illuminate the central shaft, the principal part of the Menorah, and have a common purpose. They all join together to bring divine light to Israel. Those to the right deal with spiritual matters and those to the left deal with worldly matters, but all are one united people trying to fulfill the will of God.

Four Questions

1) Why is the Menorah such an important focal point in the Torah and in Judaism?

2) What is it about the shape of the Menorah which leads Rabbi Sforno to make his comment about those to the left and those to the right? To what may he be referring metaphorically?

3) In what ways can Jews who are considered "conservative" and those thought of as "liberal" cooperate together?

4) On what issues do you see yourself being on the "left" and in what ways on the "right"? Do you see yourself as a conciliator or a polarizer? Can one (you) be both? Explain.

D'var Torah - Kee Tisa

"Moshe pleaded: 'Adonai, do not let Your anger burn against Your people, whom You redeemed from the land of Egypt with great power and a mighty hand."

Exodus 32:11

After the sin of the golden calf, God wanted to destroy the Jewish People (v. 10), but Moshe pleads on their behalf. On what basis can Moshe ask for pardon? Rabbi Moshe Alshikh (b. Turkey 1508, d. Damascus, Syria 1593), envisions Moshe acting as a lawyer in court, using the "environmental" argument. Moshe pleads with God - You, Adonai, have to forgive these people, because they still have a slave mentality. They lived for generations in a land of horrendous idolatry and other abominable practices; a land with no values or morals. If you take all that into account, you absolutely must forgive them, and ignore their sin.

Harvard law professor Alan M. Dershowitz recently published a book called *The Abuse Excuse, And Other Cop-Outs, Sob Stories and Evasions of Responsibility* (NY: Little, Brown). Dershowitz wants people to be responsible for their deeds, regardless of their upbringing or environment, and not blame the past for present crimes.

Four Questions

1) Did God forgive the people? How did the story turn out? (See verses 30-35).

2) Did you think God took into account the slave mentality & idolatrous background from which the Israelites had come? Would you have?

3) What is the difference in role between Moshe in this story and a lawyer in an American Court?

4) Is background or environment ever a valid excuse for misbehavior? Have they influenced your own life in causing you to err? Are they legitimate excuses?

D'var Torah - Vayakhel

"You shall not kindle a fire in all your habitations on the day of Shabbat." Exodus 35:3

Rabbi Samson Raphael Hirsch (Frankfurt, Germany, 1808-1888) raises the question of why **fire** is forbidden on Shabbat in Jewish homes (In the **Bet Mikdash**, however, it was permitted to kindle the Menorah and the fire on the altar.) Generally speaking, the things that are forbidden on Shabbat are acts of creation and creativity, or acts of productivity. Kindling a fire, he says, is basically a **destructive** activity. He then explains that making fire is what gave Adam and Eve true mastery over the physical world, enabling them to create tools, and synthetically probing into the nature of objects. This makes fire also **constructive**.

The "do's" and "don'ts" of Shabbat have frequently puzzled people. Sometimes matters of significant effort (walking a far distance to synagogue) are permitted, while things of little physical effort (driving a vehicle) are prohibited (depending on the deciding rabbinic authority and the destination). Rabbi Hirsch tries to unravel the mystery of the prohibition of Shabbat work.

Four Questions

1) Is the nature of fire more destructive or constructive?

2) What difference is Rabbi Hirsch trying to make between fire as destroyer and as useful tool? Why?

3) Do you think that the prohibitions on Shabbat relate to work that is constructive rather than

destructive? (Cleaning the kitchen after Shabbat dinner, for example, is permitted) Explain.

4) What is your own personal position about lighting a fire on Shabbat? Using electricity? Turning on lights, using the telephone, television, computer, etc.? Explain your position.

D'var Torah - Pekuday

"These are the records [accountings - **Pekudim**] of the Mishkan which Moshe had drawn up...." (Exodus 38:21)

The Midrash (Tanhuma) asks an interesting question. Moshe was the leader of the Jewish People, fully trusted by God. Later the Torah quotes God as saying "Throughout My household, he is trustworthy" (Numbers 12:7). Why, then, must Moshe give an accounting of the materials used in the Mishkan (the portable Sanctuary in the Wilderness) - the amount of gold, silver, copper, yarns, stones, linen, woven work, etc.?

Whenever the rabbis raise a question, they do so because they have their own answer ready. They claim that the skeptics of the generation were gossiping about how Moshe might have enriched himself by utilizing some of the leftovers of the wealth of materials used to build the Mishkan. Thus, Moshe decided to give a full accounting to make perfectly clear how all the materials were used and spent, and put an end to all the gossip about him by his contemporaries.

Four Questions

1) Is it human nature to criticize, to be skeptical of leadership?

2) Should someone in a position as high as Moshe have to be accountable to the People of Israel, especially in matters so holy as building the Mishkan?

3) What are the benefits of accountability in government? Is anyone above accountability? Explain.

4) What rules, laws or practices would you recommend for any institutions, or governments, which you are a part of, that would help preserve their integrity and appearance of total honesty?

D'var Torah - Vayikra

"When anyone brings from yourselves (Hebrew: **meekem**) an offering unto Adonai...." Leviticus 1:2

Several commentaries point out the special usage of the Hebrew word **meekem** - of yourselves, or from yourselves, which might be seen as superfluous in the verse. The simple translation is: "If anyone of you brings...." The way the verse is seen by the commentaries is with an enhanced meaning. **Meekem**, of yourselves, can suggest that all sacrifices include not simply the animal offering, or the meal offering, but it must also include something **of yourselves**.

Those who contribute of their funds, their time, their energy or their advice, to the community, to the synagogue, or to the Jewish People, should do so by making sure that their contribution comes from inside, from the heart. The sacrifice offered on the altar of community welfare must include part of you, your essence, not just your means. Any sacrifice or gift one brings should reflect the sincerity, awareness and consciousness of what that gift means to the giver and to the receiver. In that way, it will have the most powerful effect.

Four Questions

1) Explain the difference between the simple translation of the verse and the nuance of difference brought by the commentaries.

2) What is the purpose of bringing a sacrifice; in the Bible, and today?

3) How can one include something of oneself in bringing a sacrifice?

4) Think of some contributions or gifts you have made. Have you been conscious of giving of yourself with the gift? How can you be even more aware of giving of your own true self?

D'var Torah - Tzav

"This is the Torah [teaching] of the guilt offering: it is holy of holies." Leviticus 7:1

The question raised by the commentators on this verse is why the sacrifice of one who has sinned is termed "holy of holies." That special, high category should be reserved for one who has **not** sinned. Not so, says the *Kli Yakar*, Rabbi Shlomo Ephraim Lunshitz (1550 - 1619, Lemberg and Prague), who explains that a perfect **tzaddik** (wise, enlightened one) is called "holy," while a person who sins and brings an offering (i.e., who repents) is called "holy of holies." This is in accord with the Talmud that states (**Sanhedrin** 99a): "A very saintly person cannot compare with the high level of those who have sinned and repented."

For proof of this, the *Kli Yakar* quotes another talmudic passage (**Yoma** 86a) that teaches that the wicked acts of a repentant person are transformed into merits! Thus, one who sins and repents thus receives credit for good deeds as well as for sins, which are now considered as merits. A **tzaddik** only has good deeds, and is thus, holy; but a repentant sinner has good deeds and merits for repentance, and thus is "holy of holies."

Four Questions

1) Why is the *Kli Yakar* surprised by the wording of Leviticus 7:1?

2) What do you know about the phrase "holy of holies"? To what else does it refer?

3) What do you think about the fact that Tradition gives a repentant sinner preeminent status, even higher than one who never sinned?

4) Think of a time you repented, or changed a harmful behavior, and think how it felt? How did your recognition of having made a mistake affect you? Did it change you?

D'var Torah - Shmini

"And the swine [pig] - even though it has split hoofs, it does not chew its cud; it is unclean for you."

Leviticus 11:7

For an animal to be kosher, it requires two qualifications: a split hoof (i.e., a "foot" which has a space in it, as if it had two large fingers), and it must chew its cud. Animals that chew their cud swallow, regurgitate and re-swallow their food. The Torah does not explain these requirements. The point of this verse is that the pig only fulfills one of the two requirements, and thus is not kosher.

The Midrash (Leviticus Rabbah 13:5) uses the pig as an example of a hypocrite. It states that the pig stretches out its legs and shows everyone its cleft hoofs, and yells out "See how kosher I am!" It hides the fact that it does not chew its cud. The typical hypocrite brags about his virtues all the time, but conceals his shortcomings. In other words, it's like the old Yiddish proverb, "A half truth is a whole lie." People who go out of their way to fudge the facts, to twist reality in their favor, who put a fancy "spin" on their situation, are "unkosher" and "unclean."

Four Questions

1) How does the Midrash derive its message from our verse?

2) How would you define a hypocrite?

3) Can you think of someone who acted hypocritically? Are people in the public eye (such as politicians) more prone to hide the truth?

4) Do you think it is a natural human trait to cover the full truth? Explain. How can society help people to be more honest and truthful? What suggestions do you have?

D'var Torah - Tazria

"He shall be unclean as long as the disease is found within him, he shall be unclean." Leviticus 13:46

There seems to be a superfluous phrase here. Why is it necessary to repeat the phrase "he is unclean"? Of course, as long as one has a disease, that person is considered unclean, and must be isolated in order not to spread the disease.

One commentator, however, the NATZIV (Rabbi Naftali Zvi Yehudah Berlin, Rosh Yeshiva of the famous Yeshiva of Volozhin in White Russia, 1817-1893) points out that one might assume that after the ceremony of purification, one might be able to be considered pure, even though the disease is still present. No, he replies, of course not. As long as the disease is present, no ritual purification can help. It is primarily the disease that must be cured.

The NATZIV then applies this same principle to moral failures. Apologizing, repenting, and going through all the moral purification necessary is not enough, he argues, unless and until the failures are removed, and made up. Unless a person changes one's character, and discontinues the mistake, it is useless to try to purify oneself through regret.

Four Questions

1) What analogy is Rabbi Berlin making?

2) Why is it necessary to repent; why is not an apology sufficient?

3) Do diseases of the body often have analogues in diseases of the spirit?

4) What are some things you would like to change about yourself? After doing so, to whom would you apologize for past errors?

D'var Torah - Metzora

"The person to be purified needs two birds, clean and alive...." Leviticus 14:4

Part of the ceremony to ritually cleanse one who has contracted leprosy was to bring two live birds, along with cedar wood, scarlet and hyssop, to the Temple. Even as great a scholar as Maimonides confesses that he does not understand the need for the birds, the cedar wood, the scarlet, and the hyssop (see the Hertz Humash, p. 470).

One commentator, the *Tzvi Yisrael*, explains that there is a connection between the birds and the leper. The ancient rabbis believed that leprosy was a punishment for gossip. Since birds normally chirp loudly and make a lot of noise without meaning, the explanation given is that the leper will be reminded that if he did not make so much useless chirping noise through gossip and slander, he would not have contracted leprosy in the first place.

Four Questions

1) What connection does the *Tzvi Yisrael* see between the birds in the ceremony and the cause of leprosy?

2) Why did the rabbis focus on improper speech?

3) Do you think gossip, slander, improper speech is a major problem today?

4) In what ways can you be more careful in your speech?

D'var Torah - Aharay Mot

"You shall keep My laws and My rules, which if a person does them, shall live: I am Adonai." Leviticus 18:5

Rabbi Meir takes note in a Talmudic passage (**Bava Kama** 38a) that the verse refers to a "person," and does not say a "*Kohen*," a "*Levi*" or an "*Israelite*." From this he draws the lesson that the Torah means to teach us that *any human being*, Jew or non-Jew, who carries out the laws and rules of the Torah, is as valued as the *Kohen Gadol*. Rabbi Meir points out that it is a person's deeds, and one's ethical and moral behaviors, that distinguish that person from others, not one's hereditary status.

Four Questions

1) Why does Rabbi Meir make special mention of the fact that the word "adam," or "person" is used in the verse, instead of specifically mentioning a Kohen, Levi, or Israelite? What lesson does he draw from this?

2) How does Rabbi Meir deduce that any ordinary non- Jew who accepts the obligations of the Torah is as important as the Kohen Gadol? Do you agree?

3) What lesson can we draw from Rabbi Meir's doctrine about the equality of Jews and non-Jews in Jewish theology?

4) If non-Jews can be considered equal to the *Kohen Gadol*, then what makes Jews different from non- Jews? In what ways do you consider yourself different from a non-Jew? Please explain.

D'var Torah - Kedoshim

"Love your neighbor as yourself." Leviticus 19:18

This verse is thought of by many, including the great scholar Rabbi Akiva (second century C.E.) as "the greatest rule of the Torah," The idea of this verse is expressed in many forms, and is sometimes referred to in its various formulations as "The Golden Rule." The famous Talmudic sage, Hillel, expressed the same thought in these words: "What is hateful to you, do not do to your neighbor. That is the summary of the whole Torah; the rest is commentary, which we must always study."

Of course, by placing great stress on love of humanity, the Torah enunciates its most essential value. Deep values, such as love of others, also contain other layers of meaning that are useful to explore. One of these ideas is that the Torah does not stop with the words "Love your neighbor," it adds "as yourself." Several wise commentators have explained this to mean that the first step to loving others is loving oneself. Self-esteem is the basis of giving respect and affection to others. In fact, psychologists tell us that without self-love, love of others is difficult or impossible. We each have a relationship with our "self" which becomes the basis of our relationships with others. As the famous British playwright, George Bernard Shaw, once wrote, "Love of others is only the spillover of love of self."

Four Questions

1) Why did Rabbi Akiva think this verse was the most important in the Torah?

2) Does it matter if the Golden Rule is stated positively, or as Hillel did, negatively?

3) Do you agree that there is a connection between love of self and love of others?

4) Can you think of times when you felt self-confident, and how it affected your feelings toward others? Can you give some examples?

D'var Torah - Emor

"The Kohanim (priests) shall be holy to God...." Leviticus 21:6

In the Sidrah of Emor we read a great deal about *kohanim* (priests) and their command to be holy. As religious leaders of the people of Israel, their duty to maintain a high level of holiness is extremely important. It is interesting to note that holiness is not, however, the sole province of the kohanim. In Exodus 19:6 we read: "You shall be a nation of kohanim and a holy people." In other words, all Israelites (Jews) are to be holy, like the kohanim.

There is a degree of ambiguity here. How should *kohanim* be holy in ways different from other Jews? If all Jews are to be holy, why is the rule of holiness singled out for kohanim? The answer may be in the **level** of holiness, but it is clear and significant that there is no religious preserve which is exclusively the domain of the priest. Kohanim should be more holy, and all Jews should be like kohanim. The rabbis believed that both ideas are true. There is a strong democratic thread that demands the highest levels of holy living on the part of **every** Jew.

Four Questions

1) What do you think holiness means?

2) How can all Jews become holy?

3) How can we **add** holiness to our daily lives?

4) What ways are you holy in your life? How can you become even moreso?

D'var Torah - Behar

"Proclaim liberty throughout the Land for all its inhabitants. It shall be a Jubilee Year for you." Leviticus 25:10

Who benefits when slaves are freed? The natural, obvious answer is: the slaves. The Stone Chumash quotes a commentary named *Pnei Yehoshua* who makes a very wise observation. Not only do the slaves benefit, but the **slave owners** benefit as well. How? One cannot appreciate freedom for oneself, unless one also appreciates freedom for others. By freeing the slaves, the former slave-owners have heightened their own awareness of the impropriety of the institution of slavery, and made themselves more sensitive to the pains of a slave's existence.

The same comparison may be made with any immoral and oppressive behavior. It hurts the person who commits the act in some ways as it does the person who is oppressed. Keeping others in slavery warps the soul of the slave-owner; discriminating against others poisons the heart of those who discriminate. The entire society benefits when human rights are recognized and distributed to all.

Four Questions

1) What words in the verse do you think prompted the comments of the *Pnei Yehoshua*?

2) How do people who do evil benefit when evil is stopped, as much as those upon whom evil is done? 3) How was American society improved after the Civil

War, when slaves were freed? Who benefited from the Emancipation Proclamation?

4) Imagine yourself freeing a slave you once owned (pretending that you lived before the Civil War). What might it have felt like to free the slave? How would you appreciate your own freedom more after having stopped treating another unfairly?

D'var Torah - Behukotai

"If you follow My statutes and observe My mitzvot....I will grant peace in the land... and no sword shall cross your land." Leviticus 26:3,6

Since peace is a many-faceted idea, and "land" also can refer to a variety of possibilities, it is interesting to see how different commentators understand these terms, and how they may apply to our world. Rabbi Haim ben Attar, a Kabbalist who lived in Morocco and Eretz Yisrael (1696-1743) in his work *Or HaHaim*, suggests that peace refers to harmony between various groups within a country. Such peace will come when all have a fair share of food and land, and hence, will not need to bicker with one another. To Rabbi Haim this applies to every country in the world, and **eretz**, or land, means the whole world.

Holding a different view is Rabbi Moshe ben Gershon Hefetz, in his commentary *Melekhet Mahshevet* (Venice, 1663-1711). Rabbi Moshe claims that **eretz** is more narrowly defined: Eretz Yisrael and its neighboring countries. He argues that even if there is peace in Eretz Yisrael, if its neighbors are fighting among themselves, the inhabitants of Eretz Yisrael will still be afraid and uneasy, not knowing when they might be affected by the nearby wars (compare Iraq and Iran).

Four Questions

1) Why do different commentaries differ on the meaning of simple words like "land" and "peace?"

2) What different interpretations are offered for these two terms?

3) How would you apply the interpretations given above, of “land” and of “peace” to conditions in the Middle East, your own country, and elsewhere?

4) Do you think you would be more prone to violence, or even a less severe form of belligerence, if your food and home were taken away? Explain.

D'var Torah - Bemidbar

In the list of marchers through the wilderness (Midbar) toward the Promised Land of Eretz Yisrael is one named **Eliasaph the son of Deuel**. Numbers 1:14

Maimonides (12th century) points out that the same person is called in the next chapter (Numbers 2:14) the son of **Reuel**. The difference may lie in the fact that the ancient scribe copied the Hebrew letter **resh** instead of a **dalet**, which are almost identical.

But Maimonides takes advantage of the difference to make an interesting suggestion: that perhaps this fine gentleman's father gave him **two names**, which, though they sound alike, have a slightly different connotation. Reuel may be related, he suggests, to the word **ra-ayon**, related to "thinking," and Deuel may be related to **da-at** which implies knowledge.(The Hebrew letters **alef** and **ayin** are sometimes interchangeable). Maimonides suggests that Reuel/Deuel's father may have named him because he wanted him to direct both his **mind** and his **thoughts** toward God.

Today we often give our children names because they sound nice, or because they begin with the same letter of the name of a deceased beloved relative. The custom of giving a child a name because of its **meaning** is an interesting one, which places a special touch on our hopes and dreams for the children that we bring into the world and launch with high visions for their future.

Four Questions

1) Do you know what your Hebrew name means?

2) Would you consider naming a child or grandchild with a name primarily because of its meaning?

3) What are your favorite names? Why do you like them?

4) Can you give examples of some names that you appreciate because their **meaning**?

D'var Torah - Naso

The most beautiful of all blessings, **Birkat Kohanim**, the priestly blessing, is included in this Sidrah. Its first words, "May Adonai bless you and keep you," have provoked an interesting comment from the rabbis. They explain and interpret each and every word. "May Adonai bless you," with all the material things that life can bring you in abundance. Judaism never looked down upon physical pleasures. It merely tried to keep them in proportion, and to use them for positive and holy purposes. The enjoyment of material blessings, the beauty of our home, our synagogue, our clothing, are not sins but blessings.

But the rabbis were quick to add a note of caution. The **Birkat Kohanim** continues: "May Adonai bless you **and keep you**." Keep you from what? Keep you from letting your possessions possess you. Keep you from the excesses which materialism often brings, from the arrogance and self-centeredness, from the abuse of power and authority which economic power permits us. Life all things in life - moderation is important. Let the world bless you with nice physical gifts, but don't become so over-focused on these gifts that you lose your sense of priorities and forget to emphasize life's spiritual values as well.

Four Questions

1) How do we know when material pleasures "possess us," instead of our possessing them?

2) How do we make certain that our lives include ample spiritual values?

3) Can you think of some examples of people who abuse their material blessings? What safeguards can they employ to check their greed?

4) What way can we, in our own lives, in this age of ecological awareness and material abundance, be more careful to spend our dollars frugally and thoughtfully?

D'var Torah - Be-ha-alotekha

"The people were as murmurers, speaking evil in the ears of Adonai. Adonai heard and was very angry; a fire of Adonai burned against them, devouring the outskirts of the camp." Numbers 11:1

The last phrase, "the outskirts of the camp," is in Hebrew **biketzay hamahaneh**. The Hebrew word **ketzay** can mean either "base" or "leader" (**katzin**). Rashi (11th century, France) paraphrases the verse to have it mean that the fire of Adonai burned the "extreme leaders" of the camp. He explains that there are two kinds of people who drag us down: the base individuals in the community, and sometimes our most respected leaders. It may be the worst among us, or the best among us.

Rabbi Stephen Chaim Listfield gives the example of the medieval renegade Jews like Nicholas Donin in France, Pablo Christiani and Joshua Lorki in Spain, and Petrus Schwarz in Germany - who all led theological attacks on Judaism, and tried to coerce Jews to convert to Christianity. All of these men were born Jewish! Sometimes those who are the "best and the brightest" can do the most damage. When leaders become egotistical and self-serving, they do themselves and those around them terrible harm.

Four Questions

1) Explain how Rashi re-translated the phrase to find new meaning in it.

2) What general principle can we derive from Rashi's explanation?

3) Can you think of any great leaders who, though well- meaning, have done great harm to their people? Any Jewish leaders?

4) Can you think of a time when you were in a position of leadership or authority, and had the potential to bring great good or harm to the situation? What happened, and how did it turn out?

D'var Torah - Shelah Lekha

In this Sidrah we read of the 12 spies, one from each tribe of Israel, whom Moshe sent to find out about Eretz Yisrael: What kind of place it was; who were the people living there; were there fortified cities, and were the people armed and prepared for battle. This is one of the first spy missions described in history.

In Moshe's charge to the spies he says (Numbers 13:17): "Go up to the Land into the Negev, and go up into the mountains." Rabbi Yehudah Leib Eger (1816-1888), a Hasidic teacher from Lublin, Poland, makes the following comment. Moshe told the spies to view the land in terms of future generations, to go to the top of the mountain and see the long view. Instead, they looked at it from a narrow, selfish, fearful perspective. The ten negative spies reported that "we were as grasshoppers in their eyes" (Numbers 13:33). The spies thought little of themselves, and their short-term, narrow-minded, fearful attitude caused them to bring back a discouraging, demoralizing report.

Four Questions

1) What is the difference in philosophy between the charge of Moshe, as stated in 13:17 and the experience of the people (13:33)? What point is Rabbi Eger making?

2) Why does taking a longer view sometimes help us overcome some of the short-term obstacles in our goals?

3) What were the consequences of the spies' not "seeing from the mountain tops"?

4) Think of your own experience. Give an example of how looking at an issue from the broader perspective gave you a better view and a more hopeful result?

D'var Torah - Korah

"And the earth opened its mouth and swallowed them up, and their houses, and all Korah's people and all their possessions." Numbers 16:32

A Hasidic master, Rabbi Sar Shalom of Belz, explains why the Torah states that to punish the rebels against Moshe, the earth "opened its mouth." He says that since these 250 rebels, Korah's cohorts, sinned with their mouths, through making false accusations against Moshe, they were punished by having the earth literally "open its mouth" and swallow them up. This is known in rabbinic literature as "**midah k-neged midah**," or "measure for measure." Punishment comes, say the ancient rabbis, in accordance with the crime. A crime committed by the mouth is punished by the mouth (of the earth).

It is difficult for us today to accept the notion that every sin is punished, measure for measure, in kind. But perhaps there is an underlying truth to this old theological notion. It is expressed in the popular adage, "What goes around comes around." In other words, somehow, though we don't know precisely in what way, when we go astray, we pay the price.

Four Questions

1) How does the Rabbi of Belz take advantage of the Torah's metaphor of the "earth opening its mouth?"

2) Explain the phrase "divine retribution." Do you believe it?

3) In what way might this Hasidic interpretation reflect a degree of truth?

4) Can you give examples of people who have paid a penalty, "measure for measure?" Has it ever happened it you? Should this be the way justice is meted out?

D'var Torah - Hukat

"And Adonai spoke to Moshe: 'Speak to the rock to yield its water' ... And Moshe struck the rock with his rod twice and water came forth abundantly." Numbers 20: 7, 8, 11

Moshe could not fulfill his life-long dream of entering the Promised Land, because he disobeyed God's orders to **speak** to the rock, and instead **hit** the rock. The Talmudic rabbis interpreted this passage, which on the surface appears to mete out a severe punishment for a seemingly minor infraction, by explaining that there is a world of difference between the two approaches described in this passage.

There are two philosophies of education implied herein. God wants Moshe to be the kind of leader who **speaks**, not **strikes**. The best way to change people, to effect change in others, is to do it with **words**, not **sticks**. Another way to express this idea is this: the gentle, caring, persuasive, approach in influencing people is more effective than using force, or employing authoritarian method. Moshe, in this unfortunate incident, espoused an educational philosophy that was opposed to what God wanted. This severe punishment was inflicted to teach him and the generations following that conflicts must be resolved by discussion not force, by speaking not striking.

Four Questions

1) Do you think the rabbis are stretching their interpretation? Is this legitimate midrashic license? 2) Can you give examples of the difference in these two

educational philosophies in a variety of settings, such as home, school, etc.? How would the philosophies be manifested?

3) What is your own preference in style for helping others to change?

4) When it is right to use force, and when to prefer words?

D'var Torah - Balak

"God said to Bilaam: 'You must not curse the (Israelite) people, for they are blessed." Numbers 22:12

Rashi, (Troyes, France, 1040-1135), creates a fictional dialog, based on the Torah, between God and the Mesopotamian prophet, Bilaam, whom the Moabite King Balak called to curse the Israelite nation. First, God tells Bilaam: You must not curse the Israelites. Bilaam answers: Then I will bless them. God: They don't need your blessing; they are already blessed.

Rashi continues with a parable. People say to the hornet: I want neither your honey nor your sting. (God says to Bilaam, we want neither your curses nor your blessings!)

In a collection of biblical commentaries compiled by Rabbi Chaim Sofer (Mukachevo, Ukraine - pub. 1886) called *Divray Shaaray Chaim*, an interesting thought is added to Rashi's dialog. Namely, that there are two ways to destroy the Jewish people - by cursing them or blessing them. Some anti-Semites think that oppression will end the Jewish People; others believe that the best way to do away with the Jews is to give them all the friendship and freedom in the world. That way they will assimilate and disappear by themselves. The answer to Bilaam and Balak, then, is "I want neither your honey nor your sting, I want neither your blessings or your curses!" Just leave me alone, and I'll find my own way to survive and thrive.

Four Questions

1) How does Rashi expand upon the words of the Torah?

2) In what way does Rabbi Chaim Sofer take Rashi's words one step further?

3) Which way have anti-Semites had more success in fighting Jews, through vinegar or honey? Explain.

4) What are you doing to help preserve the Jewish People? Can you give some examples?

D'var Torah - Pinhas

"Thus (says God) I give to him (Pinhas) My covenant of Shalom." Numbers 25:12

In acting with spontaneous and passionate zeal, Pinhas killed an Israelite man, Zimri ben Salu, and a Moabite woman, Cozbi bat Tzur, who were engaging in lewd idolatrous acts, together with other Israelite men and Moabite women. Post-biblical commentators take a mixed view toward Pinhas' zealous act, many viewing it as rash and thoughtless, filled with pure emotion and religious fury. Though the Torah gives him great reward for his deed, the rabbis qualify and diminish his credit. One rabbi in the Talmud (Tractate **Sanhedrin** 82b) wanted to excommunicate Pinhas for his act. Despite the passionate love of God and Israel which motivated him, in his view, the means did not justify the end.

One talmudic rabbi points out that the Hebrew letter "vav" in the word **Shalom** is cut in half in the Torah text. He points out (**Kiddushin** 66b) that this "***vav ketee-ah***" - amputated vav - is intentional to show that the reward of "peace" (Shalom) given to Pinhas was not complete. It was only a partial peace, because the act of Pinhas was not an unqualified gesture of success. Zealotry is not looked upon favorably by Jewish tradition, and the rabbis tried to find ways to explain the Torah's reward to Pinhas without letting him become a hero whom others would want to emulate?

Four Questions

1) According to the Talmud, why is the Hebrew letter "**vav**" in the word "Shalom" cut short?

2) Why would some rabbis not approve of the passionate act of Pinhas?

3) Can you think of other biblical heroes who faced similar threats and yet held back from extremism? 4) To whom would you compare Pinhas today? When would you feel yourself justified in acting like Pinhas?

D'var Torah - Matot

"Adonai spoke to Moshe: Avenge the Israelites on the Midianites.... And Moshe said to the people: Send armed men to battle.... The Israelites made war on the Midianites and slew every male." Numbers 31: 1,7

This brutal war presents difficulties for religious readers who wonder why God would command such total destruction and killing. Rabbi Hertz in his commentary notes: "We are no longer acquainted with the circumstances that justified the ruthlessness with which (this war) was waged, and therefore we cannot satisfactorily meet the various objections that have been raised...."

Rashi (1135-1204 - Troyes, France) makes an interesting comment on the directive of Moshe to send armed men to battle. Men, Rashi explains, who are righteous people. Why righteous people? Perhaps because war is brutal, under any circumstances, even a so-called "clean" war, or a justified war, such as the war against Hitler. There is no way a soldier can emerge from battle exactly the way he was before. War makes people callous and less sensitive to killing and destruction. Perhaps if they start out as **righteous** people with high morals, they will suffer less negative effects of participating in a war.

Four Questions

1) Why do both Rabbi Joseph Hertz and the medieval commentator Rashi find difficulty with the kind of war the Torah commands to wage with Midian?

2) Why does going into battle necessarily affect one's personality?

3) What wars do you know of which were more justified, or less justified?

4) When is it permissible to fight in a war, and when (if ever) should one refuse? Under what circumstances can you see yourself fighting (or refusing) in a war?

D'var Torah - Mas-ay

"You shall provide cities of refuge to which a manslayer, one who acted without intention, may flee."

Numbers 35:11

Rabbenu Bahya ben Asher (Saragossa, Spain, 1255-1340) notices the importance which this verse attaches to one's **intentions**. The law that a person who commits murder can flee to a city of refuge for protection applies only to one who did not commit premeditated murder.

Rabbenu Bahya then carries this thought to the next step. He emphasizes that **all** the mitzvot (commandments) and transgressions listed in the Torah are connected to the **intention** of the person who carries out the act involved.

Four Questions

1) What importance does Rabbenu Bahya see in the word "intention"?

2) Do you believe that all commandments and sins are heightened if they are done with intention (**kavvanah**)?

3) What effect does **kavvanah** (intention) have on the performance of an act?

4) In what ways can you bring more **kavvanah** to the acts you perform?

D'var Torah - Devarim

"Adonai, your God, has multiplied you so that you are as numerous as the stars of heaven." Deuteronomy 1:10

In the last month of the 40th year after the Exodus from Egypt, Moshe summarizes the Israelites' journey and the laws that were commanded during that time. During the years preceding this momentous time - just weeks away from entering the Promised Land - Moshe reminds the people how they grew in number. They are now so many that, as the stars, they are beyond counting.

Rabbi Samson Raphael Hirsch (Frankfurt, Germany, 1808-1888) notes the various nuances of the metaphor of stars. The Jewish people are large in number, as the stars. But, he warns, do not be misled by the enormity of the multitude of the stars. One might think that since there are so many stars in the sky, that each individual star has no special importance. Rabbi Hirsch points out that the comparison of Israel to stars means that each individual member of the nation is important, just as each star is important. Each star is a world unto itself. It is by no means insignificant. Similarly, each Jew has a crucial role to play in the history of Israel. God has assigned to each of us a special mission and helps us achieve it, thereby helping us perform a special role and a unique purpose on earth.

Four Questions

1) Explain the Torah's phrase "as numerous as the stars."

2) Why is it considered a blessing for the Israelite People to be as numerous as the stars?

3) In what ways is the People of Israel similar to the stars in the sky? Is the number of Jews in the world at any given historical moment important in any way?

4) Do you think each Jew on earth has a unique role? What might yours be?

D'var Torah - Va-et-hanan

"Hear, O Israel! Adonai is our God, Adonai is One." Deuteronomy 6:4

We all know that the Sh'ma is recited twice daily by the traditional Jew, "when you lie down and when you rise up." It is also customary to recite the Sh'ma on the deathbed. A new light has been shed on this practice by people studying near-death experiences. The connection between the unity **(ehad)** of the universe , and the experience of a brush with death has received a novel interpretation in recent times.

Joan Borysenko, a cell biologist, psychologist, spiritual teacher, and author of many best-selling books, recently was interviewed by *New Age Journal* (May/June 1993, p. 129), and said this:

I...think that, as time goes on, we're going to see a growing interest in the spiritual…and I think this will come about in part by people who've had near-death experiences.…One man I met said it very clearly: … that when he was out of his body, it was obvious to him that he was connected to everything, that we're all interconnected.… He cannot look at a tree without feeling a kinship with that tree.

We now have these new mystics, who strangely enough are a result of our medical technology - they should have been dead but got resuscitated. That man I just mentioned…said that the secret of happiness is… recognizing that all things are connected, and sending out love along those connections. If you go through your life acknowledging all the things around you for their magnificence and recognize that you're part of it, then you're going to be healed.

Four Questions

1) What is the tie between the Sh'ma and spirituality?

2) Do you believe reports of near-death experiences?

3) Does the report above connect the first line of the Sh'ma with the first paragraph of the Sh'ma? (Hint: Unity and Love).

4) What do you think of when you recite the Sh'ma?

D'var Torah - Ekev

"And if you obey My mitzvot which I command you this day to love Adonai your God and to serve God with all your heart and with all your soul."

Deuteronomy 11:13

The famous commentator *Sfat Emet* (Rabbi Yehudah Aryeh Leib Alter of Ger, 1847-1905, Poland) explains that the word "if" is important here, because it implies that there is a choice in how we Jews approach the **mitzvot**, (the rules, obligations and rituals) of the Torah. If we approach them with happiness and a warm feeling, we will succeed in understanding and enjoying them. Further, "if" we obey God's laws and obey the traditions of Judaism with satisfaction and happiness, then we will love God with all our heart and all our soul.

The Gerer Rebbe further quotes the Mishnah in *Pirke Avot* which says that "The reward of a **mitzvah** is a **mitzvah**." In other words, through the pleasure and joy of the **mitzvah**, we are likely to keep the **mitzvah** in all its facets - and derive the intended benefits from it. This sense of pleasure, anticipation and joy should precede our performing the **mitzvot**, and by doing so, we will consequently reap the benefits of doing them. This is why, he explains, we say a **b'racha** before we perform a **mitzvah**, to acknowledge the joy and appreciation we feel in our heart before doing a **mitzvah** (commandment).

Four Questions

1) Why does the Sfat Emet focus on the word "if?"

2) Why is Judaism often seen as a religion of sadness and persecution instead of satisfaction and joy?

3) How can we increase our enjoyment of performing **mitzvot** by saying a "**b'racha**?"

4) Does Judaism bring joy to your life? Or is it more of a burden? How can you make it bring you more joy? What philosophy of Judaism will make it a burden, and what attitude will make it bring joy?

D'var Torah - Re-eh

"Be sure that you do not partake of the blood; for the blood is the life, and you must not consume the life with the meat." Deuteronomy 12:23

Being victims for so much of our history, the Jewish People has had a long history of hatred of bloodshed. But it is not just because of our unfortunate history of anti-Semitism and being the target of many enemies who found Jewish blood very cheap. There is a more fundamental reason.

In the Sidrah of **Re-eh**, we are told that when animals are sacrificed on the altar, no blood must be eaten. In Deuteronomy 12:23 we read: "Make certain that you do not eat of the blood, for the blood is the **life**, and you must not consume the life with the flesh." Our ancestors sensed that blood is the essence of a living creature. We often use the expression "life-blood," when referring to the essence of life. When someone is dying, we say s/he is "bleeding to death." Because blood is the *sine qua non* of life, it represents the sanctity of human life, and it must not be consumed. Kosher meat must have the blood removed before it can be eaten.

This abhorrence for eating blood, and for blood altogether, is the biblical, ethical root of the Jewish hatred for violence. Those who are familiar with Jewish law and tradition, and who understand and respect our long history of observing the laws of Kashrut, will grasp the reason for our hatred of violence and bloodshed. It flows from our deep and historical reverence for the holiness of life.

Four Questions

1) What are some reasons for our abhorrence of blood?

2) Is this more true in the 20th century, or less true?

3) Is the shedding of blood in self-defense permissible?

4) Have you every considered being a vegetarian - and thus avoiding any possibility of consuming blood?

D'var Torah - Shoftim

"When you go forth to battle...." Deuteronomy 20:1

The Torah lists a group of people who are exempt from battle, such as one who was recently married. In America today, even when the draft was in existence, there have always been legal exemptions for valid personal situations, including conscientious objectors (people who believe war is never an option).

The Talmud adds one more category: "One who talks between the placing of the *tefillin* of the hand and the *tefillin* of the head" (**Sota** 44b). This seems like a strange reason for an exemption from military duty. The meaning seems to be this: The *tefillin* on the head represents thought, and the *tefillin* on the hand represents action. When there is an interruption between thought and action, there is inconsistency - or, if you will, hypocrisy. There is no room for a hypocrite in the military. Motivation and sincerity are prerequisites for a good soldier and an effective army. This is a good lesson for all of us. There should never be a gap between our profession and our implementation, between what we say and what we do. Too many people in every society think and talk one way, and act another way. This can lead to inaction at best, and hypocrisy at worst. There is an old Hebrew folk expression: **Ehad ba-peh echad ba-lev**, which expresses a similar thought. That is, one should be consistent in both heart and mouth, in what we feel and what we say.

In other words, an authentic and honorable person is congruent in feelings, thought, speech and action.

Four Questions

1) Why do the rabbis add another category to military exemptions?

2) Does it seem to fit into the other categories?

3) Can you think of some examples when speech and action have not been consistent?

4) How can you be more consistent in your feelings, your speech, and your deeds?

D'var Torah - Kee Teze

"When you go forth to war against your enemies, Adonai your God will deliver them into your hands, and you will take them captive." Deuteronomy 21:10

On the verse above, Aharon Yaakov Greenberg, in *Itturay Torah*, quotes several commentators from several different countries and generations, and yet many of them give the same interpretation. The "enemy" referred to in the Torah is none other than our "**Yetzer Ha-Ra**" - the evil inclination. In other words, as Pogo once said in an unforgettable line, "We have seen the enemy and it is us!" We are our own worst enemies.

The pressure we bring on ourselves with our frantic schedule, the perfectionism we foist upon ourselves (and our children), the out-of-control chase for material things is something we, not our neighbors the Jones (Goldbergs?) do to us. Yes, the **"Yetzer Ha-Ra,"** our neurotic blind spots, and the gaps in our spiritual and emotional maturity, are without doubt our worst enemies.

The commentators suggest that the solution is to "go to war" with our "**Yetzer Ha-Ra**", don't just sit back and let it control our lives. Work on doing the unfinished business of growing up that we all left behind in pursuit of other "more important" goals.

Four Questions

1) What is the "**Yetzer Ha-Ra**?" Explain it in your own words.

2) How does it grow on us and in us? How can we do battle with this "enemy?"

3) Give some prominent examples of the way the "**Yetzer**

Ha-Ra" affects the average American.

4) How does it trick you in your life? How can you try to overcome it?

D'var Torah - Kee Tavo

"These are the terms of the Covenant which Adonai commanded Moshe to conclude with the Israelites in the Land of Moab, in addition to the Covenant which God made with them at Horeb (Mt. Sinai)." Deuteronomy 28:69

Rabbi Naftali Tzvi Yehudah Berlin (known by the acronym of his name, the **NETZIV** - 1817-1893, Poland), in his commentary on the Torah called *Ha-amek Davar*, asks a simple, yet obvious question: Why did God have to make a **second** Covenant with the People of Israel in the Land of Moab? Did not the Sinai Covenant, with all its majesty and numinous transcendence, suffice?

He suggests that each Covenant had its own purpose. The Covenant at Sinai was so that the People could study the Torah, learn the laws of the Torah and become familiar with its contents. The Covenant at Moab was for another reason - to **renew** the Torah, to expand its teaching, to apply its laws to modern conditions, to find new applications for the old laws and customs. Only by renewing the Torah would it be understood, practiced, and kept relevant to the masses.

Four Questions

1) What is a "Covenant," and why did the **NETZIV** find it necessary to suggest renewal for the Covenant?

2) Is the commentator reading back into the Torah the need for updating and application? Did the Torah actually recognize such a need?

3) What examples of laws in other legal systems, such as American Constitutional Law, can you think of that have needed, or still need, updating in later ages?

4) If you could modify or adapt any law that is on the books today, which one would you change? Why?

D'var Torah - Nitzavim

"Neither is the Torah beyond the sea...." Deut. 30:13

In 30:ll-14 Moshe impresses upon the people that the Torah is not far away, not beyond their reach either physically or in degree of difficulty. It is possible for every Jew to perform the **mitzvot**. The greatest risk is not in trying to fulfill the Torah, but rather in **not** trying.

Rabbi Saul Teplitz, tells the following story: A group of sailors was floating on a raft, about to sink, and thirsting to death. Drifting along, refusing to drink the ocean water because they knew it would be worse than not drinking, they were near death. Suddenly a boat appeared, and rescued them. Their first request was to ask for a drink of fresh water. They were informed that the water around them was not ocean water, because they were in the middle of the Amazon River, where the water is fresh. All they had to do was lower their buckets and drink!

It is the same with the Torah. It is all around us, and yet for some reason we are afraid, or ignorant of its contents, or intimidated because we think it is too difficult. Our fears are unfounded. The fresh life-giving waters of the Torah are close to us. They are "not too baffling, nor beyond our reach. They are not in the heavens or beyond the sea." (Deuteronomy. 30: 11-13). "No, the Torah is close to us, in our mouths and in our heart, to observe it." (v. 14).

Four Questions

1) Why is the water in the Amazon River compared to the waters of the Torah?

2) Why do people think the Torah is too difficult, too risky, too complicated or complex for them?

3) What are the two or three things that are the most common barriers to the observance of the Torah?

4) Are there any laws in the Torah which you find too difficult? How can you make them easier?

D'var Torah - Vayelekh

"Write this song for yourselves...." Deuteronomy 31:19

In the rabbinic tradition this last of the 613 mitzvot of the Torah is a command for each Jew to write a copy of a **Sefer Torah** for oneself (or have one written) (cf. Rambam, **Hilkhot Sefer Torah** 7). One way to fulfill this mitzvah is to write one letter of a Sefer Torah with the help of a **Sofer** (scribe). According to the logic of the Rambam (Spain and Egypt, 1135-1204) in his *Mishneh Torah* (Code of Jewish Law), even the absence of one letter makes a Sefer Torah invalid for public reading. Thus, by adding one letter an individual gets credit for writing (or completing) a whole **Sefer Torah**.

The *Sefer Ha-Hinukh*, written in 13th century Spain by an anonymous author who explains each of the 613 **mitzvot** of the Torah, offers another possibility. If one establishes an ample Jewish library with many commentaries on the Torah, this is the equivalent of writing a **Sefer Torah**.

Four Questions

1) How do you think the rabbis were able to read into this verse the mitzvah for each Jew to write and own his/her own **Sefer Torah**?

2) Have you ever seen a **Sofer** write a **Sefer Torah**? Can you describe some of the requirements and procedures for the proper writing of a "kosher" **Sefer Torah**?

3) Why is it important for each Jew to own his/her own **Sefer Torah**?

4) Why did the *Sefer Ha-Hinukh* consider owning a good Jewish library equal to writing a **Sefer Torah**? Do you think that you fulfill this mitzvah? Explain.

D'var Torah - Ha-azinu - Shabbat Shuvah

Shabbat Shuvah, the Shabbat between Rosh Hashanah and Yom Kippur takes its name from the first word of the Haftarah for the day: "**Shuvah Yisrael**," "Return, O Israel...." (Hosea 14:2).

Rabbi David Hartman, pioneer Israeli philosopher, orthodox Rabbi, wrote in his book, *Conflicting Visions - Spiritual Possibilities for Israel* (Schocken, 1990), about the possibility for reconciliation between Israel and the Palestinians:

"Rosh Hashanah and Yom Kippur are...a corrective to the despair that pervades so many Jewish hearts today. The spirit of Rosh Hashanah and Yom Kippur should inspire Jews to proclaim clearly to the Palestinians that they are our brothers in creation, that we share a deep moral reverence for the sacredness of human life. Jews have come home to Israel because of their deep historical sense of community. However, in coming home, we do not seek to weaken or destroy our profound sense of brotherhood with the Palestinian people. It was imperative that our respective histories and traditions not destroy our common humanity born of our shared belief in God as Adonai of Creation and majestic moral king of all humanity."

Four Questions

1) What is the connection between the High Holy Days and reconciliation with the Palestinians?

2) Do you support reconciliation?

3) What next steps should be taken to bring Israel and the Palestinians closer together?

4) How can **you** contribute to peace in the Middle East?

D’var Torah - Ve-Zot Ha’Brakhah

“Moshe commanded to us the Torah, an inheritance of the community of Yaakov [Israel].” Deuteronomy 33:4

These beautiful words have been set to music in a song that is taught to young children, to help them recognize the importance of the Torah. The Ramban (Nachmanides, Spain, 1194-1270) pays special attention to the fact that the text does not use the word “the house of Yaakov” or “the seed of Yaakov.” The word **kehillah**, or **community**, is used. Ramban points out that not only those who are **born** into the family of the People of Israel will receive the Torah, but others who **join** our people will also. He quotes, for example, Isaiah 56:6, which talks about those “who join with Adonai.” Thus, Jews-by-choice are also recipients of the Torah.

Four Questions

1) How does the Ramban explain the use of the word “community” of Yaakov?

2) How is a “community” different from a “race” or other biologically related group?

3) Why should Jews-by-choice, whose ancestors were not Jews in biblical days, receive the Torah?

4) How can you help to make Jews-by-choice feel more comfortable and part of the “community” of the Jewish People?

BOOK TWO

D'var Torah - Bereshit

"And God created a human in the Divine image. In the image of God was the human created." Genesis 1:27

Commentators have debated for centuries the meaning of the Hebrew word "tzelem," image. They gave many interpretations to the phrase which states that humans were created in God's "image."

The Mishnah (Tractate Sanhedrin 4:5) gives this explanation: When a mortal sovereign stamps the royal image on a coin, every coin made from that image is exactly alike. However, when Adonai put the stamp of the first human on humanity, every person deriving from the original one ("Adam" in Hebrew) is different from every other one.

The Mishnah is comparing the creation of the first human with a mold or stamp with which coins are shaped. The distinction it makes is that coins stamped from one original are all identical. Humans, made in God's image, created from the original "mold" of the first human, are all different.

Topics for Discussion:

1) What do you think the Torah means by saying that humans are created in the image of God?

2) How does the Mishnah understand the expression "image"?

3) Why is it important that each human being is born unique, different from all others?

4) What lessons do you derive from the fact that you are a totally unique creature? How does this idea affect your life?

D'var Torah - Noah

"These are the generations of Noah.... Noah walked with God." Genesis 6:9

Commentators throughout the ages have had mixed feelings about Noah. While the Torah declares that he was righteous and blameless, the Talmud interprets the phrase "in

his generation" as possibly meaning that in another generation, one in which more good people lived, Noach might not have been such an outstanding paragon of virtue.

Rabbi Moshe ben Hayim Alshekh (Safed, Eretz Yisrael, 1507-1600) suggests that Noah's problem was that he was concerned solely with pleasing himself and God, but did nothing to help humanity. The righteousness displayed by Noah was for show, for selfish purposes, to look good in the eyes of the Creator, but he did not show sufficient concern for the human race. For this reason it was left to his descendent, Abraham, to become the father of the Jewish People.

Topics for Discussion:

1) Why do some commentators praise Noah, and others criticize him?

2) What is the Torah's intention in saying that Noah "walked with God?" How does Rabbi Moshe Alshekh interpret this phrase?

3) How can a person strike a balance between serving God and humanity?

4) In what ways do you serve God? In what ways do you serve your fellow humans and the planet in which

we live? Are you satisfied that you do both sufficiently? How might you do better?

D'var Torah - Lekh Lekha

"And Adonai said to Avram...'Lift your eyes and look up from where you are..., for all the land that you see to you I give it, and your children, forever."

Genesis 13:14-15

Throughout Jewish history Eretz Yisrael was considered to be "higher" than other places. In these *p'sukim* (verses) we find Adonai telling Avram to "lift" his eyes to see the Land. When a person makes a pilgrimage to Eretz Yisrael it is called in Hebrew *aliyah le-regel* — going, or walking **up**. Today when a person settles in Israel we call it "making *aliyah*".

From the time of Avraham Avinu to our own day, Jews have considered Eretz Yisrael to be on a higher plane than other places. It possessed a special holiness. Whenever one is located in the Land that person is considered to be fulfilling a great mitzvah just by virtue of visiting or living there. The Talmud says that the very air of Eretz Yisrael brings special wisdom to those who reside there.

Topics for Discussion:

1) What is the significance of Adonai's command to Avram to "lift" his eyes and look out upon the Land?

2) What other phrases does the Hebrew language use to teach us that Eretz Yisrael is considered to be **higher** than other places?

3) Why is Eretz Yisrael considered to be on a higher plane than other places?

4) Imagine that you are now in Eretz Yisrael. In what ways do you feel higher, or more holy? In your

imagination think of ways in which your visit or your life in Eretz Yisrael would bring you a sense of **elevation**. Explain.

D'var Torah - Vayera

"And the angel of Adonai said to Avraham, 'Do not raise your hand against the boy, or do anything to him." Genesis 22:11

A standard principle in rabbinic interpretation of the Torah is that any repetitive phrase is not merely rhetorical, but carries some specific lesson. In our verse, the angel could have sufficed by saying "Do not raise your hand against the lad." The seemingly extra (repetitive) phrase, "or do anything to him," must be there for a reason. Rashi (11th century, Troyes, France), Prince of commentators, says that the Torah is giving us just a summary of the conversation between the angel and Avraham. First, the angel said "Do not raise your hand...." Then Avraham replied "Did I come here for nothing? How about if I just make a small wound, and let a drop of blood flow?" The angel then replied "Do not do anything to him." Rashi gets reinforcement for his imaginative interpretation by reading the Hebrew for "anything," "m'umah," as "mum," "a wound." Thus, Rashi reads the angel's reply: "Do not even make a small wound!"

Why would Avraham want to even wound his only beloved son? Is there a strain of narrow-minded, single-focused fanaticism to serve God peering through Rashi's re-make of Avraham? Is Rashi telling us that even the best of us sometimes gets so caught up in what we think is God's will that we lose our senses?

Topics for Discussion:

1) How does Rashi expand the Torah's story of the conversation between the angel and Avraham? How does the commentator's version differ from the Torah text?

2) Why and how have fanatics throughout history lost their moral direction through a passion for their cause?

3) Explain this definition of a fanatic: Someone who, when he loses sight of his goal, redoubles his efforts."

4) Is Rashi saying that **anyone** has the potential for fanaticism? Do you? Explain.

D'var Torah - Hayay Sarah

"Let the young woman to whom I say, 'Please lower your pitcher so I may drink,' and she replies, 'Drink and I will also water your camels' - she will be the one whom You have chosen for Isaac." Genesis 24:14

Avraham's servant Eliezer is sent to find a bride for Isaac. From the story we learn that Eliezer's criterion for a fitting bride is that she is asked to give drink to Eliezer, but she goes one step further and offers drink also to his animals. Her kindness to animals is proof that she is worthy of being an "em b'Yisrael" a mother in Israel, and one of the mothers of our people.

Rabbi Ovadiah Sforno (1470-1550, Bologna, Italy) offers a related explanation to prove Rebekkah's worthiness. He says that a person should always ask for less than is needed, and the person asked should also give more than is asked for. These are examples of traits of kindness and consideration which every human being should espouse. Since Rebekkah possessed these traits, she was such a worthy person.

Topics for Discussion:

1) What are the two qualities which made Rebekkah a worthy person to be an ancestor of the Jewish People?

2) What category of qualities was Eliezer seeking in a wife for Isaac?

3) Why was it important for Rebekkah to have these qualities?

4) How important does Judaism consider these qualities in judging the worth of a person? Do you

consider these qualities important in your character? Are you pleased with your efforts in this direction? Explain.

D'var Torah - Toldot

"The boys grew up and while Esav became a skillful hunter, a man of the outdoors, Yaakov was a quiet man who stayed indoors." Genesis 25:27

The ancient rabbis (Midrash Rabba 63:10) suggest that Esav and his descendants (Romans and other military powers) loved to track and kill animals, and thus became warlike. Yaakov and his descendants (the Jewish People), on the other hand, preferred study and intellectual pursuits. It is true that when Jews were not in their own land they did not fight wars. They were powerless, and became accustomed to matters of spirit and mind. Since the year 70 C.E., until the return to Eretz Yisrael in the late 19th and 20th centuries, Jews have had a history of eschewing conflict whenever possible.

This was not always true of Yaakov's descendants however. In the days of the biblical kingdoms, and since the re-establishment of Medinat Yisrael, Jews have done their share of fighting. In the past half-century Israel's wars have been mostly in self-defense. From the perspective of the entire panorama of 4000 years of Jewish history we Jews have considered ourselves as basically not a war-loving nation. It is our hope and ideal that our Torah values have kept us from fighting and preoccupied with study and matters of the spirit.

Topics for Discussion:

1) How does the Torah distinguish between the twin brothers, Esav and Yaakov?

2) How does the Midrash embellish the differences between them?

3) Do you think it is true that Jews have generally avoided warfare and bloodshed?

4) Do you believe that studying Torah can influence a person to be peace-loving, and hating war and fighting? Can it influence an individual to be more gentle and less aggressive? Has Torah study influenced you that way?

D'var Torah - Vayeze

"Jacob dreamed: a ladder was set on the earth, and its top reached to Heaven; and angels of God were going up and down on it." Genesis 28:12

Freud wrote that dreams are the royal road to the unconscious. They tell us a great deal about ourselves. From the days of the Tanakh to our own time, people have paid attention to what they dream, and often attempted to interpret their dreams, and find in them many important meanings about their lives.

One of the famous Hasidic masters, Rabbi Meir of Promishlan (Ukraine, 18th century), notes that an individual's personality is reflected in his dreams. Long before Freud, Rabbi Meir understood that what we dream is a part of who we are. Our dreams, says the Hasidic teacher, reflect our ideals and aspirations. He compares the dreams of Jacob with those of Pharaoh in the Book of Shemot. In Jacob's dream he saw a ladder reaching into Heaven, whereas Pharaoh dreamed of cows!

Topics for Discussion:

1) What message did Rabbi Meir of Promishlan find in one's dreams?

2) What do we learn about Yaakov's dream at Beth El? How has it been interpreted in history? (Hint: where is the bottom and the top of the ladder?)

3) Do you believe that dreams tell us about one's personality? If so, what kind of person was Yaakov? What kind of person was Pharaoh? About what did the late Rev. Martin Luther King, Jr. dream?

4) Have you ever paid attention to your dreams? Ever written any down for further reflection? What have you learned about yourself from your dreams?

D'var Torah - Vayishlah

"The man [angel] who was wrestling with Yaakov said to Yaakov: 'Your name shall no longer be Yaakov, but Yisrael, for you have wrestled with both divine and human beings, and you have prevailed.'" Genesis 32:29

Bestowing a name on someone in Jewish tradition is a very significant event in one's life. Names are considered more than just what people call you. They represent the values you stand for, the ideals you strive to achieve. When Jewish children are formally named, in synagogue or at home, they are often given names of family members whose lives their parents want them to emulate. Parents hope that a baby named after a grandmother, for example, will live up to the high ideals of the life of that grandmother.

When Yaakov ("the supplanter") becomes Yisrael ("wrestles with God"), the alteration in the name seems to imply that it will be the task of Yaakov from then on to struggle with divine matters, and be a loyal teacher of divine principles. Other commentators say that Yisrael may originally have meant "May God rule," perhaps implying that Yaakov must help spread God's rule. In either case, Yaakov (Yisrael) now has a lot to live up to.

Topics for Discussion:

1) What is the significance of one's name in Jewish tradition?

2) Under what circumstances might one change one's name? For what purpose?

3) Why did the angel wrestling with Yaakov *bless* him with a new name? What task falls upon the Jewish people because we are all the "children of Israel"?

4) Do you know the meaning of your Hebrew name? After whom were you named? What ideals emanate from the meaning of your name, or from the ideals of the person for whom you were named?

D'var Torah - Vayeshev

"Yosef's brothers brought the *k'tonet pasim* ('coat of many colors'; or 'ornamented tunic'), dipped in blood, to their father, and said, 'We found this. Is it your son's?' And Yaakov recognized it, and answered: 'Yes, it is my son's. A wild beast devoured him!'" Genesis 37:32-33

The favoritism shown by Yaakov to his youngest son, Yosef, made his other 10 sons jealous. Rabbi Pinhas Peli (*Torah Today*, p. 39) suggests a novel interpretation. Perhaps Yaakov knew what the brothers had done because of their jealousy. In their anger at both Yosef and their father, Yaakov, they refer to Yosef as "your son." They deny him his very name. Yaakov, understanding their jealousy, and the evil deed they committed against him, fights back and replies: "Yes, this is *my son's* tunic. Wild beasts - namely, you evil and jealous brothers - have devoured Yosef!"

Topics for Discussion:

1) Do you think Yaakov really knew the true story of what happened to Yosef? How does Rabbi Peli explain this conversation? How does his interpretation differ from that of the Torah?

2) What failures in Yaakov and in his 11 sons brought about these terrible events?

3) Is it fair for a parent to favor one child over others? In what ways might it sometimes be "normal" and in what ways "unjust"?

4) Are there times when you favor one parent/child over another? If you have, how have you dealt with these

feelings? If not, how have you prevented yourself from doing so? How can one avoid the dangers of favoritism that can lead to problems such as those in the story of Yaakov, Yosef and his brothers?

D'var Torah - Miketz

"Pharaoh dreamed that he was near the Nile when seven beautiful and robust cows came up, and they grazed in the reed grass." Genesis 41:1-2

As we learn later the beautiful and robust cows in Pharaoh's dream symbolize seven years of plenty which will come to Egypt. Two separate commentaries come to a similar conclusion. The Midrash (Bereshit Rabba 89:4) notes that the Hebrew word for reed grass (*ahu*), in which the fat cows grazed, is similar to the Hebrew word *ahvah*, friendship. The seven cows grazing in the reed grass thus remind us that when people are prosperous, during years of plenty, they behave toward each other in **friendship**.

Rashi reaches the same point by noting that the cows are referred to as "beautiful." He says the beautiful cows remind us of how **beautifully** people behave toward each other when everyone is well fed and satisfied with their material status.

Topics for Discussion:

1) What is the Hebrew word for **reed grass**, and how does the Midrash interpret it?

2) What do the seven beautiful cows represent, and how does Rashi interpret the fact that they are "beautiful"?

3) What theory of human nature are both commentator espousing? Do hunger and poverty sometimes increase a nation's chances of going to war? Explain.

4) Do you behave more pleasantly when you are not hungry, and when your material needs are met? What control can we, or should we, exercise when our unmet physical needs put us in a bad mood? Can you give some personal examples?

D'var Torah - Vayigash

"Yaakov's household of seventy persons went down to Egypt.... They settled in the region of Goshen." Genesis 46:27-28

This is the first time and place in history when the Jewish People were living together as a separate community in the Diaspora. Goshen has been called the first "ghetto" in Jewish history.

In the Middle Ages Jews were forced to live in certain regions of their countries of habitation by their gentile oppressors. In Spain it was called the *Juderia*, and in Germany the *Judengasse.* In 1516 the Jews of Venice were forced into an area called a "ghetto" which in Italian means "foundry," a place where metals are cast. From that time on the concept of the *ghetto* has had the connotation of a segregated Jewish community in the Diaspora. Until the Nazis restored forced ghettos (restricted areas of certain towns) the ghetto had been abolished in 19th century Europe. Today **ghetto** also refers to a **voluntary** Jewish neighborhood.

In the Middle Ages the ghetto had the advantage of enabling Jews to preserve their religious, cultural and communal life, but made them vulnerable to overcrowding, disease and physical attack.

Topics for Discussion:

1) Does the Egyptian region of Goshen in *Bereshit* qualify as a "ghetto"?

2) What were the advantages and disadvantages of living in a ghetto?

3) In the modern world is it good or bad for Jews to live in distinct neighborhoods and communities? What are the advantages and disadvantages?

4) Do you prefer living in a heavily-populated Jewish community, or to have a more "integrated" community, with peoples of all faiths, creeds and ethnic backgrounds? Why?

D'var Torah - Vayehi

"Yissakhar is a strong-boned donkey...." Genesis 49:14

Rashi, following the Midrash (Bereshit Rabba 98:12) interprets this to mean that Yissakhar carried the burden of Torah study, while his brother Zevulun (blessed in the preceding verse, 49:13) did physical labor. Both are children of Yaakov and Leah, and were close in birth order, territory and other ways. The relationship of these two brothers has come to symbolize the sharing of financial and cultural/spiritual duties. It often happened in history that within a Jewish family one or more siblings earned money for the family, while the other(s) could have the luxury of studying Torah full time.

Maimonides (Rambam), for example, studied Torah while his brother David earned a living for both families by trading precious stones with India. When David drowned in a shipwreck, Rambam practiced medicine to support himself, and could only spend part of his time studying, teaching and writing. In today's world we use the metaphor of the Yissakhar-Zevulun relationship to refer to one in which some support the study of Torah financially while others devote themselves more fully to actual study.

Topics for Discussion:

1) On what does the Midrash base its understanding of the relationship between Yissakhar and Zevulun?

2) Do you think there is fairness in this kind of relationship? Does it make sense?

3) Can you give examples of people who support Torah study financially and others who spend their entire vocation in study of Torah?

4) If you had a choice, which brother would you prefer to be? Explain.

D'var Torah - Shemot

"[Pharaoh said:] The Israelites are too numerous for us. Let us deal cleverly with them, lest they increase.... But the more the Egyptians oppressed them, they more they increased...." Exodus 1:9, 10, 12

Rashi, based on the Talmud (Sotah 11a), says that it was God's intention to teach Egypt a lesson. When Pharaoh said "lest they increase," the Holy Spirit said "so will they increase." It seems that God plants within people the power to resist oppression. The more the oppressors inflict pain and punishment on their victims, the stronger becomes the will of the oppressed. The metaphor of the battle of wills between God and the Egyptians is symbolic of the struggle between all oppressors and their victims. Increased oppression merely hardens the will of the downtrodden to resist and end the oppression.

Topics for Discussion:

1) How does Rashi explain the words of Pharaoh about his fear of the increase in number of the Israelites and the Torah's comment that the Israelites continued to increase?

2) Why do oppressed peoples continually resist their oppressor? Does their resistance come in some way from God? Is oppression against God's plan for the world?

3) What groups of people in our own day have shown resistance to prejudice and discrimination, and have successfully overcome them? Did the power of

their enemy urge them on to resist? Does oppression therefore carry the seeds of its own destruction?

4) Have you as a Jew felt resistance toward anti-Semitism against yourself or other Jews? Have you felt an urge to fight against this unfair treatment? What happened?

D'var Torah - Va-ayra

"I [God] have now heard the moaning of the Israelite people because the Egyptians are keeping them enslaved...." Shemot 6:5

When we read of the suffering, groaning and moaning of the Israelite people we feel a deep sense of sorrow and compassion for these slaves. However, there is another side to reading in the Torah about their moaning. The famous Hasidic rebbe, Rabbi Yitzhak Meir Alter of Ger (Poland, 1799-1866), the founder of the Hasidic dynasty of Gerer Rebbes, takes the Israelites' complaints to be something very constructive. He notes that the first step in redemption is to know and feel the problems of living in Exile (*Galut*). For a long time the Israelites seemed to accept their lot, and not feel their internal alienation from the foreign culture and religion under whom they were forced to live. Once they recognized how detrimental it was to be living outside their Homeland (Eretz Yisrael), it was possible for them to begin working toward a solution - namely, the Exodus and settling the Land of their own.

For this reason, explains Rabbi Yitzhak Meir Alter, when we eat *maror* (bitter herbs) at the Pesah Seder, we mix them with the sweet *Haroset* (nuts, apples and wine), to show that even the bitterness of slavery had a "sweet" side to it. It was the first step to Redemption.

Topics for Discussion:

1) What is the Gerer Rebbe's interpretation of the word "moaning"?

2) When can moaning be helpful, and when is it harmful?

3) Do you think that all difficult situations bear the seeds of something positive?

4) What example can you think of in your life in which a difficulty turned into something helpful, useful and positive? When have you found something sweet coming out of something bitter?

D'var Torah - Bo

"You shall guard the Matzot...." Exodus 12:17

Rashi (France, 1040-1105) explains that guarding, or carefully watching the matzot (unleavened bread), is so that the matzot will not become sour. When bread is left for too long it rises (leavens) through the souring process. Were the matzot to rise, they would then be **leavened** bread, and unfit for Pesach use.

The Hasidic sage, Rabbi Naftali of Ropshitz (Galicia, Poland, 1760-1827) gives an interesting interpretation of Rashi's comment. When Rashi writes that "they should not become sour," Rabbi Naftali says it refers to the **persons** who perform the mitzvah of eating matzah. In other words, says Rabbi Naftali, when a person does an important mitzvah such as eating matzah, it should be done with a sense of joy and celebration, and not with "sourness," or a "sour face." The Torah is thus teaching us to "guard the matzot" from being eaten with the wrong attitude, with a sense of heavy obligation and drudgery instead of with pleasure and satisfaction.

Topics for Discussion:

1) Explain the difference between the explanation of "guard the matzot" given by Rashi and that of Rabbi Naftali.

2) What is the connection between the idea of souring of bread, and souring of a face?

3) Do you agree that it is preferable to perform mitzvot out of love and joy than out of pressure and drudgery?

4) What are some ways in which you can add joy to the performance of the mitzvot you perform, and reduce any feeling of routine and dissatisfaction which may arise in the performance of mitzvot?

D'var Torah - Be-shalah

"When Pharaoh let the people go, God did not take them through the land of the Philistines, even though it would have been nearer. God said, 'The people may change their minds when they see war, and return to Egypt.'" Exodus 13:17

Had the Israelites taken the shorter route to Eretz Yisrael, it would have been a journey of several weeks instead of forty years. God intentionally led them away from the main road to avoid war with the Philistines.

Rabbi Moshe Feinstein, one of this century's leading traditional interpreters, asks the question: Why did not God, who is all-powerful, transform the Philistines into timid people, so they would not want to fight the Israelites? After all, if God hardened Pharaoh's heart, God could also change the Philistines' heart.

Rabbi Feinstein answers that the Philistines were by nature a war-like people, and to make them timid would mean that God would have had to take away their Free Will, and transform their essential nature. God was not inclined to remove from the Philistines their most precious gift of Free Will.

Topics For Discussion:

1) Why did God lead the Israelites through the long path around the Sinai desert?

2) How does Rabbi Moshe Feinstein answer the question as to why God did not simply make the Philistines more placid and less war-like?

3) Do you think Free Will is an important part of human behavior? What relationship does it have to ethical actions?

4) Does Rabbi Feinstein's answer supply you with answers to other difficult questions about God's power? Have you ever prayed that people not harm you, and by so doing, ask God to influence another person's Free Will? In your opinion is that a valid prayer? Explain.

D'var Torah - Yitro

"Six days shall you labor and do all your work." Exodus 20:9

The Midrash (Mekhilta, chapter 7) raises an interesting question. Why could not the Torah have said "Six days shall you labor and do your work"? Why is the word "all" included? Is it possible for a person to totally finish all of one's work in six days? Is there not more to do when the Shabbat is over?

The answer given by the rabbis in the Midrash is that one is commanded to rest on Shabbat by being in a state of mind that feels *as though* all one's work were completed. Even though it is in fact impossible to complete all one's work in six days, when Shabbat comes we must put out of our mind any unfinished business, and think and act as if all our work had been completed.

Topics for Discussion:

1) How does the Midrash explain the use of the word "all" in the command to keep Shabbat?

2) Is it possible to change how we feel on Shabbat? Is it possible to change our feelings and consciousness at will?

3) Why do the rabbis think it is important to be in the proper emotional frame of mind to celebrate Shabbat properly?

4) Has the thought about "unfinished business" or matters of school or work ever interfered with your Shabbat mood? Do you think you can let go of such matter on Shabbat and put them out of your mind?

D'var Torah - Mishpatim

"If two people quarrel, and one hits the other with a stone or a fist... the one who hits must provide for healing." Exodus 21:18-19

The Hebrew for verse 19 contains a repetition of the word for healing (**rapo ye-rapey**). Repetition is often used for emphasis, but the commentators, believing that the sacred Torah would never use an unnecessary word, find special meaning in every instance of repetition. What then does the two-fold mention of the word "to heal" refer to?

Rabbi Menahem Hakohen, in his collection of comments on the Torah called *Torat Am - Shemot* (Tel Aviv: Modan, 1996, p. 202), suggests that the two-fold healing refers to emotional/spiritual healing and physical healing. He points out that all physical ailments have some root in a wound to the soul. For that reason when we pray for healing in the "Mee-she-bayrakh" during the Torah reading, we always mention "healing of the soul and healing of the body" (refuat hanefesh u'refuat haguf). Notice that healing of the **soul** comes first. Thus, if the soul is healed, it stands to reason that the body will then also be able to find healing.

Topics for Discussion:

1) Why do the commentaries find it necessary to comment on a repetitive word?

2) What is the interpretation of the repetition of the word "to heal"?

3) Do you believe that the condition of one's spirit and emotions have an effect on the body?

4) Have you ever noticed that being sad, angry, hurt or afraid helped bring on a physical ailment? Was healing your feelings (your soul) a part of healing your body?

D'var Torah - Terumah

"And let them (B'nai Yisrael) make me a *Mikdash* (Sanctuary) so that I may dwell among them." Exodus 25:8

One would expect this verse to read as follows: "Let them make me a *Mikdash* so that I may dwell ***in it.***" The fact that the verse informs us that God will dwell **among the people**, rather than saying that God will dwell in the *Mikdash*, causes several commentators to take notice and give an explanation.

Rabbi Moshe ben Haim Alshekh (1508-1593, Safed, Eretz Yisrael) suggests that the verse implies that every Jew must make a *Mikdash* (sanctuary) in his/her own heart. Every Jew must find a place within where the Shekhinah (God's Holy Presence) may dwell. In other words, when every Jew builds a *Mikdash* in the heart, then Adonai will be able to dwell within every one of them.

Topics for Discussion:

1) Why does Adonai want B'nai Yisrael to make a *Mikdash*? When the Sanctuary is built, where will God dwell?

2) How does Rabbi Moshe Alshekh explain the end of the verse, that Adonai will dwell among the people, instead of saying "in the Sanctuary"?

3) How can one make a place for God in one's heart?

4) Can you give some examples of times when you felt that Adonai was dwelling inside of you?

D'var Torah - Tezaveh

"You shall create an Altar on which to burn incense." Exodus 30:1

Incense was an important part of ancient worship. It is made from the resin and gums of certain trees. When burned, it gives off a fragrant odor. It helped to mute the unpleasant smell of burning animal flesh. In our passage it is described as a regular part of the sacrificial system, burned twice daily on the golden altar inside the sanctuary.

In Psalm 141:2 incense is used as a metaphor for prayer: "Let my prayer be as an offering of incense before You." The Talmudic sages note (Tanhuma, Tezaveh, 14) that each of the consonants in the Hebrew word for incense (*ketoret*) stands for one of the qualities associated with sincere prayer: *Kedushah* (holiness), *Tohorah* (purity), *Rahamim* (compassion), and *Tikvah* (hope).

Topics for Discussion:

1) What is the purpose of an incense offering in the Torah?

2) How did the ancient rabbis use the Hebrew word for incense to explain the qualities of sincere prayer?

3) Do you think these four concepts illuminate the purpose of prayer? Are there any other words you would add?

4) When you pray do you think you are able to encompass these four qualities in your prayer? Explain.

D'var Torah - Kee Tisa

"This is what every registered Israelite should give: a half-shekel...as an offering to Adonai." Exodus 30:13

Why should every Israelite contribute a half-shekel to the Sanctuary? Rabbi Hanokh Heinikh of Alexander (Poland, 1798-1872) answered by using the method of *gematria* (numerology, or assigning each Hebrew letter a numerical value). He calculated that the word *shekel* and the word *nefesh* both equal **430**. We contribute a half-shekel in order to recognize that God gives us only a half-soul when we are born. It is our sacred task in life to complete the other half of our soul through prayer, contributions, and good deeds. When we give the half-shekel we help raise ourselves to fulfill our full soul and make ourselves more complete spiritual human beings.

Topics for Discussion:

1) What is the purpose of contributing a half-shekel as an offering to Adonai?

2) How does Rabbi Hanokh Heinikh of Alexander explain the meaning of the half-shekel?

3) In what other ways can each human being fulfill him/herself spiritually in life?

4) In what ways would you like to complete your own soul? What spiritual tasks can you think of which would make your soul more full and fulfilled?

D'var Torah - Vayakhel

"On six days work is permitted, but on the seventh day there shall be to you a holy day, a Shabbat Shabbaton [or: a Shabbat of total rest] to Adonai...." Exodus 35:2

Whenever a word is repeated in the Torah, the commentators look for additional nuances of understanding and embellished meanings. In this verse the expression "Shabbat Shabbaton" appears, meaning a day of complete and total restfulness. Since the word *Shabbaton* is so similar to *Shabbat* it appears to be an unnecessary repetition.

Rabbi Yaakov Tzvi Meklenburg (Koenigsberg, Russia, 1785-1865), in his commentary, *Ha-Ktav*

Ve-ha-Kabbalah, notes that there are two aspects of Shabbat which are included in the expression "Shabbat Shabbaton." First is **physical** rest, rest of the body from labor and effort. Second is **spiritual** rest, rest of the mind, heart and soul from worrying about making a living and finding sufficient income to supply one's material needs.

Topics for Discussion:

1) Why does the Torah seemingly repeat the word "Shabbat" in the command to observe the seventh day?

2) How does Rabbi Yaakov Tzvi Meklenburg explain the expression "Shabbat Shabbaton"?

3) What are some of the ways one can rest on Shabbat: a) physically, and b) spiritually?

4) In what ways can you make your own Shabbat a day of complete rest both physically and spiritually?

In which way do you normally rest more (physically or spiritually)? How can you increase your rest in the other aspect of Shabbat rest (physical or spiritual)?

D'var Torah - Pekuday

"When Moshe saw that they Israelite people had finished all the work [of building the Mishkan- portable Sanctuary]… Moshe blessed them." Exodus 39:43

Since the Torah does not specify what words of blessing Moshe used, the Midrash fills in the missing blanks. Rashi (Troyes, Frances, 1040-1135) suggests that these words were Moshe's blessing: "May God's Holy Presence be upon us, and let the work of our hands prosper." (Rashi borrows some of the phrases from Psalm 90, which is called "A Prayer of Moshe").

Rabbi Simcha Raz of Jerusalem, in his commentary *Shivim Panim LaTorah*, further explains that use of the phrase "work of our hands" implies that God's presence should be among us not only in the Sanctuary, but also in our places of work, business, financial matters; and not only in our heart, mind and soul, but in our **hands** - in other words in our jobs and professional work. Not only in our relation with God, but in all our relations between us and other human beings.

Topics For Discussion:

1) At what occasion did Moshe bless the people, and why?

2) What kind of blessing did Moshe offer, according to Rashi?

3) How did Rashi fill in the missing words from Torah?

4) How did Rabbi Simcha Raz expand the meaning of Rashi's words? Why is it important to feel God's

presence in our work and in relations with people, as well as with God?

D'var Torah - Vayikra

"No meal offering which you shall offer to Adonai shall be made leavened...."

Leviticus 2:11

The commentators differ as to the reason for prohibiting leaven (flour that has fermented, or risen, as opposed to *matzah*, which is **unleavened**), as an offering to the altar. In *Sefer HaHinukh*, an anonymous thirteenth century compendium of explanations of all 613 mitzvot, the author admits the difficulty of finding a clear explanation of this command. Nevertheless he suggests that "leaven," or bread that has risen, represents two qualities which are abhorrent to God.

First, leaven symbolizes procrastination. Bread rises slowly, takes its "good old time." One must not perform God's will slowly and carelessly, but rather with alacrity, excitement and enthusiasm. Secondly, leaven represents the "swelling" of the bread; in other words, the pride and haughtiness in one's heart. Arrogance is the source of sin, and humility is the source of awe and reverence for God.

Thus, leaven must be kept separate from a sacrifice whose purpose is to bring us closer to God.

Topics for Discussion:

1) What are the two suggested reasons offered by *Sefer Ha-Hinukh* for the prohibition of leaven in a sacrifice?

2) Why are these two qualities to be avoided in service to God?

3) With the Festival of Pesah coming soon, can you think of any connection between eating *matzah* and the great Festival of Freedom, in light of this verse?

4) In what ways will developing more humility help you become a more spiritual person?

D'var Torah - Tzav

"If one brings an offering of *todah* (thanksgiving)...." Leviticus 7:12

Since the destruction of the Bet Mikdash (Temple) in Jerusalem in 70 C.E. by the Romans, scholars have had different opinions about the likelihood of the resumption of animal sacrifice at some future time. One ancient midrash (Tanhuma, 4th century, Eretz Yisrael) says that in the far off future all sacrifices will be abolished except for the Thanksgiving (*Todah*) offering.

In the twelfth century Maimonides (Spain, Egypt, 1135-1204) argued that Moshe had the biblical Israelites offer sacrifices only because their pagan neighbors did so, and he wanted to wean them away from idolatry gradually. By letting them worship one God in the same manner in which their neighbors worshipped idols, the transition would not be as difficult for them. The implication is that Maimonides did not believe that sacrifices would be a permanent method of divine worship.

Topics for Discussion:

1) Do you think the Bet Mikdash will ever be rebuilt? If so, what kind of worship might take place in it?

2) Why do you think the rabbis of the midrash selected the **thanksgiving** offering as the only one which would survive in the future?

3) What are the different ways in which we worship God? Is there one way that is better than others? Explain.

4) Would you bring a thanksgiving offering if the Temple were rebuilt? What are some things for which you are thankful?

D'var Torah - Shmini

"The following birds shall be an abomination [unkosher] - they shall not be eaten: ...the stork...." Leviticus 11:13,19

The Hebrew word for "stork" is **hasidah**, which means that it is a kind bird (from **hesed**, kindness). The Talmud (Hullin 63a) explains that the stork has a natural instinct to be kind to other members of its own species. Maimonides teaches that what we eat, including its moral nature, is absorbed into our character. Why then should the stork be declared unkosher to eat?

Rabbi Avraham Ibn Ezra (Spain, 1089-1164) has an interesting explanation. He suggests that the stork is seen only at certain intervals during the year, implying that the stork performs acts of kindness only at its own pleasure, when it is convenient for its own needs. Others suggest that the stork is kind, but only to those of its own species, not to others. This limitation of its kindness is a serious flaw. For kindness to be sincere and authentic, it must apply to one's own group **and** to other groups, on a consistent basis. Limited and restricted kindness makes a mockery of true kindness.

Topics for Discussion:

1) Why is the stork called in Hebrew **hasidah**?

2) What is wrong with being kind on a selective basis?

3) Why is the stork, which is kind to its own species, not considered kosher to eat?

4) How do you restrict your own acts of kindness? Are you as kind to people of other religious, racial and

ethnic groups as you are to your own? Do you think you should be? Explain.

D'var Torah - Tazria

"And on the eighth day the flesh of his foreskin will be circumcised." Leviticus 12:3

At the ceremony for Brit Milah the following prayer is recited: "Just as this little child has now entered the Covenant of circumcision (Brit Milah), so, in later life, may he embark upon the study of Torah, marital joy and the performance of good deeds."

This brief, lovely prayer, recited (in modified form) for baby girls as well as boys, at the Jewish naming ceremony, summarizes some of the most important of all Jewish values. The Covenant of circumcision perpetuates the bond between God and Israel that goes back to the very beginnings of our people's history. The study of Torah is the goal of Judaism for a mature, enlightened and involved Jew. Knowledge of Torah permits one to carry out its precepts and demands. Through marriage one can create a family, produce children, and perpetuate the Covenant between God and Israel to the next generation. Ultimately the performance of good deeds is the way of life that God desires for those bound in the Covenant. A life filled with good deeds is the ideal of Jewish saintliness and righteousness.

Topics for Discussion:

1) Why does Jewish Tradition associate Brit Milah with other mitzvot, such as study, marriage and good deeds?

2) What connection do you see between each of these four mitzvot: Brit Milah, study of Torah, marriage, and the performance of good deeds?

3) Why are these corollary mitzvot (study, marriage, deeds) so important in our Heritage?

4) What ways can you suggest to increase study of Torah and the performance of good deeds, by you and others? Be as specific as possible.

D'var Torah - Metzora

"This shall be the ritual regulation of the leper…."
Leviticus 14:2

The rabbis of the Talmud connected the Hebrew for leprosy (**metzora**) with the Hebrew word **motzee shem ra** - slanderer, making the assumption that leprosy was a punishment for slander and gossip.

The Talmud has an abundance of advice about care in speech. For example: "Your friend has a friend, and your friend's friend has a friend, so use caution in your speech" (Ketubot 109b).

Rabbi Alexander Zusia Friedman, in his collection of commentaries called *Wellsprings of Torah* (NY: Judaica Press, 1969, Vol. II, p. 234), brings this comment: One may think: "Of what importance are my words? A word has no substance, neither can it be seen or touched." However, even though words have no substance and are invisible, like the wind they can nevertheless cause entire worlds to crash.

Topics for Discussion:

1) How do the commentators connect slander with the disease of leprosy?

2) Why does Jewish tradition focus so much attention on harmful speech?

3) What is the point of the Talmudic comment about friends having other friends . . . ?

4) What are some ways you can think of to help yourself and others be more careful about avoiding gossip and slander?

D'var Torah - Aharay Mot

"On this day [Yom Kippur] atonement shall be made for you to cleanse you of all your misdeeds. You shall be cleansed before Adonai." Leviticus 16:30

This verse repeats the phrase about being "cleansed," or forgiven by God. The second phrase mentions specifically that you shall be forgiven by God, "cleansed before Adonai." In the Talmud (Yoma 85b) Rabbi Elazar ben Azariah (of Haggadah fame) said: "The phrase 'cleansed before Adonai' is explicitly mentioned to teach that *only* misdeeds between humans and Adonai are forgiven. However, for misdeeds committed against other human beings (called in Hebrew *avayrot she-bayn adam la-havero*) Yom Kippur does not atone until the perpetrator of the misdeed asks forgiveness from the person against whom the misdeed was committed.

Topics for Discussion:

1) Why does the verse repeat the phrase about being cleansed, and why is the name of Adonai added in the second phrase?

2) Can you give some examples of misdeeds committed against Adonai, and other examples of misdeeds against other human beings? What is the difference?

3) Why does Yom Kippur not cleanse us for misdeeds committed against other people?

4) For what misdeeds do you have to ask forgiveness, and from whom? Should you wait until Yom Kippur, or can you ask for forgiveness now?

D'var Torah - Kedoshim

"You shall rise in the presence of the aged, and you shall honor the presence of a sage. . . ." Leviticus 19:32

According to the Stone Humash there is a difference of opinion about the meaning of this verse. Rashi says that both halves of the verse complement one another. In this view, one who is both elderly and pious is to be treated with honor and respect. Another view is that this verse includes two separate commands. One is to rise and honor anyone over age 70 (including an unlearned person), and the other is to rise and honor a sage, even one who is young. This interpretation translates the Hebrew word *zaken* as a sage, rather than as an old person.

According to the *Shulhan Arukh* (Yoreh Dayah 244:1), written by Rabbi Yosef Karo in Safed in the sixteenth century, the second view is the halakhah. Thus, we are commanded by the Torah to respect the elderly, and revere the sage of any age. Among Jews the aged and the learned person deserve a special measure of respect and deference.

Topics for Discussion:

1) What are the two different views about the meaning of the words "aged" and "sage" in this verse?

2) Which makes more sense to you? Which view do you prefer?

3) Why is it important in Jewish tradition to respect the elderly and the sage?

4) What are some ways in which you carry out these mitzvot in your life?

D'var Torah - Emor

"You shall keep My mitzvot, and do them: I am Adonai." Leviticus 22:31

The Prince of medieval commentators, Rashi (known after the acronym of his names, **R**abbi **Sh**lomo **I**tzhaki, 1040-1135 C.E., Troyes, France) selected the best of the ancient midrashim for his brief explanations of the Torah. For our verse he quotes from the **Sifra**, a midrashic collection written on Leviticus, edited in the 4th century C.E., in Eretz Yisrael. The question that is raised by the midrash is the seemingly unnecessary repetition in the verse. Why does God command us both to "keep" the mitzvot, and to "do" them? Are not "keeping" the mitzvot and "doing" them the same thing?

Here is the answer of the midrash: **Keeping** the mitzvot means **studying** them. You keep, or "preserve" them in the mind and heart as a first step to carrying them out. The second step is actually **doing** the mitzvot, so that we can live a life of mitzvot, and follow God's Covenant made at Mt. Sinai.

This reflects an old debate in our Tradition as to whether **study** or **action** is more important. The Talmud answers that study is more important, because it leads to action. This non-answer is the rabbis' way of choosing **both**. Study alone does not go far enough. Yet, if we practice the mitzvot, and don't plant them firmly into our brain and heart, it is not likely that our practice will be self-perpetuating. Thus, one must study **and** practice, the only combination that will successfully assure the continuity of the Torah.

Topics for Discussion:

1) What question does the midrash (and then Rashi) try to answer?

2) What is the answer to the question, and what sense does it make?

3) Do you agree with the answer of the midrash?

4) Which part of the two-step (study/practice) plan do you enjoy more? Which do you think is ultimately more significant in preserving the biblical Covenant?

D'var Torah - Behar

"If your brother becomes impoverished, and he thus comes in your charge, let him live with you." Leviticus 25:35

Rabbi Joseph H. Hertz, in his famous commentary on the Humash, compares Tanakh (biblical) law with ancient Roman law. In Roman law the creditor could put the debtor in prison, chain him to a block, sell him into slavery, or even kill him. By contrast, the Midrash points out that it is the obligation of one Jew to help another Jew at the very earliest signs of poverty, so that the person does not continue to slide down the slope of abject poverty and despair, when it would be much harder to help him. Even though the person is poor, he is still your brother!

Topics for Discussion:

1) What is the approach of the Tanakh toward an Israelite who has fallen on hard times financially?

2) What is the reason for calling the person becoming poor "your brother"?

3) How does Jewish Law compare with Roman Law, according to Rabbi Hertz?

4) In what ways does this tradition of caring for the poor continue today? What things do you and your family do to help those who have fallen on hard times?

D'var Torah - Behukotai

"I, Adonai, am your God, who brought you out from Egyptian bondage to be slaves no more; I broke the bars of your yoke and caused you to walk erect."

Leviticus 26:13

The most important spiritual benefit of God's freeing the Israelite nation from Egyptian slavery was so that they could walk erect, head held high, in pride and dignity. Slaves and oppressed peoples can easily feel an inner sense of shame that they do not have any control over their lives.

In the Siddur the prayer which precedes the Shema uses the same Hebrew word as this verse: erect. The prayer says: "Gather our people in peace from the corners of the earth, and lead us erect and in dignity to our Holy Land. You are the God Who does mighty acts of deliverance...."

Topics for Discussion:

1) Why does the verse repeat the idea of "breaking the bars of the yoke," and "causing you to walk erect"? Are they not the same thing?

2) What are the different effects which liberation from oppression have upon people?

3) Why do you think the authors of the Siddur use the word "komemiyut" — erect — or in dignity, in the paragraph just preceding the Shema? What is the connection?

4) Can you describe a time when you were "freed" from a difficult situation, your sense of self-esteem was restored, and you felt more "free"?

D'var Torah - Bemidbar

"Take a census of the entire Camp of Israel, arranging them according to their clans and tribes...." Numbers 1:2

Taking a census occurred several times during the forty years of marching from Egypt to the Promised Land. The question arises about this verse, Why does the census need to be taken with each person counted within his own clan and tribe?

Rabbi Ovadia Sforno (1475-1550, Italy) explains that it was the original intention of God to have the Israelite People enter Eretz Yisrael immediately, and not have to wait for forty years of wandering. When they entered, it was the expectation that the peoples then occupying the land would voluntarily leave and make room for them (as seems to have been the case with certain tribes who in fact did leave voluntarily - cf. Isaiah 17:9). Unfortunately, the episode of the ten spies who spread pessimism and anxiety among the people caused God to delay the entrance for forty years (read Numbers 13 and 14), and in that period the inhabitants of Canaan became more rebellious and resistant.

According to this interpretation many unfortunate occurrences could have been avoided, all of which are traced to the foolish behavior of a small group of leaders (the ten spies who returned with an "evil" report).

Topics for Discussion:

1) How does Rabbi Sforno infer from the text that it was God's original intention to have the Israelites enter the Land soon after their departure from Egypt?

2) Is it likely that the seven peoples in Eretz Yisrael might have left voluntarily?

3) Does it ever happen that a small group of poor leaders can cause great harm to a large people or nation? Can you give some examples?

4) How do you personally deal with the notion that there are so many different, and often opposing, views of the events (and beliefs) in the Torah?

D'var Torah - Naso

"When Moshe went into the Ohel Moed (the Tent of Meeting) to speak with God, he would hear the Voice speaking to him...." Numbers 7:89

Rashi (France, 1040-1135) explains that the word "the" before "Voice" is used to mean that this is the same loud, strong Voice which God used when speaking at Mt. Sinai. However, when speaking with Moshe, the Voice went no farther than the door of the tent, and no one but Moshe heard it, even though the Voice was very loud. God's voice, as it were, was "blocked" at the door.

Rabbi Moshe Feinstein, recognized as one of the leading American Orthodox scholars of this century, in his book *Darash Moshe*, explains Rashi's explanation. (It is normal for one Jewish commentary to explain others - especially Rashi, whose words are considered so important). Rashi explains that the Voice need not go outside the door, since any true student of Torah can hear God's voice by merely being diligent in the study of Torah. If, in this case, no one but Moshe heard God, it was because the Voice was intentionally blocked, so only Moshe could hear it. Reb Moshe then explains that while some believe that in the modern world, long past biblical days, we no longer hear God's Voice, it is not so. We hear God's Voice today by practicing mitzvot and internalizing Torah, and not by study alone.

Topics for Discussion:

1) Reb Moshe Feinstein's "comment on a comment" is somewhat complex. How would you re-state his idea in simple terms?

2) What does the Torah mean when it speaks of "God's Voice"?

3) What distinction is made between studying and practicing Torah? Why?

4) Do you know anyone who has heard God's Voice? Do you believe that person? Do you think it's possible? Have you ever heard God's Voice? Explain.

D'var Torah - Be-ha-a-lotekha

"When the Aron (Ark of Testimony) set forward, Moshe would say: Arise, Adonai!...."

Numbers 10:35

This is the verse which we sing as a congregation today when the Aron Kodesh is opened and the Sefer Torah is about to be removed. In the desert, Moshe was to recite these words when the Aron was carried forward from one position to another, in preparation for battle. The presence of the Tablets of Testimony (containing the Ten Commandments) reminded the people of their Covenant with God at Mt. Sinai, and of God's promise to protect the people against their enemies. The Aron and the Tablets inside it gave them confidence to win their battles when they faced enemies in the desert.

Hasidic interpretation looks more closely at the words "Arise, Adonai!" and suggests a novel (and perhaps a bit heretical) idea. This explanation is that human activity brings forces to work in Heaven. In other words, God responds to the actions of humans. Because the Israelite People were moving forward into battle, their action "encouraged" God to go forward with them, as it were. The Midrash hints that whoever is an enemy of justice is also an enemy of God, and thus, the enemies in the verse may refer to enemies of God because they are enemies of justice. When the Israelite people go out to fight injustice, it is not out of the question to suggest that God is also "aroused" to stand behind this just cause.

Topics for Discussion:

1) What does "Arise, Adonai" mean in the Torah?

2) How do the Hasidic commentaries interpret the phrase?

3) Can human action produce a similar action on God's part?

4) When you do a good deed, do you think God responds by supporting you? Explain.

D'var Torah - Shelah Lekha

"Attach a thread of **tekhelet** (blue) to the **Tzitzit** (fringe) at each corner.... Look upon it." Numbers 15:38-39

Rabbi Mordecai M. Kaplan, founder of the Reconstructionist Movement, who died in the 1980s at age 104, pointed out that when the Torah says "look upon it" - the Hebrew for "it" is masculine (**oto**), while the noun **tzitzit** is feminine. He suggests that "it" refers to the blue thread (**p'teel tekhelet**), not the **tzitzit**. The important part of the **tzitzit** was the **blue color**, in his opinion. Why?

The Talmudic rabbis suggest that the dye for this color came from a snail (**hilazon**) that became extinct. Rabbi Kaplan says that there is another, historical, reason. The Roman government forbade the use of this color blue (**tekhelet**) because it was the symbol of royalty, and wearing it was considered to be treason against the Emperor. Thus out of fear of death, the rabbis eliminated the color blue. The lesson Rabbi Kaplan teaches is that the real purpose of the **tzitzit** is to remind us of our true loyalty to the Ruler of the Universe, **melekh malkhay ha-m'lakhim** - to whom our ultimate obedience is due - above that of any human ruler.

Topics for Discussion:

1) What are the various explanations for wearing **tzitzit** on four corners of the tallit?

2) Do we have any reminders today of the "thread of blue" on our tallitot?

3) How does Rabbi Kaplan derive his interpretation, and do you think it has merit?

4) What does it mean in your life to have loyalty to God, a loyalty higher than that of any mortal leaders?

D'var Torah - Korah

"Now Korah took men...." Numbers 16:1Translators and commentators throughout the centuries have had great difficulty understanding the opening phrase of this Sidrah. The Hebrew merely says: "Now Korah took." But what did he take? The Torah does not say. Rabbi Abraham ibn Ezra (Spain 1089-1164) adds the word "men" - i.e., Korah took other people along with him in his rebellion. Most translators follow ibn Ezra and also add the word "men," even though it is not in the original.In the second century (C.E.) official Aramaic translation of the Torah done by Onkelos (and thus called Targum Onkelos - "The Translation of Onkelos"), we read: "Korah separated himself."In modern English we sometimes call a person who is selfish and power-hungry, a "taker." Maybe what the Torah intended to say was that Korah was a "taker." "Now Korah took" might simply not need any further elaboration, translation or commentary. It may be an apt description of a person who wants to be a community leader merely for the purpose of "taking," and not really interested in **giving**. Avraham, Moshe, and all great biblical leaders, are described as **givers**, and not **takers**. That was Korah's downfall, and led God to have the earth "take him" where he belonged.

Topics for Discussion:

1) What is the problem with the phrasing in the opening sentence of the Sidrah?

2) How do the commentators deal with the problem? Is their solution satisfactory?

3) From reading the rest of the story about Korah and his followers, what gives us the impression that he is a "taker" and not a "giver"?

4) Tell about other leaders, past or present, who can be described as "givers" or "takers"?

D'var Torah - Hukat

"This is the statute (**hukah**) of the Torah." Numbers 19:2

The late Rabbi Moshe Feinstein, a leading 20th century Orthodox thinker and interpreter, points out that in another passage the same Hebrew word for statute (**hukah**) is used, but with a significant difference. In Exodus 12:43 we find: "This is the statute (**hukah**) of the Pesah offering." If the phrase in our Sidrah were meant to be similar to the one in Exodus, the Torah would have said "This is the statute of purification." Instead, it says: "This is the statute of the Torah."

Rabbi Feinstein derives an important lesson from the difference. He claims that the Torah does not mean here just to introduce the new statute, as in the Exodus passage, but to imply that this is a statute of "the Torah." In other words, in a certain important way, the statute of the Red Cow, about ashes which purify the impure and make impure the pure, can be said to apply to the **entire** Torah. This means that **every character trait**, both positive and negative, can be used either positively or negatively. Every human quality can be turned to serve God or to sin against God, as the ashes of the Red Cow. For example, humility can be used either in the service of God, or to sin against God. If one acts humbly in his/her own life toward others, the trait of humility is good. If one acts too humbly when it is necessary to treat a friend with glory and honor, then humility is not good. The same with any human trait. Its use is good or bad depending on when and how it is applied, just as the ashes of the Red Cow. The lesson is to find a way to use all of our qualities in the service of God.

Topics for Discussion:

1) What lesson does Rabbi Feinstein derive from comparing the two passages which use the Hebrew word **hukah**, or statute?

2) How do human qualities resemble the ashes of the Red Cow?

3) Give an example of how the quality of assertiveness can be used for good or evil.

4) What other qualities can be used for good or bad? Think of one from your own life experience. How could you have turned a bad action into a good action?

D'var Torah - Balak

"How beautiful are your tents, O Yaakov,

Your dwelling places, O Yisrael !

Like gardens planted by a river. Numbers 24:5-6

The Talmud (Sanhedrin 105b) understands the word "tents" as "tents of Torah," or schools; and "dwelling places" as the place of God's dwelling - synagogues. Why, then, are they planted by a river? Another Talmudic passage (Megillah 29b) tells us that in the Messianic days of bliss all the Jewish schools and synagogues in the Diaspora will float to the Land of Yisrael. With a river right next to them, it will be easy for them to stream toward the Holy City and the Holy Land.

Topics for Discussion:

1) What did Balaam's blessing mean literally?

2) How does the Talmud understand the blessing?

3) In the poetic blessing of the foreign prophet, Balaam, why does he mention streams? What message is the poem trying to convey?

4) Describe in fuller detail what the Talmud means when it says schools and synagogues will stream toward Eretz Yisrael. Do you agree? When might this happen?

D'var Torah - Pinhas

"The Land [of Israel] shall be apportioned according to the listings of their ancestral tribes." Numbers 27:55

The Torah tells us that when the Twelve Tribes of Israel enter the Promised Land, each tribe will be granted a section of the country according to the number of grandchildren, over the age of 20, of the generation of people who took part in the Exodus.

Rabbi Samson Raphael Hirsch (Frankfurt, Germany, 1808-1888) explains that the descendants of that generation inherit property because of the merit of their ancestors. In Rabbi Hirsch's words: "The greatest and most precious acquisitions of parents and grandparents are children and grandchildren who prove themselves loyal and true to their heritage." Rabbi Hirsch comments further that though the descendants were worthy of receiving the Land on their own merit, the Torah gives it to them on the merit of their ancestors. This shows the reciprocal relationship between the generations, and testifies to the merit of the grandparents to the grandchildren and vice-versa. Grandchildren inherit land because of the goodness of their ancestors, and grandparents are blessed and forgiven their sins because of the good deeds of their grandchildren.

Topics for Discussion:

1) What is the simple meaning of verse 55?
2) Explain the difficulty of dividing up the Promised Land in a fair and equitable fashion.

3) How does the Torah choose to divide up the Land?

4) What merits have you received from your parents and grandparents, and what privileges do they have because of you?

D'var Torah - Mattot

"Moshe became angry with the commanders of the army…." Numbers 31:14

"Elazar HaKohen said to the army: This is the law which Adonai commanded Moshe…." Numbers 31:21

The Talmud (Pesahim 66b) draws an interesting conclusion by reading these two verses from the same chapter, only a few verses apart within chapter 31.

The rabbis say that anger causes a wise person to lose his knowledge. The proof comes from the fact that in 31:14 Moshe became angry, and then only a few verses later (31:21), Elazar HaKohen had to repeat a law that had been given already in chapter 19. Were it not for Moshe's anger, says the sage Resh Lakish, it would not have been necessary for Elazar to repeat a law that was already taught.

Topics for Discussion:

1) How does the Talmud prove that angry can causes forgetfulness?

2) What can we learn from the talmudic rabbis about their views of Moshe, the greatest prophet and teacher of all of Jewish history?

3) Why should anger make even wise people forget information?

4) Have you ever noticed the effects that anger has on your memory? Explain. What lessons should we thus learn?

D'var Torah - Mas-ay

"Thus commanded Adonai regarding the [five] daughters of Zelophehad: They may marry anyone they choose, as long as the man they marry is a member of their father's tribe." Numbers/Bemidbar 36:6

In dealing with the division of Eretz Yisrael into tribal sections, the question arose regarding the inheritance of daughters who have no brothers, when their father dies. A second question is whether they may marry someone in another tribe and still keep the land inherited from their father. The Torah answers by aying that they may inherit their father's land, but only if they marry someone in their own tribe. The Talmud (Bava Batra 120a) says that this applied only to the generation entering the Land, to keep each tribe's territory intact at least for that generation.

The Talmud questions why the Torah did not simply say: "They may marry anyone they choose in their tribe." The repetition of the word "marry" comes to teach a new lesson: that this advice is good for **any** marriage, namely to make sure that a person marries someone "in their father's tribe," that is, someone with their parents' values.

Sparks for Discussion

1. Why does the Torah discuss the issue of women's inheritance?

2. What decisions does the Torah give, and why?

3. How do the rabbis derive the idea that shared values are important in a
relationship?

4. If you are not married, what kind of values are important in the person you will choose to marry? If you are married, what values were important in your choice of a mate?

D'var Torah - Devarim

"In the fortieth year of wandering, on the first day of the eleventh month of wandering..., when they had killed Sihon, the King of the Amorites in Heshbon...." Deuteronomy 1:3-4

When Moshe was in the last year of his life, the forty years of wandering was coming to an end and the people were ready to enter Eretz Yisraël. Rabbi Avraham Yitzhak Kook, first Chief Rabbi of Eretz Yisrael (d. 1935), translates the name of the place in our verse, Heshbon, and uses it in its normal meaning - **calculations**. He says that only when all the calculations are behind you (killed, resolved), are you ready to enter Eretz Yisrael.

Rabbi Kook was an avid Zionist who was born in Russia and dreamed from the time he was a child of settling in Eretz Yisrael, which he did as a young man. He uses the word "calculations" to mean that people are always using "calculations," or excuses, to explain why they are not ready to move to Eretz Yisrael. They talk of having children finish school, making enough money to buy an apartment, waiting until they have learned enough Hebrew, etc. etc. Only when they put away (kill) all their "calculations" (excuses) can they bring themselves to take the great step to "go on Aliyah" - immigrate to Israel.

Topics for Discussion:

1) How is Heshbon used in the biblical verse?
2) What clever twist does Rav Kook give the word?

3) Why does Rav Kook think people who don't make aliyah are using excuses?

4) Have you ever thought of making aliyah? What "calculations" must you put behind you in order to do it? What do you think living in Eretz Yisrael would be like for you?

D'var Torah - Va-et-hanan

"You shall not add anything to what I command you, or remove anything from it [The Torah], but just keep the mitzvot of Adonai your God that I command you." Deuteronomy 4:2

Throughout Jewish history, sages and rabbis were afraid to have the general population veer even an inch from the exact details of the law which God commanded to Moshe. Just as removing certain laws could be dangerous to the system as a whole, so could adding things that were considered strange or unusual be threatening to those who wanted to preserve the system in tact. Today some rabbis may feel differently about specific mitzvot, but all agree that the laws of the Torah are the basis of our tradition and continuity.

In the collection of commentaries called **Itturay Torah**, Rabbi Alexander Moshe Lapidot is quoted as saying that the most prudent fashion in preserving the Tradition is to follow the Golden Mean of Maimonides. Those who would weaken and dilute the Tradition are prone to shrink the number of obligations and "remove" some of the commandments. It can also be dangerous, suggests Rabbi Alexander, to be super pious and keep adding more and more restrictions, obligations, and innovations, and make it impossible to fulfill the Tradition. This too is a threat to preserving the heritage of our past, one which we are less prone to recognize.

Topics for Discussion:

1) Why does the Torah command not to remove or add to the mitzvot God gave us?

2) Which is more common: to add or to subtract from obligations and mitzvot?

3) Which can destroy the continuity of the Tradition more easily? How can a righteous person harm the collection of mitzvot by overdoing them?

4) Have you ever tried to be more pious than the Torah warrants? Can you give some examples? Was it helpful or harmful to preserving the Jewish heritage?

D'var Torah - Ekev

"When you have eaten, and are full, then you shall give thanks to Adonai your God." Deuteronomy 8:10

When do most people pray? When they are in difficult times, or having some kind of trouble, or are hungry or are stricken by poverty. This verse commands us to thank and to bless God, not when we are hungry, but when we are full, when our needs have already been met.

A modern commentary suggests that we ought to thank God for our blessings, not only for our lacks and needs. An obvious time to pray to God is a moment of need or danger. That is called petitionery prayer - i.e., praying to God to **ask for something**. Another kind of prayer, a less obvious one to some people, but on a higher level on the ladder of prayer, is the prayer of thanksgiving. This is the kind of prayer which is suggested in this verse.

Perhaps many people are disillusioned by not having their prayers answered, because most of their prayers are asking for things. Perhaps if we view prayer not always as a request or a petition, but as an opportunity to say "thank you" to God, we would not need an answer. The prayer itself is sufficient by itself.

Topics for Discussion:

1) Why does the verse command us to bless God after we have eaten, and are full?

2 What standard prayer is recited after eating a full meal with bread?

3) Why do people tend to pray to God when they are in need, rather than when their needs are already met?

4) In your prayer life, how often do you use petitioner prayer, and how often do you bless and thank God, by "counting your blessings"? Which kind of prayer is found more often in the Siddur?

D'var Torah - Re-eh

"If there is a needy person among you, one of your own country... do not harden your heart and shut your hand to the needy person, but open your hand...." Deuteronomy 15:7-8

Tzedakah (righteousness, the moral obligation to help the poor) has always been the hallmark of the Jewish People. To illustrate this ancient, noble ideal, the late Rabbi Pinchas Peli of Jerusalem tells the following story. In an army morning roll call, each recruit was to answer to the shout of his name. The corporal called out "Kelly," and "here" was the response. "Armstrong." "Here." Next came Private Cohen's turn. "Cohen." Being habituated to charity appeals so often in his life, Private Cohen yelled out "Twenty-five dollars."

The rabbis in the Talmud (Bava Metzia 71a) derived from our verse that there are priorities in charity giving. A Jew must give to those of his/her own city before those of another city. In other words, in a series of concentric circles, givers of Tzedakah must contribute to those closest to them (immediate family, kin, other Jews, the community), and only after these primary obligations are met do we give to those farther away in relationship and in place.

Topics for Discussion:

1) What is the point of the story about Private Cohen?

2) How do the rabbis of the Talmud derive from our verse the lesson about priorities in Tzedakah?

3) Do you agree that a Jew must make giving to other Jews a higher priority? Can you make a case for Judaism being both particularistic and universalistic?

4) If it happened that you were temporarily needy, would be expect more help and generosity from the Jewish community than from others? What priorities do you have in your giving of Tzedakah?

D'var Torah - Shoftim

"Justice, justice shall you pursue, that you may live and that you will possess the Land which Adonai your God is giving you." Deuteronomy 16:20

Rabbi Samson Raphael Hirsch (Frankfurt, Germany, 1808-1888) points out that the verb "you will possess" is in the future, even though the Torah is referring to a time when the people will already have taken possession of the Land of Israel and completed its occupation. He explains that the people of Israel must not only possess the Land during its conquest, but at all times. It must constantly re-conquer the land by earning the right to live in it. How? By acting justly, as the beginning of the verse commands. Only when the people will pursue justice, thoroughly and constantly, will it win the right to keep owning the Land.

In modern times some critics of Israel say that its methods of treating terrorists is not according to international law. In its defense others argue that terrorists must be dealt with harshly in order to extract information from them which will prevent new terrorist attacks and save Jewish lives. This is a difficult dilemma for the Israel Defense Forces (IDF) and the Israeli government, since it must protect its citizens' lives and at the same time live by the high moral code of Judaism.

Topics for Discussion:

1) How does Rabbi Hirsch explain the fact that the verb "You shall possess" is in the future tense instead of in the past?

2) What is the connection between acting justly and possessing territory?

3) Must the State of Israel live by the high moral standards of the Torah?

4) How would you answer critics of Israel who claim it is being too harsh with terrorist prisoners? What would you do if you were head of the IDF (Army)?

D'var Torah - Kee Teze

"If you see your neighbor's ox or sheep which are lost, do not hide yourself from them.... So shall you do with other animals, or a garment, or anything your neighbor loses which you find. You must not remain indifferent."

Deuteronomy 22:1-3

Jewish Law (Halakhah) deals extensively with the subject of the responsibility of a person to return a lost article found in the public domain. Starting from the Mishnah (Bava Metzia, chapter 2) down through the ages, there is hardly a commentator who does not have some thought to add on the subject. The Mishnah elaborates on the Torah's verse by adding that one may not gain from investing a or using a found object, and if one does, the gain should be turned over to the owner. The finder must advertise and seek everywhere until the owner is found.

The reason for the extensive elaboration on this verse seems to be more than the return of property, important as that is. The anonymous author of **Sefer Ha-Hinukh** (13th century, Spain) explains that the very fabric of society is tested when a lost article is found. There needs to be universal trust among people for the world to function, and knowing that a lost article will be returned and not kept (stolen) by the finder is an example of that very basic sense of trust.

Topics for Discussion:

1) Why does the Torah elaborate to such an extent on the issue of returning lost articles?

2) Why is it the obligation of the finder to seek out the owner rather than the owner to seek out the finder?

3) How does **Sefer Ha-Hinukh** broaden the meaning of this verse?

4) If you found a very large sum of cash in an unidentified envelope, what would be your first thought? What would you do with the money?

D'var Torah - Kee Tavo

"Moshe and the Levi'im charged all the Israelites, saying: Today you have become the people of Adonai your God.... Observe God's mitzvot and laws."

Deuteronomy 27:9-10

In Moshe's final speech before the people enter Eretz Yisrael, he reminds them that the acceptance of the laws of God's Covenant is what makes them a people. Rabbi Samson Raphael Hirsch (Frankfurt, Germany, 1808-1888) points out that it is not the crossing into the Land by itself which makes Israel a people, but rather that they have promised to live by the Torah.

Rabbi Hirsch stresses his point since one can read this verse to mean that it is the Land which makes Israel a nation. Writing in 19th century Germany, Rabbi Hirsch realizes that the people of Israel had been living outside its Homeland for 1900 years. Since the Jewish people was able to maintain its identity for almost two millennia outside the Land, the question arises: How did we do it? The answer: through keeping the ethical and ritual commands of the Torah. Rabbi Hirsch teaches that Moshe is emphasizing the Torah as the focal point of our identity. The Land, important as it is, is not sufficient if the people forget the Torah.

Topics for Discussion:

1) Why does the Torah say: "**Today** you have become the people of Adonai"?

2) What is the connection between the first part of the verse (becoming God's people), and the second part (observing the Torah)?

3) Why does Rabbi Hirsch think that keeping the Torah is even more important than living in Eretz Yisrael? How are these two mitzvot related?

4) Put the following mitzvot in order of importance according to your own values: a) living in Eretz Yisrael, b) keeping the Torah, c) keeping the Torah while living in Eretz Yisrael. Explain your priorities.

D'var Torah - Nitzavim

"You shall return [from the Hebrew root: **shuv**] to Adonai your God, and you and your children shall obey Adonai's voice with all your heart and soul, as I command you this day." Deuteronomy 30:2

In the first ten verses of chapter 30 the Hebrew root **shuv** (return, repent) appears seven times. We know that the number seven is a special, repetitive number and theme in Jewish tradition. Before Moshe bids farewell to the people — he is about to die and they are crossing the Jordan River into the Eretz Yisrael — he leaves the people with the message of **teshuvah**. Teshuvah can mean returning to God, to the ways of the Covenant between God and Israel, to truth and righteousness, and to the origins of the Jewish faith.

Rabbi Abraham Isaac Kook, first Chief Rabbi of Eretz Yisrael (1865-1935) described Teshuvah as the illumination of the darkness when we return to our true selves, to the root of our soul, and thus to God, the Soul of souls. We have, he writes, the ability to return to who we were meant to be, and to our Maker. When we return to ourselves, we can change our life and change the world.

Topics for Discussion:

1) Can you find all the places in chapter 30, verses 1 to 10, in which the Hebrew word **shuv** appears (in various Hebrew forms)?

2) What is the reason for the word **shuv** to be repeated seven times in ten verses?

3) What is the connection between the idea of **teshuvah** and Rosh Hashanah, which follows soon after this sidrah?

4) What are the various possible meanings of **teshuvah**, including Rav Kook's? How are they different? Which do you prefer? Explain.

D'var Torah - Vayaylekh

"Moshe went and spoke all these things to the entire nation of Israel. 'I am 120 years old....' " Deuteronomy 31:1

The entire Book of Deuteronomy is made up of the final speeches made by Moshe to sum up the duties of the people of Israel who are now about to enter the Promised Land. They are recited in the final three weeks of Moshe's life.

The 20th century Hasidic teacher, Rabbi Avraham Yaakov of Sadigora, notices that Moshe is still teaching at age 120, a remarkable feat! He takes special notice that Moshe is persistent and determined enough to continue teaching Torah, according to verse 1, to the **entire** people of Israel, even at age 120. The ceaseless life of teaching, says this Hasidic teacher, is what kept Moshe alive and active. He derives this from the beginning of the verse - "And Moshe went." Moshe was always coming, going, running around finding more and more students to teach Torah.

Topics for Discussion:

1) What connection does Rabbi Avraham Yaakov make between the beginning and end of our verse?

2) What special name is Moshe known by in Jewish tradition? Can you explain this in light of Rabbi Avraham Yaakov's explanation?

3) Why is teaching such an important idea as we come close to the end of the Torah?

4) In what ways can you increase the time you spend in studying (and teaching) Torah? How can you increase the number of people who learn from you?

D'var Torah - Ha-azinu

"Ask your father, and he will explain to you,
Your elders, and they will tell you." Deuteronomy 32:7

The verse stresses the importance of continuity and history. We Jews must never forget our past, from which we always learn many important lessons. However, Rabbi Hillel Silverman gives the verse an interesting twist. He suggests that "your father" may refer to previous generations, and "your elders" to today's world. In past generations a child could turn to his father, ask a question about Judaism, and expect a proper answer. Today, on the other hand, when a child asks a parent something about our heritage, the parent says: "Ask your grandparents." Only if there is a grandparent available, can the child expect an informed answer to a Jewish question from the immediate family.

The question we have to ask ourselves today is, as the words of a popular Yiddish song suggest: "Who will be the grandparents of our children?" Will we be able to answer the questions of our children, as previous generations of children could ask their own parents?

Topics for Discussion:

1) What is the plain meaning (**peshat**) of the verse, and what is Rabbi Hillel Silverman's **drash** (midrashic interpretation)?

2) Is there a difference in levels of Jewish knowledge between the generations of your grandparents and their parents, and that of the generation of today's parents?

3) Do you agree with those who claim that the "return" to Judaism on the part of many young families will stem the tide of assimilation?

4) How would you answer the question asked above? Will you, or your children, be able to answer their children's Jewish questions? What can be done to insure the continuity of Jewish learning? What are **you** doing to insure it?

D'var Torah - Ve-Zot Ha-Brakhah

"Adonai came from Sinai, and came up from Seir; God appeared from Mt. Paran, … At God's right hand was a fiery law." Deuteronomy 33: 2

The Torah traces the path that God traveled from Mt. Sinai where the Torah (here referred to as "the fiery law" in one translation) was given to Moshe.

The rabbis in the Mishnah (Tractate Avodah Zarah 2:2) derive a message from the fact that the Torah lists several places which God passed on his way to giving the Torah to the people of Israel. Rabbi Yohanan taught that God offered the Torah to many peoples before it was finally accepted by the Israelite nation. The point that the ancient rabbis were making is that it required a high degree of readiness and commitment to accept the high moral standards of the Torah. They are expressing the pride of our people that we have striven to live by the Torah from the time of Moshe to the present day.

Topics for Discussion:

1) Why does the Torah mention places like Seir and Mt. Paran after Sinai? If you have a biblical map, you might look up these places.

2) What point do the sages make in saying that it took God a while to find the right people to accept the Torah?

3) Do you think that Jews are better than other peoples because we accepted the Torah?

4) Have you lived up to the Torah's high standards more than other people you know? Have the Jewish

people generally lived according to higher standards than others?

BOOK THREE

RASHI'S RIDDLES

D'var Torah – Bereshit

"They [humans] shall rule the fish of the sea, the birds of the sky, the animals, and the whole earth…." Bereshit/Genesis 1:26

The Hebrew word for "rule" in this pasuk uses the exact same letters as the Hebrew word that means "to descend" (yirdu). It is especially easy to read the Hebrew word as "they shall descend" if one understands that the original Torah text had no vowels. The Hebrew for "they shall descend" is *yerdu* – using the same letters, but different vowels. Rashi thus contends that the word in this pasuk can be read in one of two ways. 1) Humankind shall rule the animal world, or 2) Humankind will descend (beneath) the animal world. Then Rashi proceeds to explain the two possible translations. He says that if humans take care of the animal world and the environment, they will be able to rule over it. On the other hand, if they neglect or abuse the animal world and the environment, they will descend beneath it.

Four Questions

How is Rashi able to interpret our verse in two different ways?

In what ways might Rashi expect humankind to treat the animal world?

In what ways might Rashi expect humankind to treat the environment?

What are some things you could do to be more respectful and responsible in treating animals and the environment?

RASHI'S RIDDLES

D'var Torah – Noah

"God scattered them over the face of the whole earth." Bereshit/Genesis 11:9

Rashi notices the seeming unfairness of the punishment of the Generation of the Flood, who all perished, as compared to the Generation of the Tower of Babel, who were "scattered," yet were permitted to remain alive. The Generation of the Flood could not control their passions – they committed robbery and other terrible crimes. But one sin they did NOT commit, which is to challenge the authority of God. On the other side is the Generation of the Tower of Babel, who challenged God! Why then, asks Rashi, should the generation that did not challenge God's authority perish, and the generation that DID challenge God's authority was permitted to live (though they were punished by being scattered)? Rashi answers by saying that the Generation of the Flood treated **each other** with disdain and hostility, robbing from one another. The Generation of the Tower of Babel, though they challenged God, had the great merit of loving one another and being united with each other. We learn this from the verse above which says that "the whole earth was of one language and unified speech" (Bereshit 11:1). The most important lesson here, claims Rashi, is that conflict and hostility are hateful, and peace among humans is wonderful.

Four Questions:

What problem does Rashi see in the fact that the punishment of the Generation of the Tower of Babel is being scattered, but that they are permitted to remain alive?

How does Rashi explain the difference in the two punishments – that of the Generation of the Flood, and that of the Generation of the Tower of Babel?

Which sin do you think Rashi sees as worse – sinning against God or sinning against other human beings?

Do you agree with Rashi? Explain and defend your answer.

RASHI'S RIDDLES

D'var Torah – Lekh Lekha

"Avram took his wife Sarai...and all their possessions...and the souls that they had acquired in Haran; and...they came to the land of Canaan." Bereshit/Genesis 12:5

The Torah uses a common Hebrew word for acquiring slaves – "asa," usually translated as "made." The Torah's word for making money, or acquiring property, such as a slave, is the same verb – to make, "asa." Rashi gives the verb an interesting twist. If one translates the verb literally – that is, "made," it means that Avram and Sarai "made" the people (souls) they took from Haran to Canaan. How did they "make" them? By bringing them into monotheistic belief. Says Rashi: Avram "converted the men, and Sarai converted the women." In other words, Avram and Sarai made these people who they were by teaching them, by making them their pupils and bringing them into the Hebrew nation, with all its beliefs about one God for all humanity. By giving the verb this new twist, Rashi adds a spiritual dimension to the process of bringing the people mentioned to the Land of Canaan. They not only joined Avram and Sarai in their journey, but became part of the Jewish nation, the Jewish people, and the Jewish religion.

Four Questions:

How does Rashi transform the meaning of the verse by giving the Hebrew verb "asa" a new interpretation?

What kinds of things did Avram and Sarai do to bring their slaves (in the Talmudic expression) “under the wings of the Shekhinah [the Divine Presence]?”

Why is teaching someone considered equal to creating a new soul?

Can you think of teachers who made you who you are, who transformed your soul? Have you done that for anyone else?

RASHI'S RIDDLES

D'var Torah – Vayera

"Lot's wife looked back, and she became a pillar of salt." Bereshit/Genesis 19:26

When God decided to destroy the two wicked cities of S'dom and Amora (also called Sodom and Gomorrah), God warned Lot (through the angels) not to look back. Lot's wife disobeyed this order, and looked back. Her punishment was that she turned into a pillar of salt. Rashi, following a midrash in Bereshit Rabbah, explains the punishment. He says that this penalty was very specifically arranged for Lot's wife. "She sinned with salt, and she was punished with salt." Rashi then relates this scenario: When guests came to their home, Lot asked his wife to give them salt. She replied by saying, "Are you going to adopt this foolish custom of hospitality?" Because she refused to act hospitably and offer salt to her guests, she was punished by becoming a pillar of salt.

Four Questions:

Why does Rashi have to explain the punishment received by Lot's wife?

Does the story about Lot's wife ring true? Why did the Midrash make up this tale?

Do you think the punishment was too harsh? Why is lack of hospitality considered such a great failure?

How can you be more hospitable in your home, and in other places?

RASHI'S RIDDLES

D'var Torah – Hayay Sarah

"And Yitzhak went out to the field to meditate towards evening...."

Bereshit/Genesis 24:63

Some of the greatest modern Bible scholars disagree on the exact translation of a Hebrew word in this pasuk – i.e. the word "la-su-a**h**." The New Jewish Publication Society translation is that Yitzhak "went out walking in the field." They have a footnote that reads "Meaning of Hebrew uncertain." Others translate: And Yitzhak "went out to meditate in the field," and still others, "to converse in the field."

Rashi bases his translation on a midrash that ascribes the three daily prayers to the three patriarchs. Avraham wrote Shaharit, Yitzhak wrote Minhah, and Yaakov wrote Maariv. The proof they give for Yitzhak is this verse, "And Yitzhak went "la-su-a**h**" in the field." Rashi's explanation of "la-su-a**h**" is that Yitzhak went "to pray." He brings proof from another place where the same verb is used (though in the different tense) – Psalm 102:1. There it is clear that the verb means "to pray." Here is the usual translation: "He pours forth his plea before Adonai." Clearly this implies some kind of prayer.

Four Questions:

What are the various explanations of the Hebrew "la-su-a**h**"?

Which one does Rashi prefer and why?

Why do the rabbis claim that Shaharit, Minhah and Maariv were written by the patriarchs, when we know (and surely they realized too) these prayers were written much later?

Is it easier for you to pray when the spirit moves you, or when tradition mandates one of the daily prayers? Explain.

RASHI'S RIDDLES

D'var Torah – Toldot

"Then Yitzhak sent Yaakov away, and he went to Paddan-aram, to Lavan, the son of Betuel the Aramean, the brother of Rivkah, mother of Yaakov and Esav."

Bereshit/Genesis 28:5

The Torah is usually very careful in mentioning names of people and their relationship to the other members of their family. Rashi claims that he does not see any reason for mentioning all the relatives of Lavan. In his words, "I do not know what these words teach us." Another commentator, who lived over a century after Rashi, Nahmanides (Gerona, Spain, 1194-1270), gives a reasonable explanation. He says that Lavan is described as the brother of Rivkah, who was the mother of both Yaakov and Esav, for a good reason. Yitzhak sends Yaakov to Lavan, but not Esav, because he knew that it was God's will for Yaakov to be the one through whom the line of Avraham's blessings will be fulfilled. Yaakov will carry on the Jewish tradition, not Esav.

For whatever reason, Rashi sees no reason for the Torah's mention of Rivkah, or her being the mother of Yaakov and Esav. While Nahmanides is one of the great commentators on the Torah, Rashi is supreme and recognized as the greatest authority on the Torah. His commentary is studied first and foremost by all students of Torah. And yet, Rashi has the humility to say: "I do not know what these words teach us." This is a remarkable admission by the Dean of all Torah commentators. In fact, there are 77 different places in Tanakh where Rashi makes the same statement. This is perhaps one of the best signs that Rashi is truly a saint.

Four Questions:

Does the fact that Rashi cannot explain this passage reflect poorly on him?

What explanation does Nahmanides give for the verse?

What quality does Rashi exemplify by saying "I do not know"? What do most people say when they do not know the answer to some question?

Are you willing to admit when you don't know something, or when you cannot answer a question?

RASHI'S RIDDLES

D'var Torah – Vayetze

"Yaakov went on his way, and angels of God met him." Bereshit/Genesis 32:2

After spending twenty years away from his family and home, having fled from his angry twin brother Esav, Yaakov now has wives and children and great wealth. He is ready to return home. God calls him to come back to Eretz Yisrael and raise his large family. He says farewell to his father-in-law, Lavan, and departs. The Torah then says that angels of God encountered him. What is the meaning of this? Rabbi Gunther Plaut (*The Torah: A Modern Commentary*) reminds us that angels met Yaakov when he first left home (28:12), and now meet him again "as if to signify that his exile for the past twenty years has always been guided by God." Rashi has a more fanciful explanation, from Midrash Tanhuma. He suggests that there are different sets of angels – some that guard us outside of Eretz Yisrael, and some that guard us inside Eretz Yisrael. Now that Yaakov was leaving the Diaspora, and return home, the angels of the Diaspora were leaving him, and the angels of Eretz Yisrael were taking over, and accompanying him home.

Four Questions:

What are the explanations of Rabbi Plaut and of Rashi for the appearance of the angels?

Which explanation do you accept? Perhaps you have a different interpretation?

When the Torah speaks of angels, what do you think it means?

Do you believe in angels? What do you think an angel is? Do you have any personal stories about your own angels?

RASHI'S RIDDLES

D'var Torah – Vayishlah

"Esau ran toward him (Yaakov), and embraced him, and fell upon his neck, and kissed him; and they wept." Bereshit/Genesis 33:4

Yaakov is returning from twenty years away from home, living with his father-in-law, Lavan, and his wives, Leah and Rachel, and children. He does not know how his twin brother Esav will greet him. The Torah tells us that even though Yaakov was fearful that Esav was coming with an army to kill him, in the end the two brothers embrace, kiss and become reconciled. The Hebrew word "and he [Esav] kissed him [Yaakov] has dots above it – something very unusual in the Torah. (If you have access to a Sefer Torah – look at the dots; or perhaps in a Tikkun). Rashi quotes two opinions about the dots. One, from a midrashic collection called Sifrei, is that Esav did not kiss his brother with sincerity, but just in a formal way, to end their estrangement. The other view Rashi quotes is that of Rabbi Shimon bar Yohai, a rabbi in the Mishnah, who wrote that in a moment of deep emotion, Esav could not restrain his warm feelings for his brother, and kissed him with all of his heart.

Four Questions:

Which of the two points of view that Rashi quotes sounds more likely?

What factors would make Esav want to reconcile with his twin brother?

Can you give an example of siblings or friends who ended a long-term disagreement? How did they do it? What was the result?

If you were Esav, would you have kissed Yaakov with all your heart?

RASHI'S RIDDLES

D'var Torah – Vayeshev

"Yosef's brothers saw that it was he whom their father loved most of all his brothers, so they hated him; and they could not speak kindly to him."

Bereshit/Genesis 37:4

Rashi, following the midrash (Bereshit Rabbah 84:8) notes that the Torah seems to repeat itself. First we read that the brothers hated Yosef, and then we read that they could not speak kindly to him. It would seem obvious that if they hated him, that they would not speak kindly to him. But Rashi learns from this something positive about the brothers – namely that they were honest. They could not feel one way and speak another way. Had they spoken kindly to him, they would be thinking one way and talking a different way.

In Jewish tradition this is considered to be inconsistent and not a positive way of behaving. Honesty would seem to demand that words should follow the heart.

Four Questions:

How does Rashi find a positive trait in the behavior of Yosef's brothers?

Is it not possible that the brothers would have acted diplomatically, and even though they hated Yosef, they could behave politely and civilly toward him?

Should one always say what is in the heart? Are there occasions when a kind word is appropriate even if it is difficult to express?

What would you do if you were one of Yosef's brothers? Would it be possible for you to speak kindly to him? Explain.

RASHI'S RIDDLES

D'var Torah – Miketz

"And they [the brothers of Yosef] said, 'If you please, my lord, we came down once before to buy food...."' Bereshit/Genesis 43:20

This pasuk appears in the middle of the cat-and-mouse story in which Yosef is testing and teasing his brothers, to see if they have truly repented for their vicious act many years ago, when they left him in a pit to die. After sending his brothers back to their father, Yaakov, to bring young Binyamin (Benjamin) with them, they finally persuade Yaakov to let Binyamin come with them. They now are conversing with Yosef's house steward and explaining to him that they had come once before, and this is their second trip. The Hebrew "we came down," is a special form of the verb "to go down" which is repeated for emphasis ("yarod yaradnu"). Rashi, following several midrashim, implies that this "coming down," has two parts – based on the double use of the verb "yarad" – to come down. First, they came down because any time one leaves Eretz Yisrael it is a "yeridah," or "coming down." So going to Egypt is the first way in which the brothers "come down." Second, they are coming down because back home they used to be the suppliers of food, and now they are on the other end – they are the recipients of food.

Four Questions:

On what Hebrew words does Rashi base his explanation. What grammatical form allows him to make this interpretation?

Why is leaving Eretz Yisrael called in Hebrew "yeridah," or "coming down?"

What is the opposite Hebrew word, and in what different ways is it used?

What lessons can we derive about Rashi's view of Eretz Yisrael, and how can you act on this view in your own life?

RASHI'S RIDDLES

D'var Torah – Vayigash

"Then Yosef fell on the neck of his brother Binyamin and wept."

Bereshit/Genesis 45:14

In Parashat Vayigash we read of the reconciliation of Yosef and his brothers. Yosef is most moved by being able to reconcile with his full brother, Binyamin, the only brother who had the same mother (Rachel) as he. Thus, the Torah says that Yosef fell on the neck on Binyamin and wept. Here Rashi introduces a completely different idea, based on several midrashim. (Many of Rashi's comments are derived from older collections of midrashim, such as Midrash Rabbah). The imaginative comment of Rashi on this pasuk is based on the fact that in the case of all the other brothers (see pasuk 15) the Torah says that Yosef "wept upon them." In the case of Binyamin it says that Yosef wept upon the **neck** of Binyamin. Since the two temples were built on the land apportioned to the tribe of Binyamin, Rashi comments that when Yosef cried on Binyamin's neck, he was crying over the two temples. ("Neck" is sometimes considered by the rabbis as a metaphor for the holy Temple in Jerusalem, since it reminds them of the Two Pillars of the Temple. Especially since the Torah says that Yosef fell on the "necks" – plural – of Binyamin – this reminds them of the two pillars.) Yosef is crying, says Rashi, over the two temples that would some day be built on the land of Binyamin, and later both would be destroyed.

Four Questions:

What is the difference in the Torah between Yosef's kissing Binyamin and kissing his other brothers?

How do Rashi and the midrash explain the meaning of the word "neck?"

Why would Rashi turn his attention from the simple meaning ("peshat") of the Torah text, to the imaginative ("drash") meaning of the Bet Mikdash?

Do you ever feel sad that we do not have a Bet Mikdash in Jerusalem today? Do you think we will ever rebuild the Bet Mikdash?

RASHI'S RIDDLES

D'var Torah – Vayehi

"The time approached for Yaakov to die, so he called his son, Yosef, and said to him, 'Please, if I have found favor in your eyes, please …do kindness and faithfulness with me – please do not bury me in Egypt.'" Bereshit/Genesis 47:29

As Yaakov is about to die, his final wish is to be buried in Eretz Yisrael, rather than in a foreign land – Egypt. Burial in Eretz Yisrael has been the longing of many pious Jews from time immemorial. Rashi pays special attention in Yaakov's request to the Hebrew phrase for "kindness and faithfulness," (hesed ve-emet). He writes in his commentary that an act of kindness which one does for a dead person is truly an act of authentic kindness, a completely faithful and truthful kindness, with no ulterior motive. Rashi refers to such an act as "Hesed shel Emet," a phrase which has become an accepted term in Hebrew for the most authentic type of kindness. Why? Because it is not possible for the recipient to return the favor. The dead cannot pay you back. Doing things for the deceased, such as preparation for burial, and all the acts associated with interment, are considered in Jewish tradition to be among the highest type of mitzvah that is possible to do.

Four Questions:

What interpretation does Rashi derive from the dual phrase, "kindness and faithfulness?"

Why are things we perform for the dead considered in Judaism to be so praiseworthy?

How are they different from kind acts that a person performs for a living person?

Have you ever done an act of kindness for a deceased person? Give some examples.

RASHI'S RIDDLES

D'var Torah – Shemot

"After some time, Moshe grew up, and he went out to his people and saw their burdens…." Shemot/ Exodus 2:11

Many comments in the Midrash and in Rashi are based on tiny linguistic and grammatical wrinkles. If one reads this pasuk literally, it says in Hebrew that Moshe saw

"b-sivlotam," or "he saw **in** their burdens. Rashi assumes, based on Midrash Shemot Rabbah 1:27, that Moshe focused his eyes and his heart on what he saw, and was distressed over the burdens of his people. It is one thing to "see" their burdens, and yet another to see, feel and empathize with them. That is the meaning that Rashi infers from the Torah. This tells us about the connection that Moshe had with his people, and the immediate response he had when he saw that they were enslaved and suffering. It also tells us about the kind of person Moshe was – not one who could go back to the luxury of Pharaoh's palace and ignore the pain of his people.

Four Questions:

What Hebrew letter changes the interpretation of this pasuk?

How does Rashi explain the meaning of the pasuk based on this Hebrew letter?

What is the difference between seeing an evil, and feeling the pain of those upon whom evil is inflicted?

Can you give some examples of times when you encountered evil and just "observed" what was happening? And other times when you took action because of what you saw?

RASHI'S RIDDLES

D'var Torah – Va-era

"HaShem said to Moshe, 'Say to Aharon, "Take your staff and stretch out your hand over the waters of Egypt; over its rivers… so that they shall turn into blood…."

Shemot/Exodus 7:19

Rashi's question on this pasuk relates to the issue of why God tells Moshe to tell Aharon, instead of telling Moshe himself to stretch his rod over the waters of Egypt, so that they become blood. Rashi explains that when Moshe was a baby, his mother placed him in a small wicker basket and put him in the Nile, hoping that he would be hidden and somehow saved. Thus, Moshe was saved by the river, and it would not be appropriate now for Moshe himself to bring punishment to the river. Therefore it is Aharon who has the river turn into blood, and not Moshe. The Midrash from which Rashi takes this comment (Shemot Rabbah 9:10 and Tanhuma 14) explains further that one does not harm anything that had once been beneficial. Likewise, the Talmud has an expression: "Into the cistern from which you drank, do not throw stones" (Bava Kamma 92b).

Four Questions:

How does Rashi explain the fact that HaShem tells Aharon, and not Moshe, to turn the river into blood?

What principle is derived from this fact?

How can we apply this principle to the environment, such as the air or water?

In what ways do you protect the air and water, that every day gives you life?

RASHI'S RIDDLES

D'var Torah – Bo

"You shall guard the matzot...." Shemot/Exodus 12:17

In the Pesah story, an important part of the tale is for the Israelite people to eat unleavened bread (matzah), since they were in a hurry to leave Egypt, and did not have time for the bread to rise. Thus, the Torah warns that it is necessary to guard the flour so that it not rise and become leavened. However, Rashi notices that the Torah does not specifically say "guard the flour," – it says, rather, "guard the matzot." Naturally, thinks Rashi, there must be a reason for using the word "matzot" and not "flour." The reason, explains Rashi, is that the Torah really means another word that has the same Hebrew letters as matzot – namely, **mitzvot**. In other words, Rashi is reading the Torah to say: Guard the mitzvot. But why would this command appear here in the story of eating unleavened bread. Rashi explains further that in this case, guarding the mitzvot and guarding the matzot are very similar in one very important way. One must guard the matzah so that it does not have time to rise. Thus, bake the matzah in haste. The same with the mitzvot. When an opportunity to perform a mitzvah comes to you, make haste, don't let it sit and "ferment." Do it immediately!

Four Questions:

What two Hebrew words can be read in this pasuk because they have the same letters?

What interpretation does Rashi offer to explain why the Torah says "mitzvot" and not "matzot?"

Why is it important to make haste in performing a mitzvah? What's the rush?

Are you a person who takes advantage of opportunities to do a mitzvah when it comes your way – or the opposite? Or both? Explain.

RASHI'S RIDDLES

D'var Torah – B'shalah

"Adonai is a Warrior;

Adonai is God's name." Shemot/Exodus 15:3

In order to understand Rashi's explanation of this pasuk, we must first understand that in Talmudic interpretation, God's names have different meanings. Whenever God is called "Adonai" (really YHVH), the Torah is referring to the aspect of God which leans toward mercy and compassion. Whenever God is called "Elohim," the Torah is referring to that part of God which exercises strict judgment. In this case God is called Adonai, and therefore Rashi's comment relates to God as a merciful and compassionate God. What puzzles Rashi is that since the beginning of the pasuk states that God is a Warrior, how is it possible for the Torah to choose to use the name of God which describes God's compassionate side? It would seem more logical that in war God would be more of a strict judge, punishing the evil enemy, than a merciful Creator. Thus, Rashi says this: "Even when God is doing battle and taking vengeance from the enemy, God exercises the quality of mercy, a God Who sustains all creatures – even evil people. This is not like earthly rulers, who, when engaged in war, can only be strict and harsh." God is so different from humans, that mercy is never omitted from God's actions.

Four Questions:

What is the question that Rashi is trying to answer in this pasuk?

How does Rashi explain the fact that God is called Adonai rather than Elohim?

Why is it normal for rulers, when fighting a war, to act without mercy?

Do you think it is possible for you to keep your sense of compassion even in a time when you are fighting a battle, engaged in conflict and confrontation, or promoting a cause which requires war-like actions? Explain.

RASHI'S RIDDLES

D'var Torah – Yitro

"Yitro, the priest of Midian, the father-in-law of Moshe, heard all that God had done for Moshe and God's people Israel – how God had brought Israel out of Egypt." Shemot/Exodus 18:1

This Parashah introduces the important figure of Yitro, father of Moshe's wife Zipporah. Yitro becomes an adviser and friend of Moshe and the Israelite nation. From this chapter we learn how impressed Yitro was with God's actions in the Exodus from Egypt. The specific words the Torah uses in describing what God did in bringing out the people of Israel are that Yitro heard what God had done for Moshe and Israel. Rashi wonders why Moshe is mentioned separately, since he is also part of the people of Israel. The Torah might have said, "Yitro heard all that God had done for Israel," – and that would have included Moshe. So why is Moshe's name mentioned in addition to Israel? Rashi's answer is that Moshe is given his own acknowledgment, in addition to being part of the nation, because, in Rashi's comment, "Moshe is equal to the whole nation." Rashi is ascribing greatness to Moshe because he was the leader of the people, the one who brought them out of Egypt, and saved the nation from destruction at the hands of Pharaoh. Moshe was also the one who received and taught the Torah.

Four Questions:

What question is Rashi trying to answer?

Why does Rashi think Moshe deserves his own mention, apart from the Israelite people?

What were some of the great accomplishments of Moshe, and which was the greatest?

In what ways can you try to follow in the footsteps of Moshe, and continue his work?

RASHI'S RIDDLES

D'var Torah – Mishpatim

"If you lend money to My people, to the poor person who is with you…." Shemot/Exodus 22:24

The entire Parashah of Mishpatim deals with specific laws that govern daily human and business relationships. These include laws about Hebrew servants, personal injuries, offenses against property, moral offenses, taking advantage of the weak, truth in justice, etc. The pasuk we are now studying is about lending money to the poor. The Torah frames the matter by saying that the occasion may arise when you lend money to the poor. It adds one Hebrew word, "imakh," which is translated as "who is with you." The simple meaning (which is called the "peshat") would have been just as clear without this word. So why does the Torah add the word "imakh?" Rashi suggests that by saying that the person is **with** you, it means "Look at yourself as if you are the poor person." In other words, "with you," means literally "inside you." Imagine **you are that person**. Put yourself in that person's position, and treat that person the same way you would want to be treated.

Four Questions:

How does Rashi interpret the Hebrew word "imakh?"

How would you see another as if you were that person?

Why do you think Rashi wants you to imagine yourself in the position of the poor person?

In what ways might you act differently if you totally identify with the poor?

RASHI'S RIDDLES
D'var Torah – Terumah

"You shall make a parokhet of turquoise wool, and purple wool, and crimson yarns, and fine twisted linen; designer's work, with kruvim on it." Shemot/Exodus 26:31

The Torah describes in elaborate detail the lavish, artistic design of the Mishkan, the portable Sanctuary which the Israelites carried all through their forty years of wandering in the Sinai desert. Mechanical engineers and skilled technical artists have made models of the Mishkan based on the description in the Torah. It is a colorful, beautiful and even exquisite Sanctuary, appropriate for the House of God.

The pasuk we are looking at describes the rich colors and sumptuous fabrics of which the Torah commands the partitioning curtain (parokhet) should be made. The parokhet is significant for several reasons. First, it is the same Hebrew word we use in today's synagogue to describe the curtain that covers the Sifray Torah (Torah Scrolls) in the Aron Kodesh (Holy Ark). This shows the direct historical line that traces the history of the modern synagogue back to the ancient House of God in the biblical wilderness. Secondly, Rashi's comment lends even greater significance to the parokhet. He teaches that its purpose is similar to the separation between a king and the people. In other words, the two tablets of the Ten Commandments, which were inside the Holy of Holies, represent God's presence (the "King"). The parokhet makes a partition between the Ten Commandments (in today's synagogue, the Sifray Torah) and the worshippers in the House of God. In the biblical Mishkan it separated the Holy of Holies from the rest of the Sanctuary. Rashi's comparison between the King and the people lends an air of supreme royalty and a special feeling of sanctity to the transcendence of the Aron Kodesh.

Four Questions:

Why must God's House be constructed with the finest and most beautiful materials available?

What feeling should a Sanctuary, with the Aron Kodesh at the front and center, convey to the worshippers?

What comparison does Rashi give which makes the role of the parokhet even more special?

What feeling do you have when you enter a beautiful Sanctuary, with the Sifray Torah gracefully hidden behind the parokhet?

RASHI'S RIDDLES

D'var Torah – Tetzaveh

"Take the vestments and dress Aaron with the tunic… and bind Aaron with the decorated belt of the ephod." Shemot/Exodus 29:5

Chapter 29 of Shemot describes the elaborate and beautiful garments worn by the Kohen Gadol (High Priest). Over the tunic (cloak) was the ephod, a close-fitting coat worn around the body under the arms, with straps over the shoulders to keep it in place. Rashi explains that all the beautifully decorated garments worn by the Kohen Gadol were for the purpose of adorning and enhancing the splendor of the appearance of the Kohen Gadol. The entire Mishkan – portable desert Sanctuary – was appointed with fabric, color and textures that lent an air of extreme beauty to the worship service. When we enter a beautiful synagogue today, and see the magnificent covers over the Sefer Torahs, or the lavish architecture, or the lovely decorations and sculptures that may be on the walls, we are following the biblical tradition that worship must be associated with beauty, pleasant to the eye of the worshiper. The beauty of garments, including a tallit or kippah in today's synagogue, add to the feeling of holiness present in the act of worship.

Four Questions:

Why does Rashi find it necessary to explain the purpose of the garments of the Kohen Gadol?

What other parts of the Mishkan are commanded to be created with beauty and splendor?

Does beauty enhance the act of worship?

What part of your synagogue, or worship garments, do you find most beautiful? Explain.

RASHI'S RIDDLES
D'var Torah – Ki Tisa

"I [God] have filled Bezalel with a Divine spirit, with wisdom, understanding, and knowledge, in every craft." Shemot/Exodus 31:3

When Rashi writes a comment on a pasuk, or a phrase or word in a pasuk, he usually has a question that he thinks needs to be answered. The first question one must ask in studying Rashi is "What question is Rashi trying to answer?" The question here is this: Why did the Torah use three synonyms for one idea, when it could have used more brief language and used only one word? The Torah, a Divine book, does not repeat just for flowery literary use. Rashi's answer is this: Each of these three words – wisdom, understanding, and knowledge, has a different source. Wisdom is information that comes from what one learns from others. Understanding is information that a person infers from what he learns from others – that which a person figures out in their own mind. And finally, knowledge is Divine inspiration – information that comes from God.

Four Questions:

Why does Rashi feel it necessary to comment on the three nouns used in this pasuk?

What are the three kinds of information Rashi describes – and how can one characterize them in different words?

Is it important to know that the information we glean comes from different sources? Why?

Does the information you possess come from some or all of these sources? In what ways does this information differ one from another?

RASHI'S RIDDLES
D'var Torah – Vayakhel

"God gave the ability to teach [to Bezalel] and to Oholiav ben Ahisamakh of the Tribe of Dan." Shemot/Exodus 35:34

The main architect of the Mishkan, the Portable Sanctuary in the Wilderness of Sinai, was Bezalel ben Uri ben Hur of the tribe of Yehudah. This verse tells us that the co-worker of Bezalel was Oholiav. A few pesukim earlier we learn that God filled Bezalel "with Godly spirit, with wisdom, understanding and knowledge" (35:31). This pasuk adds that these artists also had the ability to teach this wisdom to others, and it adds the name of Bezalel's chief colleague. Rashi points out that while Bezalel was of the Tribe of Yehudah, one of the most prominent tribes, Oholiav was of the Tribe of Dan, one of the least important tribes (Dan's mother was not one of Yaakov's two wives, Leah or Rahel, he was the son of Bilhah, handmaid of Rahel). The lesson in this appointment, says Rashi (quoting Midrash Tanhuma 13) is that "The nobleman is not given preference over the pauper."

Four Questions:

According to Rashi, why did God place Oholiav on the same level as Bezalel, even though Bezalel was from a more prestigious tribe?

What role should wealth and status play in appointment of Jewish leaders?

Do you think Oholiav was less capable or inferior in any way to Bezalel? What relationship does background have to ability?

If you were to select someone to an important position, would their status or eminence play any role? Explain.

RASHI'S RIDDLES

D'var Torah – Pekuday

"Bezalel ben Uri ben Hur, of the tribe of Yehudah, did all that Adonai commanded Moshe." Shemot/ Exodus 38:22

Rashi discusses an issue brought up in the Jerusalem Talmud (Peah 1:1) about whether and why God commanded that the furnishings be constructed first, or the Mishkan (portable Tabernacle) be built first. One important point made in this complicated discussion is that Bezalel was to follow what God said, regardless of what he thought. Bezalel claims that in the normal course of events, one builds a building, and after that the furnishings. Whereas in the case of the Mishkan, it is the furnishings that God commands to build first. Rashi emphasizes that in the end it is the will and command of God which is determinative. His proof: Bezalel's name means "Be-zel-el" – in the shadow of God. All the work of the Mishkan is done under the direction (or shadow) of God. There is an underlying point of view here that all good architects follow the natural contours of God's world – that everything we build is built in "the shadow of God."

Four Questions:

What interpretation does Rashi derive from the Hebrew name of Bezalel?

What architectural principles can be learned from the meaning of the name of the great architect of the Mishkan, Bezalel?

What architectural structures or styles do you know that follow the earth's shapes and contours?

How do you see architecture as reflecting the work of God?

RASHI'S RIDDLES

D'var Torah – Vayikra

"When a soul ["a person"] brings a meal-offering to God, the offering shall be of fine flour…." Vayikra/ Leviticus 2:1

Rashi is known to have a very discerning eye in reading the text of the Torah. This is part of what makes him the Prince of Commentators, and a Master Teacher. Like a poet, he sees things that no one else sees, and expresses his vision in a way that is unique. Sometimes he gets his inspiration from the Midrash, but even then his ability to select just the right Midrash is uncanny. In our pasuk Rashi notices that in other places in the Torah the word "Soul" (Hebrew, "nefesh") is not used with a gift of a meal offering. He further reasons that meal offerings are usually the gifts of poor people. Wealthy people would be more likely to offer livestock, but poor people have none, so they offer something less expensive – flour. Since the expression "Soul" is used only in connection with meal offerings, there must be a reason. That reason, teaches Rashi, is that when a poor person brings a meal offering, even though it is a very modest gift, God considers it as if the person offered his own soul. The lesson Rashi teaches is that it is not the amount of a contribution that defines it as being "charitable," but the spirit of the gift, and the level of giving that is appropriate to one's ability to give.

Four Questions:

How does Rashi connect in this pasuk the word "soul" and "meal offering."

What lesson does Rashi draw from the connection of these two phrases?

How can we tell whether a contribution is generous or not? Is it the amount?

Do you consider yourself generous? Explain.

RASHI'S RIDDLES

D'var Torah – Tzav

"This is the law of sacrifice of well-being that one may offer to Adonai: If one offers it for thanksgiving…." Vayikra/Leviticus 7:11-12

Rashi ties this verse to Psalm 107, and notices that verses 8,15, 21, and 31 repeat the same phrase: "They should give thanks to Adonai for God's kindness and for God's wonders to humanity." Since this pasuk is repeated four times, and follows various situations of danger, Rashi sees four different examples of miracles people experience, based on this Psalm, which are reasons for giving thanks to God: such as those who are seafarers, who travel across deserts, who were confined in prison and released, and who were sick and were healed.. These seem to be the four most dangerous kinds of acts people engaged in during the Middle Ages (Rashi lived from 1040 to 1105 C.E.). To us moderns these reasons might seem rather antiquated. However, in the global village in which we now live, with violence, war and terrorism rampant, dangers from crossing the sea, traveling in the desert (Iraq), being confined in prison (in any war zone) are almost as common today as they were in Rashi's day. And being healed from illness is something every human being experiences. Rashi's attempt at making this act of thanksgiving relevant to his medieval world is equally relevant to us moderns.

Four Questions:

How does Rashi bring the verses of the Tanakh into modern times?

What other dangers do we face in the 21st century?

Why is it important to give thanks for the daily miracles we experience from God?

What ways could you be more appreciative of God's miracles in your life?

RASHI'S RIDDLES

D'var Torah - Sh'mini

"Moshe said to Aharon: 'Approach the altar…." Vayikra/Leviticus 9:7

The kohanim were about to be consecrated, and Aharon, the Kohen Gadol, is to be inaugurated into the exalted service of High Priest. Rashi comments, following the midrash in Sifra, and explains that Aharon was embarrassed and diffident, afraid to approach the altar. Otherwise, Moshe would merely have had to say: "Bring the offerings." Moshe is trying to boost up the morale and confidence of his older brother during this momentous occasion. We always assume that important people are fully confident and poised when they are about to approach the stage and perform. This gives us an insight into the more probable mood of many famous people. Actors, diplomats, and many others share these feelings of hesitation and anxiety.

Four Questions:

1) According to Rashi, what was the reason why Moshe had to tell Aharon: "Approach the altar"?

2) Why would someone as important as Aharon feel embarrassment or fear?

3) How does this insight of Rashi help us understand the sector of people who are famous and powerful?

4) Have you ever experienced fear or anxiety when about to perform or appear in public? If so, was there anyone there to encourage you?

RASHI'S RIDDLES

D'var Torah - Tazria

"As long as the disease is upon him he shall remain impure. He shall stay in isolation; his dwelling shall be outside the camp." Vayikra/Leviticus 13:46

Those persons who are afflicted with disease are to be separated from others. This is natural with a communicable disease. However, most of the time all persons who are afflicted, and isolated from the main camp of the people, can be with one another. In the case of one who has leprosy (Tza-ra-at), such a person must not only be isolated from the camp but from other afflicted persons as well. Why should this be so? Rashi says that since Tza-ra-at is brought on as a punishment for malicious gossip, this person caused a separation between a man and his wife, or between a person and a friend, the punishment is that that person too shall be separated.

Four Questions:

1) How does Rashi explain the fact that the person with Tza-ra-at is separated from the main camp as well as from others afflicted with the same disease?

2) What is the conventional explanation for the affliction of Tza-ra-at?

3) Do you think there is any connection between Tza-ra-at and immoral behavior?

4) Have you ever participated in gossip? How can you reduce the amount of gossip you (and others) participate in?

RASHI'S RIDDLES
D'var Torah – Metzora

"The Kohen shall order two live pure birds, cedar wood, crimson stuff, and hyssop to be brought for him who is to be purified." Vaykra/Leviticus 14:4

When a person who contracted leprosy is verified by the Kohen as having been cured, there is a ritual that the cured person must undergo before returning home. This ceremony gave the cured person a sense of renewal, physically and spiritually. Included in the ritual are a number of items which are reminders to the person about the future. Since the biblical mind associated illness with moral failure, the items involved in the ritual are connected with the failures associated with that particular disease, such as malicious gossip and arrogance. The birds remind the patient of the verbal twittering and chattering the person engaged in. The cedar wood is included because the cedar is a tall and beautiful tree, reminding the person that he acted in a way that was "high and mighty." The wool is used because the Hebrew word for wool is the same word as "worm," (cf. Exodus 16:20) – to remind the person to be low like a worm, and not high and arrogant.

Four Questions:

Why is it necessary for a cured person to undergo a ritual of purification?

How are the items in the ritual tied to the disease of leprosy?

Is it necessary to remind a person of one's moral failures? For what reason?

Would going through such a ritual be helpful to you to improve yourself?

RASHI'S RIDDLES

D'var Torah – Aharay Mot

"Aharon did as God commanded." Vayikra/ Leviticus 16:34

Chapter 16 describes the elaborate ritual which Aharon performed on Yom Kippur in his role as Kohen Gadol. The chapter ends with the phrase, "Aharon did as God commanded." There are many mitzvot listed in which the Torah does not point out that they were in fact carried out. It is merely assumed that what is commanded by God is followed. In this case, regarding the intricate ritual of Yom Kippur, the Torah specifically mentions that it was carried out. Rashi wonders why the Torah mentions that the command was carried out in this pasuk, and not in many other places. His answer is that the Torah is praising Aharon, that he did not wear his elaborate and attractive garments (see verse 32) on this solemn occasion for his own glory and greatness, but rather he did it because God commanded him to do so.

Four Questions:

1) What is unusual about this pasuk that prompts Rashi to raise a question?

2) What does Rashi's answer tell us about Aharon's devotion to God?

3) Is it really important why one carries out a command, as long as the command is fulfilled?

4) Would you prefer to obey an authority because it is the law, or because you desired to do so out of your own heart? Explain.

Rashi's Riddles

D'var Torah – Kedoshim

"You shall not steal, and you shall not deal falsely, and you shall not lie to one another. And you shall not swear falsely by My name…." Vayikra/Leviticus 19:11-12

What is the connection between the various prohibitions in these p'sukim? Is there is relationship between stealing, dealing falsely, lying, and swearing falsely by God's name? Rashi sees a connection. He writes: If you have stolen, you will then deal falsely by having to deny your act of stealing. Then you will likely weave a web of lies to support your false denial. In the end you will swear falsely when challenged in court. In short, Rashi's good advice is: do not lie, or you will end up telling more and more lies to cover up your original lie.

Four Questions:

Does the Torah make a connection between the various prohibitions in these p'sukim? Or does Rashi see this on his own?

What is the connection that Rashi sees?

What are some of the problems with lying?

Have you ever caught yourself in this web of lies, or known someone who did? What was the result?

RASHI'S RIDDLES

D'var Torah: Emor

"He shall be holy to you…." Vayikra/Leviticus 21:8

The special status of kohanim has been recognized since earliest times. They were to receive the highest respect because they were, in a sense, channels, or facilitators, by which the people approached God. They offered "the food of your God" on the altar. After the destruction of the Bet Ha-Mikdash by the Romans in the year 70 C.E., kohanim no longer had that same role, but did maintain a special status in the community. Rashi reminds of us of that special status by writing in his commentary "Treat him [a kohen] with holiness, that he should take priority to be the first in all matters. For example, he should take precedence to lead Birkat HaMazon." Other things which reflect the status of kohanim in our day are honors such as having the first aliyah at the Torah, officiating at a Pidyon HaBen, and chanting the Birkat Kohanim in the ceremony known as "duchaning" in congregations where that is still done.

Four Questions:

How does Rashi explain the holiness of the kohanim?

What ways do kohanim still reflect special exalted status?

Since there is no Bet Mikdash in existence today, should kohanim retain their special roles?

Should kohanim insist on maintaining these special privileges today?

RASHI'S RIDDLES

D'var Torah: Behar

"For the Land is Mine, and you are only strangers resident with Me"

Vayikra/Leviticus 25:23

This passage discusses the famous Jubilee Year (Hebrew Yovel, meaning "shofar," since the shofar is blown to announce the onset of this special year). When the Jubilee Year comes, every fiftieth year, all land reverts to its original owner. This is done to prevent any one person from accumulating massive amounts of property, and causing the original owners to become impoverished. The plan is remarkable in its innovative approach to providing fair distribution of land and property. The underlying belief supporting this plan of re-distribution of the Land is that God is the ultimate Owner of all the land. While one person owns the land for a while, that person should not consider that she/he is the permanent owner. It is God who is the real Owner, the permanent Owner, and God can distribute the land in a way that seems fair by divine standards. Rashi teaches that when the person holding the land has to return it to its previous owner during the Jubilee Year, that owner should not return it begrudgingly, because it is really God's land anyway.

Four Questions:

What is the underling purpose for returning land to its original owner during the Jubilee Year?

Why should the present owner be forced to return the land to its original owner? Is that fair?

Explain the meaning of words in the verse that say that we are "strangers" with God.

How does it make you feel to know that you are only a temporary guardian of all your property, and that the true owner is God?

RASHI'S RIDDLES

D'var Torah: Behukotai

"If you will go in my decrees…." Vayikra/Leviticus 26:3

Rashi's commentary on this pasuk delves into the word "go," and he wonders what it means. By reading the rest of the pasuk, "and observe My commandments and do them," one might think that the second half merely repeats the first half. What then is the reason for stating it twice? First, "to go in my decrees," and then "to observe My commandments." So, claims Rashi, there must be another, different meaning of the word to "go" in my decrees. It means, argues Rashi, to study the Torah diligently, and to labor in the study of the Torah. In this interpretation Rashi is following the midrash Sifra which states that "going" implies that the process of Torah study is "going" from one level to the next higher level of understanding. "Going" also means putting forth effort and labor, which is included in the process of delving deeper and deeper into the meaning of God's commands.

Four Questions:

Why does Rashi question the meaning of the word "go" in this pasuk?

What conclusions does he reach?

Why is it important to constantly reach higher and deeper levels of understanding of the Torah?

What ways can you be assured that your study of Torah becomes ever deeper and deeper?

RASHI'S RIDDLES

D'var Torah: Bemidbar

"Those who encamped before the Mishkan (Tabernacle) in front, before the Tent of Meeting on the east, were Moshe and Aharon and his sons, guardians of the Sanctuary...." Bemidbar/Numbers 3:38

The first Sidrah in Sefer Bemidbar deals with the census of the people, and how they were to encamp around the Mishkan. Each tribe is given its proper place, which they held whether they were in camp, or marching through the Sinai Wilderness. Rashi observes that Moshe was on the east of the Mishkan, right next to the tribe of Judah. He points out that the proximity of Moshe to the Tribe of Judah was beneficial for the Judah-ites because being close to Moshe they gained from his wisdom. Just as Moshe studied Torah, so too did the members of the Tribe of Judah study Torah. Rashi brings a biblical proof from the Book of Psalms (60:9), where Judah is called God's "Lawmaker." By the same token, Rashi says that the tribes of Issachar and Zevulun were also positively influenced in this direction because they too were close to Moshe, on the east side of the Mishkan. Being close to a scholar influences one's own interests in learning.

Four Questions:

What lesson does Rashi learn from the location of Moshe and the tribes of Judah, Issachar and Zevulun?

Why is it important to have neighbors and friends who have good values?

In what ways do good neighbors and friends influence us, and we them?

What close friends of yours have you been influenced by? How can you make sure to maintain friendships with people who will have a good influence on you?

RASHI'S RIDDLES

D'var Torah: Naso

"May God endow you with grace." Bemidbar/ Numbers 6:25

There are two different ways to translate this pasuk. The new Jewish Publication Society translation says "May the Lord deal... graciously with you." Both translations are possible, but they mean different things. There are two ways God could bless a worshipper – first by bestowing Divine grace, or dealing graciously with the person. This is how JPS has it. Rashi sees it differently. His comment is: "may God give you grace." In other words, not that God will be gracious toward you, but that God will endow you with the quality of grace. That YOU will have grace, not that God will be gracious to you.

Four Questions:

What are the two ways this pasuk can be understood?

How does Rashi understand it?

What is the difference between the two interpretations? What is meant by "grace?"

Which would you prefer – that God treat you with grace, or that God give you grace so that you yourself possess the quality of grace?

RASHI'S RIDDLES

D'var Torah: Be-ha-alotekha

"God said to Moshe: Gather for Me seventy men from the elders of Israel…. And I will draw upon the spirit that is on you and put it upon them…."

Bemidbar/Numbers 11:16-17

This is the second time in the Torah that a council of 70 sages is appointed to assist Moshe in the leadership of the large throng of Israelites. Rashi is interested here mainly in the process of endowing these seventy leaders with spiritual wisdom. God declares that some of the spiritual wisdom of Moshe will be shared by God with these seventy wise people. Did God take away any of the spirit of Moshe? Rashi says that the language indicates that God shared the wisdom of Moshe with the elders, without Moshe having to lose any of it. Moshe can be compared, says Rashi, to a lamp that gives light to other lamps without losing any of its own fire. This is what happens when a wise person shares wisdom and inspiration. In the process of sharing the person does not lose any of their own, but the others gain from it just the same.

Four Questions:

What question does Rashi focus on in this pasuk?

When God confers some of the spirit of Moshe on the 70 elders, does Moshe lose any of his own? Why not?

How is giving money to someone different from giving knowledge and wisdom?

Have you received inspiration from someone? Did that person lose any of their spirit? Explain.

RASHI'S RIDDLES

D'var Torah: Shelah Lekha

"They shall make themselves tzitzit on the corners of their garments…and you shall remember all the mitzvot of Adonai …." Numbers/Bemidbar 15:38-39

Rashi wants to know what the connection is between wearing tzitzit and remembering the mitzvot. Basing himself on Midrash Tanhuma, he uses the system called "Gematria," in which each letter of the Hebrew alphabet has a numerical value. For example, alef is one, bet is two, gimmel is three, etc. If one takes the five letters of the word "tzitzit," and add them up, we have 600. Rashi then says that we should add the eight strings of the tzitzit and the five knots, and behold – we have 613 – the number of mitzvot in the Torah! So by wearing tzitzit, we are enabled to remember all the mitzvot of Adonai.

Four Questions:

How does Rashi connect the idea of remembering with wearing the tzitzit?

What is the connection between the tzitzit, the number 613, and the mitzvot in the Torah?

Is remembering the mitzvot sufficient? What is the next step after remembering them?

When you see or wear tzitzit, does it help you remember the mitzvot? How can you make sure that it does?

RASHI'S RIDDLES

D'var Torah: Korah

"Moshe summoned Datan and Aviram b'nai Eliav; but they replied: "We will not go up."

Bemidbar/Numbers 16:12

Rashi pays special attention to the answer given by Datan and Aviram to the plea of Moshe for them to come and discuss their problem. Moshe is apparently trying to open the lines of communication and persuade them to put an end to their rebellion. But their own words, says Rashi, trip them up. Today we would call this a "Freudian slip." What we would have expected from Datan and Aviram is "We will not come." Instead they say, "We will not go up." Rashi says that their own mouths led them to stumble by saying that they have nothing in store but failure. They cannot "rise" to the occasion. "We will not go up!"

Four Questions:

What phrase leads Rashi to give his interpretation?

What Freudian slip did Datan and Aviram make?

What effect do our inner thoughts and feelings have on our speech?

Have you ever said something which you did not mean to say, but which reflected an inner truth that you may have been holding inside? Explain.

RASHI'S RIDDLES

D'var Torah: Hukat

"There was no water for the assembly, and they gathered together against Moshe and against Aharon." Bemidbar/Numbers 20:2

The verse before this one tells of the death of Miriam. Talmudic tradition always looks for connections between themes that follow one another. The question in Rashi's mind, thus, is "What is the connection between the death of Miriam and the fact that there was no water?" Obviously there was water for most of the forty years of wandering, since it now says that the water ceased to be available. Rashi's answer is as follows: During the forty years of wandering, there was a well that followed the people from place to place, and this well was there through the merit of Miriam. Many people today put a special cup on the Pesah Seder Table, parallel to Elijah's cup, but instead of wine, it is filled with water, in honor of Miriam's important role in the Exodus.

Four Questions:

What connection does Rashi see between the death of Miriam and the absence of water to drink?

Why would the presence of water be symbolic of the merit of Miriam?

Do you think that the role of women is under-recognized in the Tanakh?

How can you and others help bring the important role of women in the Tanakh to our awareness?

RASHI'S RIDDLES

D'var Torah: Balak

"Lo, a people who arises like a lion and leaps up like the king of beasts...." Bemidbar/Numbers 23:24

There are several places where the Tanakh uses the image of the lion, mostly as a metaphor of physical power. In these cases, the image is of a lying or crouching lion (Genesis 49:9, 24:9, Ezekiel 19:2). However, in this pasuk we see a picture of a lion *rising*, not *lying*. Rashi notices this and makes the following comment. The people of Israel is like a lion, rising from their sleep in the morning, like the king of beasts, ready to perform mitzvot, to wear a tallit, to recite Shema, to put on tefillin. Rashi thus uses the image of the rising lion as one of spiritual strength instead of physical strength.

Four Questions:

1) How does Rashi see the image of a lion used in various places in the Tanakh?

2) How is the lion image used here differently than other places?

3) What spin does Rashi infer from the *rising* of the lion, as opposed to the *crouching* of a lion? What is the connection between a lion and the mitzvot?

4) When you do mitzvot, like reciting the Shema in the morning, or other mitzvot, do you ever feel like a lion? Explain.

RASHI'S RIDDLES

D'var Torah: Pinhas

"Moshe spoke to HaShem saying, 'May HaShem, Source of the breath of all flesh, appoint someone over the community, who will go out before them and come in before them, who shall take them out and bring them in; and let the community of HaShem not be like sheep that have no shepherd." Bemidbar/Numbers 27:15-17

Rashi pays great attention to the proximity of passages in the Torah. This passage follows the section in which God tells Moshe that he is soon to die. Rashi notices that immediately after he hears about his own death, Moshe begins to worry not about his own fate, but about the welfare of others around him. This, says Rashi, is the sign of a righteous person, who worries more about the community, and the future welfare of his followers, than he does about himself. "They [such righteous persons] put aside their own needs and deal with the needs of the public."

Four Questions:

Why does Rashi pay attention to the passages that come before and after certain p'sukim?

What connection does Rashi see between the p'sukim above and the ones that come before?

What is the lesson that Rashi learns from this connection? Why is placing concern for the community above one's own personal needs considered praiseworthy?

Do you know people who put the needs of others before their own? Talk about them. Have you ever put the needs of others before your own? Explain.

RASHI'S RIDDLES

D'var Torah: Matot

"Moshe spoke to the people, saying, 'Arm men from among you for the army so that they may fight against Midian to inflict God's vengeance on Midian."

Bemidbar/Numbers 31:3

The Israelites are told to attack the Midianites, who brought the prophet Bilaam to curse them and lead them astray. What interests Rashi is the final clause of the pasuk which says that they are to inflict God's vengeance on Midian. In the previous verse (31:2) we read that they are to take vengeance for the Israelite nation. In this pasuk it states that they are to take God's vengeance. Why the difference? Rashi learns a lesson from this – that "One who fights Israel is as if he is fighting against the Blessed Holy One." Fighting against God's people is the same as fighting against God.

Four Questions:

1) What difference does Rashi notice between pasuk 2 and pasuk 3?

2) What conclusion does he draw from this difference?

3) What does it mean to be "fighting against God"?

4) Is there an implied protection of Jews by God in Rashi's lesson? Why would God protect the Jewish People? Do you feel special protection of God since you are a Jew?

RASHI'S RIDDLES

D'var Torah: Mas'ei

"These are the journeys of the Israelite nation, who started out from the land of Egypt…."

Bemidbar/Numbers 33:1

This chapter lists some 42 stations that the Israelites traveled from Egypt to the Promised Land of Eretz Yisrael. Rashi calculates that if you deduct the first 14, during the first year – before the decree to wander for 40 years - and then deduct 8 more after the death of Aharon in the last year – we are left with only 20 places that the Israelites stopped. Rashi's conclusion is that this long list of stations is to show God's kindness, "For even though God decreed upon Israel to move them about and make them wander in the wilderness, one cannot say that they constantly moved around the entire forty years without rest." In fact they only moved on an average of once every two years.

Four Questions:

1) What explanation does Rashi give for the Torah's listing all 42 places the Israelites camped in the Sinai Wilderness?

2) What does Rashi say about God's relationship with Israel in this connection?

3) Why does Rashi want to soften the picture of the punishment God gave the people?

4) When you give or receive punishment, should it be given with strictness or gentleness? Explain.

RASHI'S RIDDLES
Parshat Devarim

"Adonai our God spoke to us in Horev, saying, "You have had much dwelling at this mountain." Devarim/ Deuteronomy 1:6

At the end of the forty years of wandering, Moshe recounts the events of the long four-decade journey from Egypt to Eretz Yisrael. When they first began their long march, they were at Mt. Sinai. After staying there for a while, God told the people to move on, that they had been there for a long time already, and it was time to proceed. Rashi interprets this verse, that "you have had much dwelling at this mountain," based on a midrash in Sifrei, in a different way. "You have had much," explains Rashi, does not mean you have been here a long time. It means much has happened to you here, and you received much greatness and reward for being here at Mt. Sinai. You built the Mishkan, the Menorah, and the holy implements inside the Mishkan. You appointed courts to establish a system of justice and the rule of law. Most important of all, you received the Torah. What greatness happened here at Sinai!

Four Questions:

What is the peshat (simple interpretation) of this pasuk? What is its midrashic (homiletical) interpretation?

What elements and additions does the midrash add to the peshat?

How does the midrash expand the Torah's literal meaning with imaginative interpretations? What is its purpose?

What do you think about the Jewish People's greatness in its accomplishments –such as building the Mishkan, establishing a system of justice, and receiving the Torah?

RASHI'S RIDDLES
Parshat Va-et-hanan

"Please let me cross and see the good land that is on the other side of the Jordan, this good mountain and the Lebanon." Devarim/Deuteronomy 3:26

In recounting the story of the forty years of wandering, Moshe reminds the people how his plea to see the Promised Land was rejected by God. How sad it must have been for the great Master who led his people out of Egyptian bondage, through 40 years of wandering in the harsh wilderness, only to be denied his life's dream. Moshe longed to see the beautiful mountainous Land of Promise, including the high snow-capped peaks of Lebanon. Rashi gives a slight twist to Moshe's plea. What would be the most important thing Moshe would want to see? – Jerusalem, of course. (Never mind that Jerusalem was not made the capital of the Israelite nation until centuries later under King David. Chronology never bothered the rabbis of the Talmud, nor interfered with any midrashic comment). Thus, Rashi interprets "this good mountain" as Jerusalem. He explains Lebanon as the Holy Temple, since Lebanon shares the Hebrew root "lavan" – or white, and it was the Temple that *whitened*, or forgave, Israel's failures, through the people's sin offerings and other sacrifices.

Four Questions:

What did Moshe refer to when he spoke of "the good mountain?"

Why would Rashi interpret this phrase differently than the Torah's literal meaning?

What importance does Jerusalem hold for Rashi, as for Judaism in general?

Have you been to Jerusalem? If not, do you plan to vist? What are your thoughts about Jerusalem?

RASHI'S RIDDLES

Parshat Ekev

"…to keep the mitzvot and statutes of Adonai, which I command you today, for your benefit." Devarim/ Deuteronomy 10:13

In the final speeches of Moshe, the great Teacher and Prophet admonishes his followers, the Israelite nation, to follow the mitzvot and laws of God. Rashi focuses on the expression at the end of the pasuk – "le-tov lakh," "for your benefit." Rashi sees many values in following God's rules, not the least of which is the benefit for the people themselves. Don't do it only for the reward which God will inevitably confer upon those who follow the rules, but for your own benefit. The teaching is that doing mitzvot is not only because God wants us to, but because we ourselves gain from doing so.

Four Questions:

What are some of the possible meanings that the phrase "for your benefit" might have?

Which one does Rashi emphasize? Why?

Is it better to obey God because God wants us to, or because we ourselves benefit from doing the mitzvot?

What is your primary motivation in carrying out Judaism's commands – because you are obliged to, or because you feel personal satisfaction from doing so?

RASHI'S RIDDLES

Parshat Re-eh

"…you will be doing what is good and what is right in the eyes of Adonai, your God." Devarim/ Deuteronomy 12:28

Moshe reminds the people that when they follow God's laws it will be good and right in the view of God. Rashi, following the Midrash (Sifre 79), teaches that the act of obeying God will be pleasing to both God and humans. Since the Torah says only that it will be good in the sight of God (and not humans), how does Rashi add the idea that good behavior will be pleasing to *both* God and humans? The assumption is that whatever is good in the view of people will also be good in the view of God. Thus says Rashi, - "Good" refers to the eyes of God; "right" refers to the eyes of humans. When we act rightly towards God, humans are pleased, and when we please God, we also please humans.

Four Questions:

Why are the words "good" and "right" both used, when they seem to mean the same thing?

Does Rashi agree with the Torah or reverse the meaning of the Torah?

How do we explain that right behavior in the view of God is also good in the sight of our fellow humans?

Explain how God will be pleased by your good behavior toward others, and how others would be pleased by your right behavior toward God.

RASHI'S RIDDLES

Parshat Shoftim

"You shall come to the …Judge who will be in those days…."

Devarim/Deuteronomy 17 9

Parshat Shoftim deals with laws and norms for the proper behavior of judges and litigants. Judges should be people of integrity, and there should be courts in every location, for every tribe. Only in that way shall laws be followed according to the dictates of the Torah. Rashi focuses on the phrase "in those days….," and explains in detail what it means. He writes: "Even if he is not like the other judges who were before him, you must listen to him. You have to obey the judge who exists in your time, even if his decision disagrees with a previous judge's decision." Rashi seems to make it very clear that a contemporary judge, a judge living in the present time, has the authority to make a decision that contradicts a past decision, and is not bound or tied to all precedents.

Four Questions:

Why is it necessary for the Torah to add the phrase "in those days?" Why does Rashi see it necessary to comment on these words?

What if these words were omitted from the Torah? What difference would it make?

How far can a judge go in making new decisions? Are there any restrictions placed on a judge, and can a judge decide something based solely on his own thoughts?

What is your opinion about present judges changing decisions that were made in the past? How far would you be comfortable in permitting a judge to make new decisions?

RASHI'S RIDDLES

Parshat Kee Teze

"You shall not muzzle an ox in its threshing." Devarim/Deuteronomy 25:4

The way farmers in biblical days got corn from the field was through threshing – that is, through having an ox pull a board with sharp studs on the bottom, over the stalks of corn. Periodically the animal would stop and eat some grain when it was hungry. If a farmer wanted to prevent the ox from doing that, to keep the animal working, or to save that amount of grain, it would place a muzzle over the ox's mouth. The Torah forbids this. It is similar to saying to a person selling candy in a candy store that they may not eat any of the candy. They can touch it, or smell it, when they sell it, but they cannot eat it. This is cruel, and the Torah is trying to establish humane practices for the Israelite nation. Many of the laws in Deuteronomy have this as their goal. One of the Torah's goals is to make people human kind and humane. Rashi expands the Torah's law by saying that the Torah uses the ox as an example, but the law does not refer exclusively to oxen. It refers to all domesticated animals that are engaged in work involved with food.

Four Questions:

What is the purpose of the law about muzzling an ox?

Why does the Torah forbid it?

What does Rashi add to the law, and why does he want to add anything to the Torah's laws?

What ways can you be more kind to animals in your own life?

RASHI'S RIDDLES

Parshat Kee Tavo

"This day Adonai your God commands you to perform these rules and laws…."

Devarim/Deuteronomy 26:16

As part of his final words to the nation of Israel prior to their crossing into the Promised Land, and prior to his death, which is about to occur, he reminds the people that the Covenant between God and the people is an important part of their life in the Land (Eretz Yisrael). He reminds them that they must obey all the rules and laws contained in the Torah, the Book which is the written record of the Covenant. Rashi notes that the words "this day" seems repetitive ("hayom hazeh"). In Hebrew just one word, "hayom," means today. Why is it necessary to add the word "hazeh," - "this?" In other words, why does the Torah go out of its way to say "This day," instead of "Today?" Rashi's answer is that "this day" refers not only to the day Moshe is reminding them of the Covenant, but rather that the people should feel that God is commanding them to follow the rules and laws of Judaism every day the same as today. The laws should never feel that the rules are old, but are brand new every single day. They will not grow stale and feel ancient if you picture yourself receiving the laws for the first time every single day of your life.

Four Questions:

What word does Rashi think seems extra, or repetitive? Why does he think so?

Why is it necessary to feel that the laws and rules are given fresh each day?

What makes people think that the laws of the Torah no longer apply?

How can you keep the Torah new in your daily life, and not let it feel old and stale?

RASHI'S RIDDLES
Parshat Nitzavim

"You are standing today, all of you, before Adonai your God...."

Devarim/Deuteronomy 29:9

There are a number of standard models of interpretation that the Midrash uses to explain words in the Torah. Rashi is an avid student of the Midrash, and he too follows many of the same methods of explanation. For example, in this verse Rashi finds a word that is not strictly necessary. Midrash assumes that whenever the Torah uses a certain word, there must be a good reason. So, asks Rashi, why is the word "standing" used? The verse could just as easily have said: "You are all here today before Adonai your God." So "standing" must have some significance. Rashi then uses a second standard method of interpretation, which is that one must see what comes before or after a verse to see it in its full context. What comes before this verse, toward the end of the previous Parashah (Kee Tavo) is the long list of curses that will come upon the people if they do not follow the rules of the Torah. Now Rashi has the answer why the word "standing" is used. The terrible curses with which God threatened the people might have frightened them, thinking that God would destroy them because of their failure to live up to all the Torah's laws. Moshe consoles the people, says Rashi, by telling them that despite the harsh warnings that God gave you, God did not destroy you – you are still **standing**! God wants to help you by encouraging you to obey God, and not do wrong by bringing upon yourselves all the terrible punishments listed in Parshat Kee Tavo.

Four Questions:

What problem does Rashi see in the first pasuk in Parshat Nitzavim?

What methods of interpretation does Rashi use to solve the problem?

Do you think it is helpful to the people to read the threats and possible punishments that God will use if they go astray? Why would such harsh threats be used?

If you have been, or are, in charge of a group of people, have you, or would you establish rules and consequences if the rules are violated?

RASHI'S RIDDLES

Parshat Vayelekh

"…this song shall speak up as a witness, for it shall not be forgotten from the mouth of its offspring…." Devarim/Deuteronomy 31:21

God tells the people of Israel that while in the future, after they cross over the Jordan River and live in Eretz Yisrael, they may not always behave properly, and when they violate God's laws, the Song of Moses (in next week's Parashah, Ha-azinu) will stand up for them. The Song testifies that God will care for the Chosen People. God is faithful to the people, and will not forsake them. The people's part is to continue to study the Song and the whole Torah in which it is found. This will help bring them back to God. Rashi reinforces this idea by saying that "This is a promise to the people of Israel, that the Torah will never be forgotten by their children and their children's children, for all future generations." This promise has come true. The proof: You are studying the Torah as you read these lines at this very moment!

Four Questions:

What promise is God making to the people of Israel?

How will the Song of Moses protect the people?

How has the Jewish People kept the Torah alive for over 3000 years?

What role do you play in keeping the Torah alive?

RASHI'S RIDDLES

Parshat Ha-azinu

"The Rock, perfect is God's work, all God's ways are just."

Devarim/Deuteronomy 32:4

The Torah and later books of the Tanakh and rabbinic literature use many words for God. The main ones are Adonai and Elohim. God is also called "Shadai" (Almighty), "HaRahaman" (The Merciful One), "Goel" (Redeemer), and by many other names. In our pasuk God is called "Tzur" (the Rock). Rashi's explanation tries to answer two questions: First, why is God called "Rock." Second, what is the connection between God as "Rock" whose work is perfect, and the second half of the pasuk, which says that "all God's ways are just." Rashi explains that the Torah uses the word "Rock" to describe God as strong. A rock is the symbol of strength. It does not break easily, and it can cause serious damage if it falls or is thrown at someone. Then Rashi explains that the strength attributed to God is not harsh or evil. God can be tough when punishment is required for those who violate the Torah, but not unfairly so. God's strength is applied in a "just way." Thus Rashi is able to explain the second half of the pasuk. God is strong, but his strength is used in a perfect way, to strongly punish, but not with cruelty, because God, being perfect, uses punishment fairly and is not vicious, mean or merciless.

Four Questions:

What questions arise in Rashi's mind regarding this pasuk?

How does Rashi answer these questions?

Is the Torah describing God in an unfair way by saying God is a "Rock?"

How do you think of God – as strong, punishing, or nurturing, loving? What other words come to mind in describing God? Which ones appeal most to you?

BOOK FOUR

D'var Torah – Bereshit

"When God [Elohim] began to create heaven and earth…." Bereshit (Genesis) 1:1

The rabbis of the Talmud paid particularly close attention to the use of different Hebrew names for the Divinity. The name "Adonai" was assumed to refer to the quality of God's mercy. The name "Elohim" was assumed to describe God's attribute of justice. The word Elohim in the Tanakh often reflects the role of "judge." (For example, in Shemot 21:6, we have the pasuk [verse], referring to a slave who was due to be released, and refused, "His master shall take him to Ha-Elohim." Some translate Elohim there as God, others as "the judges").

So why does our verse use the word "Elohim" rather than Adonai? Rashi (acronym for **R**abbi **Sh**lomo **I**tzhaki – 11th century, Troyes, France) explains that God first intended to create the world with the Divine attribute of Justice. But , thought God, Justice without Mercy would be too harsh. On the other hand, Mercy without Justice is too lenient. Thus, in perek (chapter) two, pasuk (verse) 4, we find that **both** words for God – Elohim and Adonai - are used. While God used both qualities, Justice and Mercy, our verse teaches that God especially wanted to add the quality of Mercy, so the world would have both qualities - Justice and Mercy.

Four Questions

What qualities are associated with God's names?

How does Rashi explain the fact that the word "Elohim" is used in Bereshit 1:1?

Why does the world need both qualities: Justice and Mercy? Why does a judge also need both of these qualities?

Have you ever judged anyone too harshly? Too leniently? Explain.

D'var Torah – Noah

"They [the builders of the Tower of Babel] said, "Come, let us build a city for ourselves, and a tower whose top is in the heavens, to make a name for ourselves…."

Bereshit (Genesis) 11:4

It seems obvious that the people of the generation who built the Tower of Babel felt inferior. Rabbi Samson Raphael Hirsch (Frankfurt, Germany, 1808-1888) comments on this verse that one's sense of insignificance can lead a person in one of two directions. A person can feel humble or arrogant. If one realizes that she is a small part of a gigantic galaxy created by God, she will be aware that her role in the universe is small, and thus owes a great debt to the Creator and to society. This sense of humility will lead one to live a life filled with acts of kindness, caring, service and righteousness.

A person who feels insignificant can also try to build oneself up by acts of pride and arrogance, seeking to achieve things that will lend fame and notoriety to himself. Such a person may do things that he thinks will cause other people to admire and respect him. These kinds of activities can include doing things that are self-serving rather than promote the welfare of the community. The generation of the Tower of Babel falls in the second category, people whose sense of inferiority led them to challenge their Creator and bring chaos into the world.

Four Questions

1) How does Rabbi Hirsch see the level of self-esteem of the generation of the

Tower of Babel?

What phrase in the verse do you think he focused on to derive his conclusion?

Which direction is a person most likely to lean towards: humility or arrogance?

Can you give examples of people who have gone each way?

D'var Torah – Lekh Lekha

Adonai said to Avram, "Leave your homeland, your birthplace, and your parents' home for the land that I will show you." Bereshit (Genesis) 12:1

Rabbi Lawrence Kushner, formerly of Sudbury, Mass., and a well-known teacher, writer and advocate of modern-day Jewish spirituality, sees the key phrase in this *pasuk* as leaving your parents' home.

This is the job of "separation," – or, as the famous Swiss psychologist Carl Jung called it, "Individuation." A child grows up, becomes his/her own person, and leaves the parental nest. This is not an easy or a rapid process. Rather, it takes a lifetime. And then the cycle repeats itself. We have children, and we have trouble letting go of our own children, as they begin their own lives. And our children's children, and so on. This important process of growing up, striking out on one's own, and taking on more and more responsibility, cannot be done in one fell swoop. We are caught, explains Rabbi Kushner, between the generation who brought us into the world, and those we ourselves launched.

Avram did not know much about this God who is asking him to leave his home, but he follows his directions, and has faith that he is doing the right thing. Maybe, argues Rabbi Kushner, this is "the land that God will show us [the land of independence], *and* what it means to be a blessing." Blessing comes, in other words, when we grow up and reach out to God on our own, in our own place, on our own terms.

Four Questions

Why did Rabbi Kushner focus on the phrase "leave your parents' home?"

Why do you think Carl Jung thought becoming independent was the primary task of life?

What does growing up having to do with the relationship between God and Avram?

In what ways have you grown up, and in what ways do you still have to "grow up?"

D'var Torah - Vayera

"Then Adonai said to Avraham, 'Why did Sarah laugh, saying, "Shall I in truth bear a child, old as I am?"''" Bereshit/Genesis18:13

God quotes Sarah in speaking to Avraham. But there is a problem. God fudges! In verse 12, what did Sarah really say? When told that she will have her first child in her old age, in a state of shock, she reacts: "Am I to enjoy marital relations with my husband, who is so old?" God then twists the truth here a bit. What Sarah *really* said was that her *husband* is too old to have a child. But when Adonai tells Avraham about the conversation with Sarah, God quotes her as saying "old as I am?" Why did Adonai twist the truth?

The Talmud (Tractate Bava Metzia 87a) explains God's "untruth." "Great is peace, for even the Blessed Holy One bent the truth to preserve shalom." Had God repeated exactly what Sarah had said, there may have come some friction between Sarah and Avraham. God obviously felt it was "the better part of valor" to protect their relationship.

Four Questions:

What did Sarah really say, and how did Adonai quote her?

Why did God allow an untruth to pass thru the Divine "lips?"

Is it acceptable sometimes to bend the truth? Under what circumstances?

Have you ever told an untruth for a good purpose? How did you feel when you did it?

D'var Torah – Hayay Sarah

"Quickly, she emptied her jar into the trough, ran back to the well, and drew water for all his (Eliezer's) camels." Bereshit/Genesis 24:20

After Sarah's death, Avraham sent his servant Eliezer to the ancestral homeland, Haran, to find a wife for his son, Yitzhak. Eliezer asked God's help in finding the right wife for Yitzhak. May it be the case, pleads Eliezer, when I ask one of the young women at the well to give me drink, that she gives me drink, and also to my camels, that will be the one who will be a wife for Yitzhak.

A contemporary teacher, Stuart Muszynski, uses this story as an example of the importance of choosing not only the proper mate, but also the right family who brought forth that mate. Rebekah was a woman who displayed kindness, and came from a family who taught her to be kind. A kind mate will have a deep influence on her spouse. The choices we make in life impact on us in ways we cannot predict at the time. Avraham wanted to make sure that his son would have the influence of positive values in his home.

Four Questions

What evidence did Eliezer have that Rebekah met his criteria for a good mate for Yitzhak?

Why did Avraham want his future daughter-in-law to come from a good family?

What are some of the values that should be present in a Jewish home?

What can you do to make sure your home is filled with good Jewish values?

D'var Torah - Toldot

"And they [the twin boys, Yaakov and Esav, still fetuses inside their mother Rivkah] wrestled in her womb…." Bereshit [Genesis] 25:22

The word translated as wrestled, usually rendered as "struggled" is interpreted by Rashi (Troyes, France, 1040 – 1105 C.E.) differently than the standard explanations. Rashi sees a sermonic lesson in this word by giving it a different slant. He sees in the word, which in Hebrew is "Vayit-rotz'tzu," the same Hebrew root as "Ritzah," meaning "to run." What are the boys, Yaakov and Esav, running after? Every time, claims Rashi, that Rivkah, while pregnant, would pass by a Yeshivah (Torah school), Yaakov would want to rush (run) and be born, so he could study Torah. And every time Rivkah passed by a pagan temple Esav, who was the supposed ancestor of the pagan nation of Rome, he rushed (ran, struggled) to be born. Rashi is thus saying that the difference between the twins is that Yaakov would one day be the Father of the Jewish People (later his name was changed to Yisrael) and wanted to study and teach Torah to his descendants. Whereas Esav's passion was to worship idols.

Four Questions

What is the difference in the character and destiny of Yaakov and Esav?

How does Rashi see this distinction in the verb to struggle, or run?

What value is ascribed by Rashi to Yaakov and his descendants?

In what way in your life do you reflect the values of Yaakov?

D'var Torah - Vayetze

"Yaakov left Beersheva and traveled toward Haran." Bereshit/Genesis 28:10

The rabbis of the midrash always assume that the Torah uses the least amount of words to make a point. Thus, the Torah might have said, "Yaakov traveled toward Haran." However, the verse begins by saying "Yaakov left Beersheva." Why was it necessary, asks the midrash (Bereshit Rabbah 68:7) to mention where he was traveling from? That was obvious. The reason, they explain, is that whenever a saintly person leaves the town in which s/he lived, a gap is created. When such a pious individual lives in the town, his splendor, his brilliance, his luster, are present. When he moves from the place he lived in, along with him go the splendor, the brilliance and the luster. The same is true when we read of Naomi and Ruth (Book of Ruth 1:7), where the Tanakh says that Naomi and Ruth left Moav to return to Yehudah (Judea).

Four Questions:

Why does the midrash assume that there is meaning in the phrase "Yaakov left Beersheva"?

What meaning does the midrash assign to this phrase, and where else in the Tanakh does the midrash find the same expression? What do Yaakov, Naomi and Ruth share in common?

Do you think a pious person has an impact on their environment? In what way?

Whom do you know who left their place of residence, and left behind an important legacy – whose town was changed after that person left?

D'var Torah – Vayishlah

"'I am not worthy of all the kindness,' said Yaakov to HaShem, 'that you have shown me.'" Bereshit/ Genesis 32:11

Yaakov is returning to Eretz Yisrael after spending twenty years with his father-in-law, Lavan, and his wives, Leah and Rahel. He has become prosperous, and feels that it is time to return home. The first item on his agenda is a meeting with his estranged twin brother, Esav. As he reaches the border of the Land, his emotions are mixed. He does not know how his brother will treat him – will he forgive him or attack him? Yaakov prays to God, asking for guidance at this crucial point in his life. As a sign of humility he turns to God in thanksgiving, telling God that he is grateful for all the good things God has done for him, and for the promises God made to him to protect him, and make his people as numerous as the grains of sand at the sea. In expressing his gratitude, Yaakov tells God that he is "not worthy of all of God's kindness." The Hebrew for "not worthy" is literally, "I am too small," ("Katontai"), or too modest.

Rabbi Alexander Zusia Friedman, in *Wellsprings of Torah*, quotes from the Musar tradition (Musar is a 19th century movement of rabbis and their followers who excelled in ethical behavior), which says that feeling humble and small is sometimes good, but not always. In this case, Yaakov feels **too** small in his own eyes, and is too fearful of his brother. The miracles Yaakov has seen God do for him, and the successes God has helped him achieve, should have given him more confidence. Instead, unfortunately, he feels small and inadequate.

Four Questions

Why does Yaakov portray himself before God as "katon" (small)?

Can this be a good thing or not? Which is it in this case?

How does the Musar interpretation explain Yaakov's sense of self?

How would you feel if you were facing Esav after twenty years? Explain.

D'var Torah – Vayeshev

"Yosef, seventeen years old, tended the flock along with this brothers, as a helper [na-ar] to the sons of his father's wives, Bilhah and Zilpah." Bereshit/Genesis 37:2

Rashi, based on the midrash, pays special attention to the Hebrew word "na-ar." While in common usage, a "na-ar" is a young lad, it has a secondary meaning as a "helper." In English we use the word "boy" in the same way. Sometimes it can mean an assistant, a helper, or a servant. While the Torah uses the word to mean a "helping-lad," Rashi makes a play on the word to interpret it as meaning "a young boy," someone who is immature, still needing to grow up. The whole cluster of verses of the beginning of this Sidrah focuses on Yosef's immaturity. He seems to be constantly doing things to arouse the jealousy and anger of his brothers. (Ironically, in Yiddish, a "na-ar" means a "fool"). Rashi implies that it was Yosef's immature behavior that brought the wrath of his brothers.

Four Questions

What are the different meanings of the Hebrew word "na-ar," and "boy" in the Torah and in other languages?

How does Rashi understand the word, and how does his comment interpret the word "na-ar"? Read verses 2 and 3 and explain how the rest of the story lends credence to Rashi's lesson?

What makes one youngster act maturely, and another maturely? Why does the same person sometimes act like a child at one time, and more like an adult on another occasion?

In what ways and in what times have you been like Yosef, the immature, self-centered person? How did you grow out of that stage in your life?

D'var Torah – Miketz

"In the morning [after his dream] Pharaoh's spirit was troubled, and he sent for all the magicians and wise men of Egypt, and told them his dreams, but none could interpret them for Pharaoh." Bereshit/Genesis 41:8

In the normal course of biblical interpretation, commentators often look for extra words, which could just as easily be left out, and the verse would have the same general meaning. In this case, the last two words, "for Pharaoh," seem needless. The verse would mean the same without them. But in the view of midrashic interpreters, no word in the Torah is "extra," since it is written carefully. In fact, since the traditional commentators believed that God wrote the entire Torah, word for word, why would there be any extra words? If that is the case, why add the words "for Pharaoh?"

Rashi says that the magicians and wise men of Egypt did, in fact, interpret the dreams, but not "for Pharaoh." The explanations were not what Pharaoh wanted to hear. Their words were not credible to him. "Their interpretations," writes Rashi, "did not penetrate Pharaoh's ears." Pharaoh may have wanted an explanation that was more sensible to him, and that fit in to his own view of what was happening in Egypt. This is an interesting example of how people often hear only what they want to hear, and block out what they do not want to hear.

Four Questions

Why do the traditional commentators pay special attention to words in the Torah that seem to be "extra?" What words in this verse seem "extra," and why?

How does Rashi interpret these "extra" words, "for Pharaoh?"

What reason do people often have to dismiss what is said to them?

What types of things do you dislike hearing? Can you explain why? What do we need to do to be able to hear things that do not fit into our present views?

D'var Torah – Vayigash

"How can I return to my father unless the youth is with me?" Bereshit/Genesis 44:34

The brothers of Yosef, speaking with the viceroy of Egypt, still do not realize that he is their brother, Yosef. Yosef asks the brothers to return to Egypt, and leave their youngest brother, Binyamin, with him. Yehudah, who pledged to his father, Yaakov, that he would guarantee that Binyamin would return, argues with Yosef that he cannot return to Yaakov without Binyamin. "How can I return to my father unless the youth (Binyamin) is with me?" he asks.

Rabbi Yaakov Yosef of Polnoye (leading disciple of the founder of Hasidism, the Baal Shem Tov, from Polnoye, Russia, 1710-1784) interprets the verse as if the "father" mentioned is "Our Father in Heaven," – God. He thus reads the verse as follows: How can one return to our Father (when our life on earth is completed) without our youth – meaning, having wasted our youth. Can I go up to my Creator without the youth that was given to me having been spent on worthwhile pursuits?

Four Questions

What is the literal meaning of the verse, and how does Rabbi Yaakov Yosef re-interpret it?

Why is it so important to spend our youth wisely? In what way does it affect our later life?

How do we define a youth well spent? What are its components?

If you are young, how can you make the period of your youth more useful? If you are an adult, how can you help your child, or any child, make better use of their time?

D'var Torah – Vayehi

"Yaakov lived in the land of Egypt." Bereshit/ Genesis 47:28

As we come to the conclusion of the Book of Bereshit, we find that there are two sidrot (weekly Torah readings – singular: sidrah) – namely, *Hayay Sarah* and *Vayehi*, which start with a form of the Hebrew word for life ("Hayay Sarah" means "The Life of Sarah," and "Vayehi Yaakov," means "And Yaakov lived…." It is ironic that both sidrot speak, in fact, about the **death** of the person mentioned in the title. *Hayay Sarah* deals with the death of Sarah, and *Vayehi* deals with the death of Yaakov.

Rabbi Moshe Avigdor Amiel (1883-1946, Chief Rabbi of Tel Aviv and prolific author) points out that it is no accident that both of these sidrot, called by the Hebrew word for "life" actually deal with "death." He explains that when great people, such as Sarah and Yaakov, die, their spirit lives on. The Talmud teaches that "Even in physical death, the righteous continue to live on" (Tractate Berakhot 18a).

Four Questions

What connection does Rabbi Amiel make between the two Sidrot, *Hayay Sarah* and *Vayehi*?

How do those who die continue to live on? What connection is there between great Jewish leaders of the past and the living heritage of Judaism which we received?

Who in your family, or among your acquaintances, died, and left an important legacy that lives on?

What legacy would you like to leave after your time on earth is completed?

D'var Torah – Shemot

"Now these are the names of the Israelites coming to Egypt with Yaakov…."

Shemot/Exodus 1:1

The English translations of this first verse of the Book of Shemot differ, since the art of translating is not an exact science. The Hebrew verb in the sentence is in the present tense, (see above translation – "coming"), although many translations use the past tense, since the Israelite nation had already arrived in Egypt years before. One astute commentator notices that the verb is in the present, and not the past, and makes an interesting interpretation. Rabbi Avraham Shmuel Binyamin Schreiber (1815-1875, Hungary), known from the title of his collection of writings as the "Ktav Sofer" – a play on words on his last name, which in German means a "scribe" – like the Hebrew, *sofer* – says the following about the verb being in the present tense. Rabbi Schreiber says that the Israelites never really felt themselves as "Egyptians," but as "Israelites." In other words, they did not see themselves as having come (in the past) – but as still arriving. Their minds and hearts were still in Eretz Yisrael. Their journey to Egypt was still taking place – so it's still happening. Being loyal to their Homeland, they were not really enslaved. It was only when the next generation arose, who forgot that their true home was in Eretz Yisrael, that they became enslaved.

Four Questions

How did Rabbi Avraham Schreiber interpret the word “coming,” differently than other translators and commentators?

How did the first generation of Israelite people feel about being in Egypt?

How would you compare our generation’s feeling about living in the Diaspora, with those living in Egypt?

How do you feel about living outside Eretz Yisrael? Did you ever think of living in our spiritual Homeland?

D'var Torah – Va-era

"It is the same Aharon and Moshe to whom Adonai said...." Shemot/Exodus 6:26

"...These are the same Moshe and Aharon." Shemot/Exodus 6:27

In the two verses we are now studying, both brothers, Moshe and Aharon, are mentioned. In verse 26 Aharon is mentioned first, and in the next one, verse 27, Moshe is mentioned first. Rashi claims that the reason is to show that both brothers were important in dealing with the oppressive Pharaoh. But Rabbi Yosef Dov Soloveichik (1903-1993, head of the Talmud faculty of Yeshiva University's Rabbi Isaac Elchanan Theological Seminary in New York) adds another wrinkle. He explains that Moshe and Aharon each represents a different quality: Moshe is the man of Law, while Aharon is the representative of kindness and peace. (We think of the Torah, the Book of Law, as Torat Moshe; we remember Aharon for the incident of the Golden Calf, the ultimate compromiser and peacemaker). Rabbi Soloveichik says that at different points in Jewish history different qualities are required. Sometimes one must be firm, and follow the letter of the Law. At other times, one should be compassionate and flexible. During the experience of slavery in the previous Sidrah (Shemot) the quality of kindness was needed. In next week's Sidrah (Bo), when the people are freed, they need firm direction, or Law. This week's Sidrah, Va-era, is the in-between time. Thus, says Rabbi Soloveichik, both qualities are always needed, firmness and compassion. In Va-era we are in a period between slavery and freedom. This, he further argues, is the period we are living in right now – We are neither oppressed, nor are we yet fully redeemed. Jewish leaders today must exercise both Law and Kindness.

Four Questions

What matter of interest does Rabbi Yosef Dov Soloveichik notice about verses 26 and 27?

What point does he raise about the order of mentioning the two brothers, Moshe and Aharon?

What reasons are there for associating Moshe with the quality of firmness, and Aharon with the quality of peace?

Have you found in your own life that sometimes you act one way, and at other times the other way? Can you give an example?

D'var Torah - Bo

"You shall observe this word as a law for all time, for you and for your children."

Shemot/Exodus 12:24

Rabbi Aryeh Ben David, a teacher in Efrat, Israel, in his book, *Around the Shabbat Table*, notes that in this week's Sidrah children are the focus. The tenth plague, the slaying of the first born of all Egyptian families, shifts the theme of the conflict between the Egyptians and the Hebrews from the leaders of the people (Pharaoh and Moshe), and their lands (the plagues affected the soil, the crops, the cattle, the water, etc.), to the next generation – the children and grandchildren – that is, from the present to the future. This punishment of the tenth plague, the death of the children of Egypt, reminds the reader of the command by Pharaoh to put to death the children of the Israelite nation when they were born (Shemot/Exodus 1:16). Pharaoh wanted to deprive the Hebrews of their future. Now it's the Egyptians whose future is threatened. When the Israelites leave Egypt, the Jewish nation will be born, and the future of the people will be assured.

Four Questions

What significance does Rabbi Aryeh Ben David see in the mention of "you and your children"?

How does he define the conflict between Egypt and Israel?

What connection do the children have to the Exodus story? Why are they important?

What importance does today's Jewish community place on the role of its children? What are you doing in your life to assure the future of the next generation of Jews?

D'var Torah – B'shalah

"Moshe said to the people, 'Do not fear! Stand fast and see the salvation of Hashem… for as you have seen Egypt today, you shall not see them again. Hashem shall do battle for you, and you shall remain silent.' Hashem said to Moshe, 'Why do you cry out to me?'" Shemot/Exodus 14:13-15

The Jerusalem Talmud (Tractate Ta-anit, 2:5) teaches that four distinct groups approached Moshe with complaints. First were the fatalists. They thought there was no hope – the sea before them, the Egyptian army behind them. To them Moshe said, "Do not fear!" The second group were the pacifists who wanted to return to Egypt and become assimilated into Egyptian culture. To them Moshe's advice was:"You shall not see them again." The Egyptian army and people will soon be no more. The third group was made up of fighters, ready to battle the Egyptians. It was life or death. To them Moshe said, "Hashem will fight for you." Don't think you can do this on your own, you must rely on HaShem. Fighting is important, but not without faith in God to assist you. The fourth and last group were protestors, screamers. To them Moshe said, "And you shall remain silent." Screaming at the Egyptians is futile. During all this time the people at large were praying to God for help. They ignore these four groups: the *fighters*, the *fearful*, the *assimilationists*, and the *politicians*. God told Moshe: "Why do you cry out to Me? The people are already praying to Me!"

Four Questions

How does the Talmud use the words of Moshe to find questions that he is answering?

Which of these four groups has the most authority on their side, if any?

Do these four groups still exist in today's world, fighting anti-Semitism?

Which group do you identify with most? Do these four groups have more correctness on their side, or do the people? How do you balance activism with faith in God?

D'var Torah - Yitro

"All that Adonai has spoken, we will do." Shemot/ Exodus 19:8

When Moshe brought the Torah down from Mt. Sinai, the Israelite nation was excited to receive it, and immediately called to him: All that Adonai asks of us, we are ready to fulfill. The Midrash fills in, out of its imagination, what might have taken place before God offered the Torah to the Israelites (Midrash Pesikta Rabba 21). First God offered the Torah to the descendants of Esau. They asked about the contents of the Torah. When God said, "Thou shalt not murder," they replied. We can't accept the Torah because Esau taught us to live by the sword. Then God offered the Torah to the Ammonites and the Moabites. When they asked about the contents, God said, "Thou shalt not be unfaithful." When they heard this they refused to accept the Torah. God finally offered the Torah to the Israelites, and they replied, "We shall accept and we shall obey."

Four Questions

What prompted the Midrash to fill in the empty blanks?

What differences does this midrash suggest exists between the Israelites and the other nations who refused to accept the Torah?

What does the readiness and willingness on the part of the Israelites to live by the Torah say about the Jewish People?

What impact does living according to the Torah have on your life?

D'var Torah – Mishpatim

"You shall not side with the majority to do wrong...." Shemot/Exodus 23:2

Rabbi Abraham ibn Ezra (b. Toledo, Spain, 1092-1167) warns against following the majority in the case where your own knowledge of the situation is insufficient, and you rely on others for your opinion. Do not say to yourself in such a case, "How could so many people be wrong?" Do not, in that situation, follow the majority and cast your vote with them, assuming they are right and you are wrong. This is a warning not to side with the majority in the absence of a clear opinion of your own, or in the absence of sufficient data in your mind to make a proper decision. Ibn Ezra's message is particularly relevant in today's world, with the coming of the Information Age, when one must master enormous amounts of facts and data to make a thoughtful decision. Demagogues in government often claim the right to decide for the masses, because they have "more information" than the average citizen. This is an easy path to dictatorship. In addition, it is easy to follow the sound bites of the media who research a complex issue, put out a one-paragraph summary to the public, and thus take control of the mind of the masses. It is the obligation of a responsible citizen in a democracy to be informed. Rabbinic Judaism always presumed an oligarchy of knowledge, not of power.

Four Questions

Why does the Torah command us not to go along with the majority?

What type of situations does the Torah refer to?

When is it the ***right*** thing to do – to go along with the majority?

Have you ever stood up to a majority? Can you give more details?

D'var Torah - Terumah

"Adonai spoke to Moshe, saying: Tell the Israelites to bring me an offering; you shall accept offerings for Me from all persons whose heart so moves them."

Shemot/Exodus 25:2

The Hebrew word for "offering" is "Terumah," which is the name of this week's Sidrah. Each Sidrah takes its name from the first important word in the Sidrah. The word "Terumah" comes from the Hebrew root "rum" – meaning rise, or elevation. (A "ramah" is a hill, or elevated surface). The Hasidic master Rabbi Tzvi Hirsh of Rymanov, Poland (1778-1847), in his commentary on the Torah, *Be'erot HaMayim* – or *Wells of Water* - makes an interesting observation about the word "Terumah." It has the same letters as the word "Torah," with one extra letter – a "mem." In Gematriah (numerology, a system in which each Hebrew letter has a numerical value – starting with "alef" for "one," "bet" for "two," etc.) the letter "mem" equals the number **forty**. So what connection does Rabbi Tzvi Hirsh make between the Hebrew words "Terumah" and "Torah?" He suggests that the extra Hebrew letter "mem" – equaling the number "forty," – represents the forty days Moshe remained on Mt. Sinai to receive the Torah. Thus, he says, the main path to raising ourselves ("Terumah" = raising) is to fulfill the values of the Torah. If we follow the ways of Torah, we will thereby raise our selves and our lives in every part of our existence.

Four Questions

What connection does Rabbi Tzvi Hirsch of Rymanov make between the two Hebrew words "Terumah" and "Torah?"

How does he interpret this connection? What message does it have?

When we live by the values of the Torah, how do we elevate our lives?

What parts of the Torah help you to elevate your own life?

D'var Torah - Tezaveh

"Aharon shall carry the names of the twelve sons of Yisrael (Yaakov) on the Breastpiece of Judgment over his heart, whenever he comes into the Sanctuary for remembrance before Adonai at all times." Shemot/ Exodus 28:29

From the Torah we learn that Aharon, the Kohen Gadol (High Priest), wore on his chest a device to use in determining God's will when questions arose. This device is called the "Breastpiece of Judgment," or, as some call it, "Breastpiece of Decision" (in Hebrew *Hoshen Mishpat*). On the outside of the *Hoshen Mishpat* Aharon was required, as our verse tells us, to have the names of all twelve sons of Yaakov, the heads of the twelve tribes of Israel. Why? Rabbi Ovadiah Sforno (Bologna, Italy, 1475-1550) teaches that it was important that God always remember the names of the founding tribal fathers of the Jewish People, to treat their offspring favorably. This idea is known in Jewish tradition as "zekhut avot," or gaining merit because of the good deeds of their ancestors. Others teach that one moves toward moral perfection by carrying the accumulated spiritual heritage of righteous ancestors. For this reason we constantly refer to the patriarchs and matriarchs of our people (Sarah, Rivkah, Rahel and Leah, Avraham Yitzhak and Yaakov) in reciting the Amidah.

Four Questions

Why does Rabbi Ovadiah Sforno think the names of the heads of the tribes should be written on the *Hoshen Mishpat*?

Is it important for a nation to recall its founding ancestors? Why?

How do you feel when you chant the names of the patriarchs and matriarchs during the Amidah?

In what way does carrying our ancient tradition in your mind and heart help you become a better person?

D'var Torah – Kee Tisa

"The People of Israel shall keep the Shabbat...." Shemot/Exodus 31:16

Rabbi Haim ben Moshe Attar (b. Morocco 1696, d. Jerusalem, 1743), in his commentary *Or HaHayim*, gives a novel interpretation of the Hebrew verb "Ve-shamru," "to keep." In some places in the Tanakh the verb *shamar* can mean "keep guard," or "wait for." In our verse Rabbi Alshekh says that the word "Ve-shamru" means that the Jewish People should "wait anxiously" for Shabbat to come. All week long we should look forward to the coming of Shabbat. Maimonides (Rabbi Moshe ben Maimon, or Rambam - Spain & Egypt, 1135-1204) in his Code of Jewish Law (*Mishneh Torah*) in the section on the Laws of Shabbat (30:2), states that a Jew should bathe on Friday afternoon, and then wear his tallit, and wait with great enthusiasm for Shabbat to arrive, just as one would welcome a king or queen.

Four Questions

How does Rabbi Haim ben Moshe Attar translate the verb "ve-shamru" differently than the standard translation?

What meaning does he give our verse, based on this translation? How does Maimonides extend the new translation?

Why is it important to look forward to the coming of Shabbat?

What things could you do to increase your preparation and excitement for the arrival of Shabbat?

D'var Torah – Vayak-hel

"And Moshe assembled all the congregation of the Israelite nation." Shemot/Exodus 35:1

As we reach the end of the book of Shemot, the Torah once again gives all the details of the construction of the Mishkan (portable Tabernacle). After the conclusion of the building of the Mishkan, we find that "Moshe saw all the work and blessed the people" (Shemot/Exodus 39:43). Why did Moshe wait until the work had been completed before blessing them? First the people had to come together in unity. According to Rabbi Avraham Yitzhak Kook, first Chief Rabbi of Eretz Yisrael (d. 1935), unity and harmony are prerequisites for a person to achieve her/his maximum potential. The same is true for a nation. Our double sidrah begins with the people coming together, and concludes with a special blessing by Moshe. When the people found harmony, they were able to build a beautiful House of God, and then find blessing.

Four Questions

Why did the Torah mention the people coming together before they were blessed by Moshe?

What is the relationship between unity, harmony and achievement?

How does Rabbi Kook's idea apply to an individual? To a nation?

Have you experienced inner harmony? Has it resulted in positive results?

D'var Torah – Pekuday

"All the gold that was used for the work, for all the holy work, even the gold of the offering…." Shemot/ Exodus 38:24

The final chapters of the Book of Shemot give minute details about the construction of the portable Tabernacle that the Israelites carried with them, housing the two tablets of the Ten Commandments. Chapter 28 enumerates the total amount of the precious metals used in the building of the Mishkan (portable Tabernacle). Rabbi Aharon Yaakov Greenberg, in his book *Torah Gems*, quotes a commentary called "Shirei Zimrah," who notices that the gold listed in this chapter is used for a sacred purpose. He points out that gold has both positive and negative uses. Sometimes it can make people wealthy and happy, and sometimes it can make people miserable. People fight over it, they gamble for it, they win it and lose it, making them happy or sad within seconds. Sometimes people even kill to get it. Yet, in the case of our verse, gold is used for a most noble purpose – to adorn the House of God. The moral value of the gold depends on how it is used. If used for Tzedakah or other holy causes, it can be a great source of sanctity.

Four Questions:

Why does the Torah list all the precious metals in the building of the Mishkan?

What special insight does the "Shirei Zimrah" see in the use of gold in constructing the Mishkan?

Give examples of how gold is used in our society for good or for evil.

What ways have you used money for good or bad purposes?

D'var Torah - Vayikra

"When anyone among you [*meekem*] brings an offering to Adonai…." Vayikra/Leviticus 1:2

Rabbi Yehudah Leib Eger (Lublin, Poland, 1816-1888) translates this verse to mean that anyone who brings an offering to God brings themselves [*meekem*] to Adonai. He thus understands the verse to mean that when anyone who brings themselves as an offering – or brings of their time, energy or ability – it should be for a Godly purpose. Anyone who volunteers their time, or who helps any cause, should do so only for causes that are high-minded and noble, enterprises that are divine in caliber. So many of us give of our time to causes that are less than divine, less important than ones that are at the highest levels of commitment, that we should use great caution in our selection, and make sure that our time and ability are reserved only for the best and the highest purposes.

Four Questions

What meaning does Rabbi Eger read into this verse?

Which causes are worthy of our time, and which ones may not be?

How can we make sure that our time is being used for the best purposes?

What high goals have you used your time for? Which noble causes would you like to serve in the future?

D'var Torah - Tzav

"A perpetual fire shall be kept burning upon the altar; it shall not go out." Vayikra/Leviticus 6:6

The Torah refers to the fire on the altar in the portable Sanctuary, the Mishkan. Even when the Israelites moved to a new location in the Sinai desert, the fire on the altar was not permitted to be extinguished. Thus, the Jerusalem Talmud comments, "The fire shall not go out, even when the altar travels" (Yoma 4:6). Later commentaries apply the idea of "traveling" not only to the fire on the altar, but also to the fire of passion for righteous values in the heart of good people. In other words, when one is at home, it is much easier to keep alive the fire of righteousness and ethical behavior, because one's family and friends, and one's environment and habitual actions all tend to help keep one in the right path. However, when one travels, and is in the presence of only strangers, and unusual conditions with which one is not accustomed, the temptation to sin is much greater. Thus, in such circumstances, it is important to keep alive the fire of goodness and right conduct.

Even when one is far from home, far from the routine and from people one knows, the fire of Torah and ethical laws should not go out, but should continue to burn in one's heart.

Four Questions

How do modern commentators interpret the Talmud's statement that the fire on the altar should not go out, even when traveling?

What kinds of "fire" are the commentators referring to?

Why is it more difficult to follow Torah laws when one is not at home?

Is it easier for you to maintain high ethical standards when home or when away from home? Give some examples.

D'var Torah – Sh'mini

"Now Moshe inquired diligently about the goat of the sin offering…."

Vayikra/Leviticus 10:16

The text of the Torah was lovingly copied century after century, with as much precision as possible. However, as with anyone copying a text from one parchment to another, differences in spelling gradually crept into the text. Thus, a group called the Masoretes (from the Hebrew word "Masorah" – or "transmission"), who worked from the 6th to the 10th centuries C.E., began to count the letters and the words, in order to protect the accuracy of the Torah text as carefully as possible. Finally, Aharon ben Asher in the year 930 C.E. in the holy city of Tiberius, established the text which was made the "gold standard." It is known as the "Masoretic Text." According to the count of the Masoretes, the very middle of the Torah, in counting words, comes between two Hebrew words in our verse. The words translated "inquired diligently" are in Hebrew "darosh darash." The Hebrew "darash" means to inquire, or to study. One 20th century commentator, Rabbi Aharon Lewin of Reisha, Poland (1880-1941), known by the title of his book, "HaDrash ve-Ha-Iyun," who was tragically murdered by the Nazis, offered a novel explanation. His interpretation of this repetition of the verb "to study" is that one must study one's own inner motivations in study and observing the Torah. That is **half** the mastery of the Torah. The other half is just learning and studying. Once one masters one's own inner sincerity and integrity, then it is possible to study the Torah with a whole heart.

Four Questions

Why was it necessary for the Masoretes to count the number of letters and words in the Torah?

How does the commentator "HaDrash ve-Ha-Iyun" explain the halfway point in the number of words in the Torah?

What is the importance of bringing one's inner sincerity to the study of the Torah?

Can you give an example of how your study of the Torah is influenced by your inner sincerity and integrity?

D’var Torah – Tazria

“The leper must call out, ‘Unclean, unclean.’” Vayikra/Leviticus 13:45

The rabbis in the Talmud declared that the person who becomes leprous is guilty of slander, defamation of another human being. They made this connection because the Hebrew for leper, *metzora*, is similar to the Hebrew for *motzi ra*, one who spreads evil. The rabbis considered slander one of the most evil of all sins. They stated that one who literally kills a person kills only one individual. Yet one who slanders another kills three: the one who speaks evil, the one who hears it, and the person about whom it is said. Since the ancients considered leprosy a contagious disease, they wanted others to know when a person contracted leprosy so that they would avoid him. He was banished from the camp of the Israelite people, so as not to spread his disease. Thus, he had to call out “Unclean! Unclean!” This was a warning to others not to come near him. However, one commentator called *Imrei Shefer*, quoted by a modern Israeli teacher, Dov Furer, claims that the call “Unclean! Unclean!” has a double meaning. The person with leprosy is not only warning others not to approach him because of his contagious disease, but is also creating his own punishment by denouncing himself morally, and yelling out to others, “I am unclean.” In other words, “I am morally sinful, because I have defamed the reputation of another human being.”

Four Questions

How did the Talmudic rabbis connect the disease of leprosy to the sin of slander?

Why did they consider slander such a terrible sin?

What is the double meaning which the commentator Imrei Shefer attaches to the leper crying out "Unclean, unclean?"

How can you be more careful in refraining from gossiping and speaking evil of other people?

D'var Torah – Metzora

"The kohen shall take some of the blood of the guilt offering, and the priest shall put it on the right ear of the person being purified, and on the thumb of his right hand, and on the big toe of his right foot." Vayikra/Leviticus 14:14

If a person was afflicted with the disease which the Torah calls "Metzora," – usually understood as leprosy, though it may be any kind of skin disease – the Kohen must examine that person after the disease has run its course. If the afflicted person is cured, then certain rituals must be carried out to be able to declare the person ritually pure. One of these rituals is that a guilt offering is sacrificed by the Kohen, since the biblical view was that the disease was the result of a sin (usually slander or gossip). During the ritual of the guilt offering, the Kohen would take some blood from the animal sacrificed, and put it on the ear, thumb and big toe of the person being purified. Why these parts of the body? Rabbi Shimshon Raphael Hirsch (Frankfurt, Germany, 1808-1888) suggests the following reasons. While the afflicted person has been cured, he must still be careful to improve himself morally in three ways. First, his ear represents the head, or mind – thus the person must improve his mind through Torah study. Second, the thumb represents action – thus the person must perform more good deeds. Third, the toe represents forward movement – thus the person must put forth more effort in self-improvement in all ways.

Four Questions:

What sin did the Torah ascribe to a person who was a "metzora?"

What steps did a "metzora" go through to become ritually cleansed?

Do you agree that a disease may be the result of bad moral character?

In what ways can you improve yourself in mind, deeds, and effort?

D'var Torah – Aharay Mot

"In the seventh month, on the tenth day of the month, you shall afflict your selves….."

Vayikra/Leviticus 16:29

The sages of the Talmud interpreted the Torah's words "to afflict yourselves" to mean abstaining from food and drink (Tractate Yoma 74b). In the twelfth century the great scholar, physician and legal authority, Rambam (often called Maimonides; Spain and Egypt, 1135-1204) in his14-volume Code of Law (*Mishneh Torah*), phrases this abstention in an unusual way. He says that one should "rest" from eating and drinking (Laws of Sh'vitat Asor1:4,5). When we think of fasting, especially since it comes from the biblical phrase to "afflict oneself," we have images of pain and suffering. Yet Rambam's phrase creates a completely different picture of fasting. It is not a "punishment," or an "affliction." Rather, it is an opportunity to serve God without the usual necessities that fuel our bodies. Humans become like angels, who are above the needs of physical nourishment. According to Rambam, the purpose of fasting is to help us reach higher spiritual levels, to be like angels, so that our repentance is free of worry about physical needs.

Four Questions:

What are the different interpretations of the Torah's phrase "to afflict ourselves" on Yom Kippur?

What point is Rambam trying to make when he chooses the word "rest" from eating and drinking?

How does fasting help a person become more spiritual?

Do you find fasting an experience that is elevating, or distracting from the goals of Yom Kippur? Explain.

D'var Torah - Kedoshim

"You must rise before the aged." Vayikra/Leviticus 19:32

Judaism has always prized the elderly, assuming that they have more experience, wisdom and knowledge than younger people. In modern American culture, young people are the ideal. Many people go to unusual, and sometimes expensive, extremes to appear youthful, trying to hide wrinkles, gray hair, and other signs of old age. The latest fad is "Botox" injections which do away with wrinkles on the face. According to our verse, and Jewish tradition, wrinkles are a sign of experience and wisdom, and are to be viewed with respect.

The Zohar, the medieval "Bible" of Jewish mysticism, has a clever twist in its interpretation of this verse. It says "Rise up and repent before you reach old age." In other words, in this explanation the "aged" refers to the reader, not to a third person. Rise up in your spirit, and return to your best self, before it's too late – before you are too old to change.

Four Questions

Why do modern people value youth over age, as opposed to Jewish tradition?

What are some of the benefits of being older rather than younger?

What new meaning does the Zohar give to this verse?

How do you feel about growing older?

D'var Torah - Emor

"A man cursed God, so he was brought to Moshe. His mother's name was Shelomit the daughter of Divri of the tribe of Dan. He was placed in custody." Vayikra/ Leviticus 24:11-12.

The Torah tells us in this passage about a man who sinned by violating the laws of Judaism – cursing God, a most awful offense. The midrash notices something unusual about the way the man is identified. Not only is he mentioned, but his mother's name and his grandmother's name, and the name of his tribe (Dan). Why go to all this trouble to trace his lineage back so far? After all, he is the one who committed the crime! In *Midrash Vayikra Rabbah* we find this interesting comparison: "Why is the people of Israel compared to sheep? Just as when you hit a sheep on its leg, or other body part, the entire sheep feels the pain, so with the Jewish people. If one Jew goes astray, all Jews feel the pain and shame." In other words, the man who cursed God is bringing disgrace to all Jews, - his family, his tribe, and the entire Jewish people. The behavior of one Jew reflects good or bad, as the case may be, on all Jews. We thus have an obligation to our entire people to bring glory and honor upon the name of Jew and Judaism.

Four Questions

Why is cursing God viewed with such seriousness?

How is the man who committed this offense identified? Why?

Do you agree that the behavior of each individual Jew reflects on all other Jews? Explain your answer.

Are you proud when other Jews achieve great things? Are you ashamed when a Jew commits an offense? Why do you feel that way?

D'var Torah – Behar

"You shall count for yourself seven cycles of sabbatical years." Vayikra/Leviticus 25:8

Very often biblical commentators notice the tiniest words, words that seem totally insignificant on which to hang a very significant moral lesson. Hebrew verbs often add a small word, a preposition, to a verb – such as in the famous call to Avraham "Go to the Land I will show you," – or Lekh Lekha – that is, literally, "go for yourself." In our verse, the Hebrew word to "count" also has the same preposition, Count "Lekha" – for yourself. The commentator known as Kli Yakar (Rabbi Shlomo Ephraim of Lunchitz of Lvov, Ukraine – d. 1619) suggests that a person's life is counted only in terms of the time one spends in doing spiritual acts, mitzvot. A meaningful life is counted only in the hours and days we spend in doing things that have purpose and benefit for others and ourselves. A wasted life is filled with counting time in trivial deeds that have no usefulness for God, Torah and the community. Thus, "count for yourself" – for the benefit of your soul.

Four Questions

Why do many commentators rest their thoughts on small seemingly unimportant words?

How does Kli Yakar interpret the phrase "count for yourself?"

Why is it important to count time in terms of its usefulness to self and others?

In what ways can you spend your time more wisely for the benefit of the community, and your own spiritual development?

D'var Torah – Behukotai

"When anyone makes a vow…." Vayikra/Leviticus 27:2

Making promises has always been a controversial subject in Jewish law and lore. A Jew has always been known to be a person who fulfills what is promised. In the traditional expression, a Jew is "a man of his word." Promises are taken seriously, as are all words that we utter, especially when made with the force of a vow. The main trend in Jewish ethics is to discourage vows, because they are often difficult to fulfill, and breaking one's word carries significant penalties. The Talmud (Nedarim 22a) says: "One who makes a vow, even if that person fulfills the vow, is called wicked." This is extreme, but the Talmud often makes extreme statements when it wants to teach an important lesson. The lesson that one's word is sacred is deemed important enough in Jewish tradition to exaggerate the threat of punishment. In the Tanakh (Kohelet 5:4) we read: "It is better not to vow than to vow and not fulfill." The Kol Nidre prayer, recited on what is deemed the holiest night of the year, releases everyone from all vows, oaths and promises so that the New Year can begin with a clean slate, with no unfulfilled vows on the record.

Four Questions:

What is the Jewish view toward vows?

Why is it considered in Jewish Law so important that one keep one's word?

What are the some of the consequences of not fulfilling a promise or a vow?

Are you a person of whom people can say: that person keeps their word! Can you improve on that score? Explain.

D'var Torah – Bemidbar

"...the tribe of Zevulun...." Bemidbar/Numbers 2:7

In English the book of Bemidbar is called "Numbers," because the content of the book deals with the census of each of the twelve tribes of Israel. As each tribe is mentioned and counted, the next one is listed. Before the next tribe we find the conjunction "and." For example, "*and* the tribe of Gad... *and* the tribe of Binyamin...*and* the tribe of Naftali...." In one case, however, the connecting word "and" is omitted – that is in the case of the tribe of Zevulun. Rabbi Yaakov ben Asher (1270-1343, Barcelona & Toledo, Spain) gives his interpretation why this is so. Zevulun, he explains, engaged in commerce, and provided the funds for its brother tribe of Issakhar to study Torah. This relationship of siblings is not uncommon in Jewish history. The brother of the famous philosopher and legal codifier, Maimonides, was a merchant who provided the money for his brother to study. When Maimonides' brother died suddenly at sea, he had to study medicine to support himself. Rabbi Yaakov ben Asher explains that providing the funds for the tribe of Yissakhar to study qualifies it to be equal in importance to its sibling tribe that did not engage in providing funds. Their division of labor made it possible for each to perform an important function. Thus, by omitting the word "and" the Torah is teaching us that both tribes are equally important. Enabling Yissakhar to study Torah gave Zevulun a level of importance that was just as high as its sibling tribe.

Four Questions:

Why is the word "and" left out in the case of the tribe of Zevulun?

Why does Rabbi Yaakov ben Asher consider financial support of Torah study so important?

Do you know of any persons or foundations that provide funds for study and research? Do you consider them to be as important as those who actually study?

Which would you rather be – the financial backer, or the researcher and student?

D'var Torah - Naso

"From wine [the Nazirite] must abstain and consecrate oneself.... A razor shall not cross one's head... neither shall the Nazir approach a dead body." Bemidbar/Numbers 6:1-6

Chapter six of Sefer Bemidbar (the Book of Numbers) deals with a special act of consecration. The Nazir (one who is specially consecrated) makes a voluntary vow not to do three things: drink intoxicating beverages, cut one's hair, and come near the dead. There is much debate in the millennia of literature on this chapter about Judaism's general approach to material pleasures, and refraining from hair-cutting or touching the dead. Ordinarily, there are no commands to refrain from physical enjoyment, as long as one does no harm to oneself or others. The case of the Nazir is unique. If a person feels a special sense of gratitude to God, such a person "consecrates" oneself for a period of time (or for life, as in the unusual case of Samson – the story in the Haftarah for this week), and abstains from these three areas of action.

While the case of the Nazirite is unusual, and no one today will likely consecrate oneself in this way – to become a Nazirite – nevertheless there is an important idea in the act of choosing to be a consecrated person to God. Rabbi Avraham ibn Ezra (Toledo, Spain, 1092-1167) argues that the central idea is to learn the art of self-discipline. In today's world of addiction to things like alcohol, drugs, smoking, overeating and overworking, self-discipline is a character trait that all of us can relate to, and need to exercise in a greater degree.

Four Questions:

What is a "Nazir?" How does one become a "Nazir?" How does Judaism generally look upon abstention from physical pleasure? Why is an exception made in the case of a Nazir?

Does the existence of the institution of the Nazir reflect a general attitude of the Jewish tradition, or is it an exception? Explain.

What are some of the positive results of being a Nazir, as Rabbi ibn Ezra sees it?

What areas of your life need more self-discipline?

D'var Torah – Be-ha-a-lotekha

"Adonai spoke to Moshe, saying: Speak to Aharon and say, 'When you kindle the lamps, let the seven lamps give light…' Aaron did so." Bemidbar/Numbers 8:1-3

The Menorah is the central religious symbol in the Jewish religion. It is symbolized today in every Jewish Sanctuary by the Ner Tamid, the Eternal Light, whose light represents truth, justice and knowledge. The Menorah is on the emblem of the State of Israel, and it is the only biblical symbol that truly represents Jewish values. The Star of David is never mentioned in the Torah, though it too has become an important symbol today. The Magen David (Star of David, or Shield of David), however, does not have the high spiritual meaning of the Menorah. This week's Sidrah opens with the command to Aharon to kindle the Menorah. The Torah relates that Aharon followed the command. Is it not obvious that Aharon would follow God's command? Why should this be mentioned? The Vilna Gaon (Eliyahu ben Shlomo Zalman, Lithuania, 1720-1797) comments that even though Aharon kindled the Menorah every single day (even Shabbat!) he never lost his enthusiasm or reverence for the holy task that God assigned him.

Four Questions:

Why is the Menorah the most important religious symbol in Judaism?

What other symbols are there, and why is the Menorah more important than any of the others?

What lesson is the Vilna Gaon teaching about Aharon's lighting the Menorah? Why was Aharon able to perform this mitzvah with consistent piety?

What religious tasks do you perform on a regular basis? Do you maintain the same level of reverence each time? Explain in detail your "yes" and/or your "no."

D'var Torah – Sh'lah Lekha

"Is the land good or bad?...Is the soil rich or poor?" Bemidbar/Numbers 13:19-20

In the first year of the forty-years of wandering in the wilderness, Moshe sends twelve spies to see what kind of Land they were commanded by God to take over and live in. An interesting question arises: If God commanded that the Israelite nation take the Land, what difference does it make what kind of land it is? Furthermore, God had already told Moshe that it was a good land. What need is there for Moshe to send spies to find out details about the land and report to the people? A famous Hasidic master, Rabbi Menahem Mendel of Kotzk (1787-1859, Poland), has an interesting solution. Moshe probably instructed the spies to give a good report, even if it were exaggerated. If they saw an infertile land, they should say it was fertile. Don't rely on your own visual perception, he said. Go beneath the surface, and show your deeper understanding that this special Land that God gave us is a wonderful land. What Moshe wanted the spies to do was not to make an objective report, but to demonstrate their faith in God. Without faith, they could never take the Land and live in it.

Four Questions:

If God had already told Moshe that Eretz Yisrael was a good land, why did Moshe send spies to examine the Land?

What is the answer of Rabbi Menahem Mendel of Kotzk to this question?

Why is faith important in significant undertakings? Can you give some modern examples?

If you were among the twelve spies, what kind of report would you have given? Explain.

D'var Torah - Korah

"Korah, the son of Yizhar….[and others] along with 250 Israelites, leaders and men of reknown… rose up against Moshe and Aharon…." Bemidbar/Numbers 16:1-3

The story of Korah and his company of rebels is sometimes called "The Great Mutiny." A group of leaders of the Israelite community rose up and demanded to share authority with Moshe and Aharon – because they too were Levites (some of them, anyway). The rabbis of the midrash and the Talmud discuss at length the reasons for this rebellion. In sum, they see Korah as a self-serving, power-hungry upstart, whose motives were insincere. One commentator, known by the name of his book *Kli Yakar*, (Rabbi Ephraim of Lunschitz, 1550 –1619, Lemberg and Prague) pays special attention to the descriptive phrase "men of renown." He notices that this phrase (in Hebrew "anshei shem" – people of name, of distinguished reputation) appears only one other time in the entire Torah – in the story of Noah and the Great Flood (Bereshit/Genesis 6:4). Based on the Genesis reference to this phrase, the commentator asks an important question: Does the Torah mean to say that these men were "persons of renown" – or that they *wanted* to become such persons – to share the wealth, power and reputation with Moshe and Aharon? He answers that their motive was the latter. Like the men in the days of the Flood, they really had done nothing to warrant sharing such high position – they were merely self-centered power-hungry power-grabbers, unworthy of sharing, and certainly not replacing the leaders chosen by God.

Four Questions:

Was the authority and position of Moshe and Aharon challenged for good reasons?

What makes the commentator, *Kli Yakar*, think that the rebels were unworthy?

When is it legitimate to try to replace the duly-appointed or –elected leaders?

If you were among the nation of Israel at that time, which side would you have taken? Explain.

D'var Torah – Hukat

"Miriam died there [in Kadesh] and was buried there." Bemidbar/Numbers 20:1

Miriam died toward the end of the forty years of wandering in the Wilderness of Sinai. This Sidrah mentions her death, and the death of her brother Aharon. One can say that she died when her work was complete. She had helped her brothers lead the people, and the time was ripe for them to cross the Jordan and enter the Promised Land, Eretz Yisrael. Rabbi Samson Raphael Hirsch (Frankfurt, Germany, 1808-1888) points out that the women among the Israelite nation were least responsible for the frequent experiences of rebelliousness among the people; and they were the most faithful to God's commands and teachings. Rabbi Hirsch notes that the Midrash (Bemidbar Rabbah 27:1) teaches that that is the reason the women were not included in God's punishment – that is, not to enter the Land themselves, but only their children. (The view of the Midrash that the women of the generation of Egypt did enter the Land, is imaginative, and contradicts the Torah. But the Midrash is fanciful, and permits itself exaggerations for teaching purposes). The idea is that the grandmothers and mothers were able to pass on the teachings of the past by helping the younger generation adjust to their new life of freedom and independence in their own land.

Four Questions:

What does Rabbi Hirsch say about the timing of the death of Miriam?

Did the women deserve to enter the Promise Land? Why would the women among the people be thought of as the best "teachers?"

Do you think women make better teachers today? Why?

Give some examples comparing male and female teachers you have had, and what qualities might distinguish between men and women as teachers.

D'var Torah - Balak

"Adonai opened the donkey's mouth." Bemidbar/ Numbers 22:28

A talking donkey? What kind of crazy story is this? Since the Sidrah of Balak is read during the summer months, when many people are traveling, or on vacation, and perhaps not in synagogue to hear the Torah reading, this story is not very well known. Few people know that there is a story in the Torah about a talking donkey! This is the story: As the Israelite people were traveling from Egyptian slavery to the Promised Land, Eretz Yisrael, King Balak of Moab (where the kingdom of Jordan is today) summoned a Mesopotamian prophet to come and curse the Israelites. King Balak had heard about the might of the Israelite nation, and that God was on their side, and he was afraid of them. Bilaam, the prophet called by Balak, was coming to curse the Israelites, riding on a donkey. But the donkey was instructed by God not to cooperate in this nasty venture. When the donkey saw angels of God, blocking his path, he swerved and did not go forward. Bilaam became angry and hit the donkey. Then God opened the donkey's mouth and had him challenge Bilaam. Of course it is very unusual for an animal to speak, and this is one of the few such stories in the Torah (another is the snake in the Garden of Eden). What is the lesson we learn from it? A commentator (named by the title of his book, *Kli Yakar* - Rabbi Ephraim of Lunschitz, 1550 –1619, Lemberg and Prague) suggests an interesting interpretation. God was teaching Bilaam a lesson, he writes. Just as it was God who commanded the donkey to talk, so it is God who permits the prophet Bilaam to speak. Thus, Bilaam cannot curse the Israelites without God's permission. *Kli Yakar* thus brings us the teaching that only God has the power to enable humans or animals to speak.

Four Questions:

What do you think about a story that includes a talking animal? Why would the Torah include such a story?

Why did God eventually transform Bilaam's curse into a blessing? Do you know what blessing it was?

In what way does God exercise the power to control people's speech? Does this deny humans freedom of speech? Could the Torah be using this story as a "metaphor," or a "teaching story?

What lessons do you derive from this story for your own life?

D'var Torah - Pinhas

"Adonai said to Moshe: Take Yehoshua bin Nun (Joshua the son of Nun), a man in whom is spirit, and lay your hands upon him." Bemidbar/Numbers 27:18

As the Israelite nation is about to cross the Jordan River into Eretz Yisrael, Moshe will die and a successor must be appointed. God tells Moshe to appoint Yehoshua as his successor. The Midrash (Bemidbar Rabbah 21:15) puts a question into the mouth of Moshe. He asks: Why Yehoshua? Why did not God ask me to appoint one of my sons, Eliezer or Gershom, to succeed me? The answer God gives is that Moshe did not train his sons in Torah and leadership. He was apparently so busy leading his people that he neglected his own family. "If you want a tree to bear fruit, you must tend to the tree," says God to Moshe. "You neglected the tree, so you have no (worthy) fruit." Joshua, on the other hand, earned the right of succession because he followed the leadership of Moshe, and studied from his master.

Four Questions:

Why was Yehoshua worthy of becoming the successor to Moshe?

What fault did God attribute to Moshe? What type of individual is likely to share this flaw?

Why is it important for a person to care for his/her own family first, before the rest of society?

How are you and the members of your family with regard to treating each other? Does each family member place one another before non-family members?

D'var Torah – Matot

"Every person who has slain a human being…shall stay outside the camp seven days…. You shall purify yourself on the third and seventh day."

Bemidbar/Numbers 31:19

The conventional interpretation for keeping soldiers outside the camp for a week after contact with the dead is that Jewish Law mandates rituals of purification after such contact. However, Rabbi Harold Kushner (*Humash Etz Hayim*) suggests another reason. He proposes that these soldiers were permitted certain normally forbidden behaviors that are necessary in war, but not permitted on normal occasions. Thus, they needed a week to decompress, to absorb the shock of the horrible experience of killing, even though it was justified and important to do. This reflects the general Jewish view that war is to be avoided whenever possible, because all human life is sacred. One who kills in wartime is permitted to do so, in fact, commanded to do so, in order to protect oneself and one's people. But that does not mean that such a person does not suffer after effects. In modern times we use the term "post traumatic syndrome" to describe the negative psychological and spiritual effects that such an experience has on someone.

Four Questions:

What possible reasons are there for the Torah to require soldiers to remain outside the camp for seven days after killing someone?

Do you think that killing in time of war is excusable?

Why would someone who did what was right and commanded – like killing the enemy in war - feel guilty and unsettled?

Do you know anyone who killed another person in battle? If so, what was that person's reaction? If not, what do you think your own reaction would be?

D'var Torah – Mas-ei

"They journeyed from Yam Suf (the Reed Sea) to the Wilderness of Sin." Bemidbar/Numbers 33:11

Normally the Wilderness through which the Israelites traveled is called Sinai, not Sin. The difference in Hebrew between Sin and Sinai is one tiny letter – Yod. Rabbi Yaakov ben Asher, known as the Baal HaTurim, after his mammoth work on Jewish Law (Germany and Toledo, 1270-1343), was one of many scholars through the ages who looked for hidden meanings in "Gematria," or "numerology." The numerical equivalent of the Hebrew letter "Yod" is ten. Says Rabbi ben Asher, the Wilderness was first called "Sin," but after the Ten Commandments were given its name was changed to "Sinai," – that is, a "yod" was added to "Sin" to make it "Sinai," because "yod" is ten, and Ten Commandments were added to "Sin." Furthermore, he says, Moshe stayed on the top of Mount Sinai for 120 days. The Letter "Sin" is spelled "Sin" "Yod" "Nun," which add up to 120. (Sin equals 60, Yod is 10, and Nun is 50 – a total of 120).

Four Questions:

How does Rabbi Yaakov ben Asher explain the name change of the Wilderness from Sin to Sinai – and why?

What value does using Gematria have in studying the Torah? Have you heard of "Torah Codes," and if so, explain what they are and give your opinion about them.

Do you believe that there are hidden meanings within the Torah that the normal eye may miss if one does not study very carefully?

Do you know of any other examples of how Gematria is used? A good study project is to do some research and find out more about Gematria.

D'var Torah - D'varim

"You said, 'Let us send men before us, that they may spy out the land for us….'" D'varim/Deuteronomy 1:22

Moshe is now recalling the events of the past forty years of wandering in the wilderness. Among the events that he recounts is the story of sending spies into the Land of Israel (Eretz Yisrael) to see what kind of land it was. Because the spies brought back a negative report, the people were punished and not permitted to enter the Land. The entire generation had to die off (except Joshua), and only their children would enter the Land. In the story as it is told in Bemidbar (chapters 13 and 14) it was God who commanded that the **spies** carry out their mission, and the spies were to blame for their report. In the account here in D'varim it is the **people** who ask to have the spies sent, and the people who are blamed for the results. A famous modern Israeli teacher of the Tanakh, Nehama Leibowitz, points out that even though it may have been God who made the initial assignment, the people accepted it, and they must take full responsibility. Each person must be his or her own leader, she claims, and that is why the people are now blamed.

Four Questions:

What is the difference between the story of the Spies in Bemidbar and the one here in D'varim?

How does Nehama Leibowitz explain the difference in the two versions? What other possibilities are there?

Why should the people be blamed, according to Leibowitz, if it was the spies who brought back a negative report?

Have you ever tried to blame someone else for something you did, because it was not your idea in the first place? Were you right? Explain.

D'var Torah - Va-et-hanan

"Take care of yourself and take great care of your soul…." Devarim/Deuteronomy 4:9

Many commentators explain that "yourself" refers to your body, or your physical dimension, while "your soul" refers to your spiritual dimension. The Torah is teaching us to be very careful in taking care of both of our material and our religious selves. We are one human being with two different aspects of our person. Each deserves attention, since we are God's creatures, made in God's image. The Baal Shem Tov (1700-1760), Founder of Hasidism, taught that both our body and our soul are important and that we must take great care of both of them. If, for example, said the Besht (abbreviation for **B**aal **Sh**em **T**ov), our body becomes weak, our soul in turn weakens. Thus, when we take good care of our bodies, we are also taking great care of our souls.

Four Questions:

What words in this *pasuk* (verse) refer to the body and to the soul?

Does Judaism recognize these two separate parts of ourselves?

Which part is more important, according to this *pasuk*? According to the Besht?

In what ways do you take care of your body? Your soul? Which part of you could use more attention than you now give it?

D'var Torah – Ekev

"Know in your heart that just as a parent disciplines a child, so Adonai your God disciplines you." D'varim/ Deuteronomy 8:5

The Book of D'varim contains the three great speeches of Moshe in the last weeks of his life, summing up what happened during the forty years of wandering in the Wilderness of Sinai, and reviewing the mitzvot the people should follow after they enter Eretz Yisrael. In summing up the four-decade journey, Moshe reminds the people that God sometimes punished them, and will continue to do so, when they go astray. In speaking to the people Moshe tells them that when they are punished, it is discipline out of love, the same way a parent disciplines a child. One of the questions we must ask about discipline is this: Should a parent discipline a child in a tough manner, to set the proper course for the rest of the child's life? Many argue that this is indeed the correct way. But Rabbi Avraham Yitzhak Kook, first Chief Rabbi of Eretz Yisrael (1865-1935 – he became Chief Rabbi in 1921) argues in a different way. While obedience and good discipline are certainly important, even more important is a strong will and the ability to make independent decisions, apart from parental guidance. This will lead a child to be one who can make the world a better place, and have the highest level of moral character.

Four Questions:

Why does Moshe tell the people that God's discipline is similar to that of a parent?

What are the two approaches to discipline (among others) that come to mind?

Do you agree with Rabbi Kook that a strong will and independent action are more important than obedience? Explain why, and under what circumstances.

With which kind of discipline were you raised? Which kind do you prefer to use if you are (or will be) a parent?

D'var Torah – Re-eh

"...You shall inherit them and dwell in their land." Devarim/Deuteronomy 12:29

Moshe tells the people that when they enter the Promised Land (Eretz Yisrael) they are to dispossess the idolatrous and immoral inhabitants and purify the land and take possession of it. The love of Eretz Yisrael, and the mitzvah to dwell in the Land begins with the Torah and continues throughout Jewish history to this day. The Midrash (Sifrei, Parshat Re-eh) reports a story about Rabbi Eliezer ben Shamua and Rabbi Yohanan HaSandlar who once left Eretz Yisrael to study Torah. They did not get very far when they remembered the verse above, realized they were violating a mitzvah of the Torah, so they wept, tore their clothing (a sign of mourning), and returned. They said "Living in Eretz Yisrael is equivalent to all the other mitzvot in the Torah."

Four Questions:

Why did God command the Israelites to take possession of the Land of Canaan?

Why did the two rabbis in the account in the Midrash tear their garments?

What is the place that Eretz Yisrael holds in Jewish Tradition?

Have you been to Eretz Yisrael? If "yes," what was it like? If "no," would you like to go? Do you have plans to go?

D'var Torah – Shoftim

"When you approach a town to attack it, you shall offer it terms of peace." D'varim/Deuteronomy 20:10

The Torah's attitude is that even though war is cruel and destructive, it is sometimes necessary, and therefore, there must be rules about how to conduct a war, to make it as least horrible as possible. The war referred to in this Sidrah is the war against the inhabitants of the Land of Canaan, commanded by God. It is the only war that God specifically commands. Yet, even in this unusual, important war, ordered by God, the Torah's position is that every effort should be made to avoid the conflict by discussing terms of resolution – and thus, peace. Rabbi Bradley Shavit Artson, in his book *The Bedside Torah*, emphasizes that peace is a supreme value in Judaism. He quotes the Talmud: "Peace is the foundation and principle of the entire Torah, and the essential element in the creation of the world." The ancient rabbis also, says Rabbi Artson, declared the Torah an instrument of peace, quoting the verse from Mishle (the biblical Book of Proverbs, 3:17) "All her ways are pleasant, and all her paths are peace." Further, many important prayers conclude with the prayer for peace, "Oseh Shalom," such as the Kaddish, the Amidah, and others. In short, the Torah is a book dedicated to Shalom, to Peace for all God's children, even when war seems like the only choice.

Four Questions:

Why is the command to offer terms of peace in this verse considered so extraordinary?

Does it make sense for there to be "rules for the conduct of war?" If war becomes necessary, should one not do anything possible to win?

How would you characterize the Torah's approach to peace?

Are there things that you as an individual, that we as a country, and as a society, can and should be doing to bring about more Shalom in the world?

D'var Torah – Kee Teze

"If a child is wayward and defiant, and listens neither to the voice of his father nor to the voice of his mother…." D'varim/Deuteronomy 21:18

The Torah deals with laws that regulate every aspect of personal, family and community life. In this pasuk, we are told that a defiant child is subject to severe punishment. Later commentators explained that the harshness of the punishment was meant to be a warning, and that the law was never intended to be carried out in its literal sense. In describing the actions of the child, there is an implicit lesson about the norms of child-rearing established by parents. The Talmud (Sanhedrin 71a) pays particular attention to the fact that both the "voice of the mother," and "the voice of the father" are listed. To the ancient rabbis this implies that parents must speak with one voice. Their values and household rules must be compatible, and the methods of treatment of their child must match. A child raised in a home where there is disagreement, conflict, and approaches to child-rearing that are too far apart, will turn out to be confused and defiant. According to this talmudic view, the law applies more to the parents than to the children.

Four Questions:

Why does the Torah mete out such harsh punishment to a defiant child?

What patterns in the home does the Talmud see that may be the cause of the bad behavior of such a child?

Do you agree that parents must agree on everything they say to their children? Explain in detail.

Can you think of an example, either as a child or as a parent, when there was inconsistency that brought about an unhealthy result? Or an example where consistency helped to raise a healthy child?

D'var Torah – Kee Tavo

"The Egyptians treated us in an evil way…." D'varim/Deuteronomy 26:6

Moshe tells the Israelite nation that when they enter Eretz Yisrael they are to perform a beautiful ritual, "The Ceremony of First Fruits," acknowledging the gifts that God gave them from their new land and home. As part of this ritual, they recite a brief history of how God took them out of bitter Egyptian slavery, where they were mistreated, "in an evil way." Rabbi Moshe ben Hayim Alshekh (Safed, 1508-1593) interprets the Hebrew word "treated us in an evil way" to mean "they made us into evil people." Either translation is acceptable, but by translating the Hebrew in this way, Rabbi Alshekh makes an interesting point. Not only did the Egyptians treat us in an evil way, but they did even worse. They made us as evil as they were. Perhaps worse than being treated harshly by an oppressor is the common situation where the victim becomes like the oppressor. Not only does one have to suffer at the hand of an evil person – that may be short-lived. But when one learns the ways of the evil, and becomes evil oneself, that is a great tragedy. This may be, argues Rabbi Alshekh, the worst thing the Egyptians did to us, and made it imperative for the Israelites to flee from Egypt to their own Land, where they could live a free and moral life.

Four Questions:

Why does Moshe command the Israelite people to perform "The Ceremony of First Fruits?"

How does Rabbi Alshekh interpret the phrase "treat us in an evil way" and what lesson does he teach by doing so?

Do you know of any person or group in history who was oppressed and then became evil, similar to their oppressors?

How can persons who are mistreated avoid turning into people like the ones who mistreat them? Can you give an example of something like that happening to you?

D'var Torah – Nitzavim

"Adonai your God will return your captivity...." D'varim/Deuteronomy 30:3

As Moshe and the Israelite people approach the end of the forty years of wandering, Moshe assures them that if they go astray, but repent, God will always bring them out of captivity, just as God took the people out of Egyptian exile. God's love for the people, and God's compassion for them, is eternal. The Talmud (Megillah 29a) notices that the Hebrew verb is not in the normal causative form (it would normally say: "God will cause you to return from captivity"). This means, say the rabbis, that God is joining the people in their return from captivity. In other words, the Talmud translates the verse as follows: "Adonai your God will return with your captivity." By this they mean to point out that God went with the people into Exile, and God will return with them when they repent and come back to Eretz Yisrael. This is a daring theological statement – that God cares so much for God's people that God even goes into exile. It shows how deep is the relationship between God and the Israelite nation, and how important is the Covenant made between God and God's People at Mt. Sinai.

Four Questions:

Under what circumstances will God bring the people back to their Land?

How does the Talmud interpret the verse about returning to the Land?

What is the nature of the Covenant made at Mount Sinai between God and the People of Israel?

Do you feel God's love and concern for the Jewish People in today's world? Explain.

D'var Torah – Vayelekh

"Gather the people – the men, women and little children…."

D'varim/Deuteronomy 31:12

There is a law in the Torah called "Hak-hel" which commands the entire nation to come together to hear the words of the Torah read aloud in public, so that their message will penetrate into their minds and way of life, and so that they will not forget the importance of the values of the Torah. This was before the custom which we observe today of reading the Torah publicly four times each week (Shabbat morning and afternoon, Monday and Thursday mornings). "Hak-hel" took place every seven years on the Festival of Sukkot. In proclaiming this law, Moshe tells the people to bring their little children with them. Rashi (Troyes, France, 1135-1204) asks an obvious question: Why bring the babies and infants to such an important occasion? Certainly they are not mature enough to understand what is being said. Rashi answers by saying that even though the little children will not understand, their parents will be rewarded for bringing them. Rashi implies in this comment that education begins at the very earliest age. Just by being there, the youngest members of the family will begin the habit of Torah study.

Four Questions:

What is "Hak-hel" and why was it carried out?

Why is it necessary to constantly repeat the reading of the Torah in public?

How does Rashi explain the importance of bringing little children to "Hak-hel?"

At what age do you think education begins in the life of a child? How old were you when you began to hear about, or study, Torah? At what age do children in your family begin to study Torah? Why is it important to start early?

D'var Torah – Ha-a-zinu

"May my Teaching fall like rain/ May my Words drip like dew…."

D'varim/Deuteronomy 32:2

Just as Moshe began the forty year march through the Sinai wilderness with a song (Shirat HaYam – The Song of the Sea – Sh'mot, chapter 15), so he ends his forty years as the leader of the people of Israel with another Song – The Song of Moshe. The two songs share a general idea – that after these forty arduous years the people will enter Eretz Yisrael, the Promised Land, and will prosper and thrive, spiritually and materially. To introduce the final Song, which, like Shirat HaYam, is crafted in poetic form, he offers a prayer that his words – the words of the Torah – will enter into the hearts of the people. Using powerful poetic imagery, he offers the hope that the Torah will be like rain that is eternal and life-giving; and that the Torah will be like dew, that, in the words of Rabbi Joseph Hertz, "falls gently and unheard, yet has a wonderful reviving power." The Midrash (Sifre) suggests another reason for the use of the metaphor of dew. While not everyone is happy when it rains – if one is traveling, for example - everyone loves dew. Dew helps water vegetation, does not interfere with travel, and it presents a shiny, sparkly surface to the flowers and the leaves on the trees. In the same way, Moshe hopes that the Torah will be loved by all.

Four Questions:

Why does Moshe begin and conclude the forty years in the Sinai desert with two songs?

What ideas does the poem try to convey by using images like "rain" and "dew"?

Is the Torah loved by everyone? Why? Why not?

What are some parts of the Torah that you love best?

D'var Torah – Ve-zot Ha-B'rakhah

"He became Ruler over Yeshurun...." D'varim/ Deuteronomy 33:5

On the last day of Moshe's life he blesses his people. Before his death he wants to offer a final word of support and affection. The journey which now comes to an end began at Mount Sinai, the major moment in the life of the people of Israel, when they became a distinctive people to God, and a covenant was made binding God together with God's special people. At that holy moment at Sinai, God formally became the "Ruler" over the people of Israel. God's part in the covenant is to love and care for the people, and the people's part is to obey, love, and be faithful to their Creator. Rashi (Troyes, France, 1135-1204) suggests that God's sovereignty over the people, as mentioned here, reminds them that they must follow God's rule book, the Torah. In Jewish tradition, the recitation of "Shema Yisrael," implies accepting the "yoke of the rule of Heaven" – "Ol Malkhut Shamayim." As Moshe is about to bless the tribes of Israel, one by one, he wants to remind them that they must always remember the Covenant, the Ruler who established it, and the book – the Torah – which contains God's rules.

Four Questions:

Why does Moshe bless the people on the last day of his life? Of what does this remind you?

How does Moshe begin his blessing, and why?

What is the nature of the Covenant between God and the people of Israel?

Do you feel bound by this Covenant even though it was made over 3000 years ago? Define the relationship you feel toward God as Giver of the Torah.

BOOK FIVE

[In Book Five, We suggest that each family frame their own questions after reading the D’var Torah.]

Parashat Bereshit

"When God began to create heaven and earth...." Bereshit/Genesis 1:1

Both Rashi and the New JPS translation understand the first pasuk in the Torah to mean: "When God began to create heaven and earth...," instead of the conventional translation "In the beginning God created Heaven and Earth." What the pasuk does is set the time frame – i.e., the following occurred when God began to create.... The main point of this understanding of the pasuk is that creation is something that is ongoing. When humans create something, they can finish it. (By the way, the Hebrew here is bara' – which is only used in the Tanakh together with God – only God can "boray" – create – there are other Hebrew words for human creation). God's creation of the world is still happening – all the time. Were it not for God's constant continuation of the creative process, creation, the world, would fall apart. Thus we say in our tefillot that God in goodness renews creation daily, constantly. Of course, Jewish tradition assigns to humans the task of being partners with God in this process of on-going creation (shutafim b'maasay Bereshit). By doing so, we are elevated ourselves, and we elevate those around us. Creation is a gift from God to us to become more like our Creator. By being creators, and partners with our Creator, we are more like our Creator. Another commentator (*Hashavah l'Tovah*) gives a midrashic twist to this thought by saying that the pasuk also means that Bereshit – at the beginning of each day – we should focus on the idea that God created the heavens and the earth. Creation is such an important part of both God and God's creatures, that the idea of creation should be our foremost thought each morning that directs us to a day filled with creativity. That we are creative beings is one of the most defining qualities of the human race.

Parashat Noah

"These are the offspring of Noah, Noah….." Bereshit/Genesis 6:9

The introductory pasuk to this section tells us that we are about to read the list of Noah's children. But we don't, at least not for a short while. First we hear about Noah himself. Why is this so? Rashi says that the Torah wants to talk about Noah ("Noah was a righteous and wholehearted man in his generation; Noah walked with God."), because the most important offspring of a person are his/her good deeds and spiritual acts. Unless a person sets an example in his/her own life, it is unlikely that that person will be able to produce righteous children.

Rashi's comment highlights the importance of being a role model to our children. A wise person once wrote that there are three important paths to raising good children: modeling, modeling, and modeling. Ralph Waldo Emerson once said that "Your actions speak so loud, I can't hear what you are saying." Our words are probably more important than Emerson makes them out to be. What we say is significant, and our children often listen carefully to what we teach and say (often, of course, they do the opposite, or ignore us, but we should not underestimate the power of words). Once a driver was lost and asked a policeman standing at the corner which way to go. The policeman pointed to the left, but said "Turn right." The driver proceeded to turn left. When asked by passengers in the car why he ignored what the policeman said, he replied: "When a person says one thing and does another, I always follow what he does."

Often we find children of famous people who don't emulate their parents' good traits. Even Moses had children who were not worthy of following his example of leadership. That only demonstrates the famous generalization that "all generalizations are false, including this one." That paradox affirms the fact that if something occurs most of the time, it is good enough. No rule, no advice, no principle, is full proof. There is a host of psychological factors in relationships that prevent normal, expected consequences to follow. But the cards are stacked in our favor if we demonstrate to our children in our lives, our deeds and in our behaviors, the noble ideals we want our children to follow. Most of the time the apple does not fall far from the tree. (All we can say is "most of the time"). Do good, and you have a much better chance that your children will follow your lead.

Parashat Lekh Lekha

"From your land, from your relatives and from your parents' home."

Bereshit/Genesis 12:1

There are three levels of spiritual growth that a person can choose in self-development. This phrase describes them. One would think that the pasuk would be in reverse order, since when parting we first leave our parents home, then our wider family, and then our homeland. The commentator "Netivot Shalom" informs us that the reverse chronological order is in ascending order of difficulty. The easiest place to leave is our country. It is harder to leave our extended family. Most difficult of all is to leave our parental homestead. .

Let's consider for a minute, the meaning of these three levels of departure. For Avraham, it was important to rise above all the influences around him in order to found a new religion, discover a new homeland, and become the ancestor of a new people. It required, in one fell swoop, a gigantic leap forward in his spiritual development. All the negative influences from his past had to be wiped clean.

If we apply these "departures" to our own lives, we can tone down the levels of change by thinking of the ways in which we can grow. We don't live in a polytheistic society, filled with superstition, a totally corrupt society, governed by a primitive moral code. On the contrary, most of us live in a modern democracy, under the rule of law, with standards of morality that are considerably higher than ancient Babylonia.

Nevertheless our society is far from ideal. The violence, corruption, selfishness and materialism are forces that we must fight against if we are to improve our own souls as well as make a contribution to society. But if we have a map, a plan, and specific goals to reach for, it will help us become better human beings, and help raise our generation and the next, to a level higher than the one before ours. If we try to apply the three levels that Avraham left behind, we can attempt to rise above a) the uncivilized habits of much of our country, b) the bad habits of some members of our extended family and community, that we inevitably ingest through psychological osmosis, and c) the ingrained unhealthy family patterns that inevitably influence us from our parents and other close relatives, We need to identify the good and the bad of these three influences that we accepted in growing up and with which we now live, and establish a hierarchy of aspirations which we would like to reach for in our life-long search for a more highly developed spiritual life.

Parashat Vayera

"God opened her (Hagar's) eyes and she saw a well of water."

Bereshit/Genesis 21:19

The Torah does not say that God created a new well, or moved a well from another place to put it in front of Hagar. It must mean that the well was there all the time but Hagar did not see it. Midrash Bereshit Rabbah draws the conclusion that there are things around us to see all the time, but unless we utilize the divine powers of awareness that God bestowed upon us, we do not see many things that are very near us.

Someone described a poet as someone who sees what the rest of us see, but with new eyes. The art of seeing is very subjective. Psychologists call this "selective perception." We see and hear only that which interests us. For example, when we learn a new word, suddenly we see that word everywhere, and are puzzled why all of a sudden the word is everywhere, when just a day or two before, it was nowhere. The truth is that the word was everywhere all the time, but we did not see it, because we were not attuned to it. We are creatures of habit, and we see only the things we are accustomed to seeing. Attaining higher levels of spirituality and creativity is the act of opening our eyes wider, with God's help, and seeing the things that we missed before.

How often do we hear rabbis say "I read this chapter, or this verse, many times before, but never noticed the following insight...." Preaching, teaching, writing, are all things which the creative person does because she is able to sit back and go through a process of thinking, feeling and becoming more aware of the (formerly) hidden things nearby. Fritz Perls, the late founder of Gestalt Therapy, claimed that the basis of all mental health was constantly increasing awareness of our environment, our feelings, and all the things that in the past we took for granted and ignored.

The spiritual person allows God to continually open our eyes to beauty, information, insights, feelings, and all of our surroundings, within and without.

Parashat Hayay Sarah

"The life of Sarah was one hundred years, twenty years, and seven years…."

Bereshit/Genesis 23:1

Many commentators and interpreters take notice that the Torah does not say that Sarah was 127 years old, but rather than the word "years" is inserted after each number: 100 years, and 20 years, and 7 years. The Midrash comments (Bereshit Rabbah) that Sarah was as beautiful at 100 as she was at 20, and as innocent at 20 as she was at 7. The commentary *Ma-ayanah shel Torah* brings another explanation. Sarah was the same at 100 as she was at 20 – how? Even at age 100 she was still filled with the passion of youth, optimism, and enthusiasm.

All of us know people in their twenties who act as if they are near death: bored, lacking interest, zeal, and idealism. We also know people in their twilight years who are still full of energy, commitment and fervor. Youthfulness is not a factor of age, but of attitude. Sarah was one who loved life, believed in herself, and sought new challenges. We all grow older, but we need not grow old. Leo Buscaglia, popular California self-improvement guru, once wrote: "People don't grow old merely by living a certain number of years. Aging is an activity of the mind, an attitude. We grow old when we give up our sense of fun. We age when we relinquish our ideals, our dignity, our hope, our belief in miracles. Age comes when we cease reveling in the game of life, when we are no longer excited by the new and challenged by the dream. As long as we celebrate the richness of the world, hear the laughter in the voice of love and continue to believe in ourselves, age is incidental." And Ashley Montague, famous anthropologist, said that "I'm going to die young…as late in life as possible."

I was once interviewed for the position of rabbi by a search committee who asked me an interesting question: "Who do you get along better with, old people or young people?" The answer came quickly, from some deep source inside me. "I get along better," I replied, "with young people of all ages." I was called to that pulpit.

Indeed, Sarah died young, at a very advanced age.

Parashat Toldot

"Adonai said to her [Sarah]: Two nations are in your womb, and two peoples shall be separated from your bowels." Bereshit/Genesis 25:23

Rabbi Simcha Raz explains (*The Torah's Seventy Faces*, p. 36) that these two children, Yaakov and Esav, are different even at birth. As they grew, the differences in their character and spirit became more apparent. "As they grew, Esau was a cunning hunter, a man of the field; but Yizhak was a plain man, dwelling in tents." Two sons – worlds apart. Both needed to be educated as the sons of one family. How is it possible to educate two different children in one home?

Says Simcha Raz: "The wisest man who ever lived, King Solomon, answers this question: 'Educate the youth according to his way,' according to each child's natural tendencies. 'According to the opinion of the son should the father teach him' (Talmud Yerushalmi, Pesahim 116:8)."

The same idea is expressed in the passage of the four children in the Pesah Haggadah. The importance of the pedagogical ideal that each child must be taught in a way that reaches her/his individual heart, mind and soul, is of prime importance. We have visual learners and audio learners; we have students with analytical minds and others with artistic tendencies; we have pupils whose memories are strong and others who must have frequent repetition. In education the rule that one size fits all does not work. It is crucial for a teacher to get to know the soul of the learner, to develop a close bond between master and pupil, in order for the learning to take place effectively. This deep relationship and mutual affection will permit one to know the other in a way that their styles will fit together, and the teacher will adapt his style to his pupil, and the pupil will adapt her style to her teacher. They will appreciate each other's unique qualities, and the learning relationship will flourish.

Our ancestors were master pedagogues, and we have much to learn from them about how to teach and to learn.

Parashat Vayeze

"A ladder was set on the earth and its top reached to heaven."

Bereshit/Genesis 28:12

The famous ladder that appears to Yaakov in his dream at Beth El is the source of much of Jewish mysticism. The bridging of the distance between heaven and earth has been the goal of pious souls throughout history. In mystical devotion, one who prays attempts to cling to God – and some say, become united with God. Some consider themselves true mystics, and others feel that they "have" mystical experiences, though not mystics themselves.

There is hardly anyone who has not had what we might call a "mystical experience." This is what the late Rabbi Max Kaddushin called "Normal Mysticism." (Normal in the sense of *usual* for everyone, as opposed to normal versus abnormal). It might be at night during a dream, or in a park or cliff overlooking a breath-taking scene in nature, especially when the sun in setting. Or perhaps glancing out at the ocean with the powerful rays of the sun cutting a bright path through the rolling waves. As a child of 7 or 8 in summer camp I remember standing at the top of a hill, staring down into the shimmering lake beyond, and at the stately tress behind the lake, feeling that special sensation that spiritual souls might dub "mystical." I said to myself, "I know that I will always remember this moment throughout my life." And I have.

The commentator "Yismah Moshe" writes that the ladder is a metaphor for a human being. Our body, formed from the earth, is set on the earth. Our soul, which is divine, reaches to heaven. We can only reach the highest spiritual heights when we let our soul prevail over our body; when the ideals of Torah overcome our bodily desires. We all possess the capacity to turn our eyes toward the ground, and the ability to raise our eyes heavenward. Yaakov's ladder points us in the direction of heaven.

Parashat Vayeze

"Yaakov dreamed; behold a ladder with its top in the sky, and angels going up and down on it." Bereshit/ Genesis 28:12

Rabbi Yitzhak Nisenbaum points out that Yaakov had two dreams. The first dream (28:12) was about the heavens and angels – since he had a propensity toward spiritual matters and a life of values. The second dream, "I had a dream in which I saw that the he-goats mating with the flock were streaked, speckled and mottled" (31:10). In this dream he exhibited a tendency toward wealth and materialism. The first dream Yaakov had in Eretz Yisrael. The second, in Aram Naharaim – in the Diaspora.

Is there any doubt that one's environment affects his thinking, his values, his aspirations and dreams for the future? In the last number of years I lived in Princeton, New Jersey. The environment of Princeton University, the Institute for Advances Studies, the quality of the intellectual life in the area, all had a profound effect on the thinking, values, and the life of the mind of Princeton residents. I have lived for short periods, on a temporary basis, in other communities since then, and one cannot compare the heights of Princeton to the lowlands of other places.

I remember my friend Professor Susannah Heschel once talked about the joy of visiting Jerusalem. Everywhere one goes in the Holy City one meets people who are writing books. Everyone in Jerusalem is writing a book. In so many other places, people are barely reading books, let alone writing one. My own experience in Israel is similar. As the Talmud says,

"The very air of Eretz Yisrael makes one wise." The large number of yeshivot, schools of higher learning, scientific, medical and technological institutions is truly remarkable. The level of discourse in Israel is so elevated that, like the high tide that lifts all ships on the sea, the level of discussion at the average table in Israel is far more serious and inspired than most other places.

Living in a community with high values and a deep commitment to learning, to Torah, to spiritual searching, impacts the life of all its citizens.

Parashat Vayishlah

"Yaakov arrived whole at the city of Shechem." Bereshit/Genesis 33:18

Our ancestors always viewed the events that occurred to the patriarchs and matriarchs as a precursor to what will happen to the Jewish People. (Ma-asay avot siman l'vanim). In this case, Yaakov's return to Eretz Yisrael is seen as a foreshadowing of the future return of our people to its Homeland.

One commentator notes that the word "whole" (*shalem*) is an acronym – shin, lamed, nun. Shin stands for Shem (name). Lamed stands for Lashon (language). Mem stands for Malbush (clothing). Despite Yaakov's being outside the Land, living with Lavan, who was not a positive influence and whose environment could hardly have helped Yaakov maintain his Hebrew identity, Yaakov overcame these negative influences and kept his Hebrew background in a strong way. He did so through the three methods in the acronym.

He kept his Hebrew **name**, and that of his family. He did not relinquish his spoken Hebrew, his native **language**. And he did not adopt the **clothing** of the local environment.

In our day these three methods still have great relevance in maintaining our Jewish identity. Every Jewish child and adult must have a Hebrew name. Furthermore, every Jew should know his/her FULL Hebrew name (Shimon ben Hayim ve-Ester, Shira bat Gedaliah ve-Shoshana). Second, every Jew should be familiar with the Hebrew language. That includes fluency in reading and understanding Hebrew literature, as well as speaking modern Hebrew. In

Eastern Europe everyone spoke Yiddish, and there was a common language among all Jews. That is such a strong binding force in the Diaspora, as well as a source of Jewish values for all who know and speak the Hebrew language.

We can take poetic license and understand "clothing" as the general mores of our surroundings – keeping Shabbat and holidays, observing Kashrut, being involved in Jewish organizations and activities – these are the "dressings" that make us Jewish.

A good lesson on Jewish survival and continuity – **name, language and clothing**.

Parashat Vayeshev

"They could not speak a friendly word to him." Bereshit/Genesis 37:4

Yosef's brothers were angry at him. Yaakov's preferential treatment to his beloved wife Rachel's son infuriated Yosef's brothers. They were obviously very jealous when Yaakov gave Yosef a "Ketonet Pasim," an "ornamented tunic," or "coat of many colors," depending on which translation you use.

Anger has a way of deepening when it is not dealt with, or expressed. If there were a way to establish open communication, perhaps the brothers could have talked through the issues among them. But they did not. "They could not speak a friendly word to him." They refused to allow him to engage them in any conversation.

The Torah has an antidote for this kind of problem. "You shall not hate your brother in your heart, but you shall reprove the other" (Vayikra/Leviticus 19:17). Once you express your feelings, and open a dialog, the process of ventilation, open expression, has a cathartic effect, and good relations can be re-established. This did not happen with Yosef and his brothers, and instead it led to the terrible consequences – of their throwing him in the pit, his being sold and brought to Egypt, having the unfortunate incident with Potiphar's wife, going to jail, etc. (We can leave aside the fact that the story ends well, with Yosef becoming next to Pharaoh in power – divine intervention turned this whole sibling hatred into something positive).

Too often our temper gets the best of us, and we are the losers for it. The Midrash teaches that "When the kettle boils, it spills hot water down its side." In other words, an angry person punishes himself more often than others. The great medieval sage Maimonides wrote this advice:

Defile not your souls by quarrelsomeness and petulance. I have seen the white become black, the low brought still lower, families driven into exile, princes deposed from their high estate, great cities laid in ruins, assemblies dispersed, the pious humiliated, the honorable held lightly and despised, all on account of quarrelsomeness. Glory in forbearance, for in that is true strength and victory.

We learn many lessons from sibling rivalry in the Torah. This is not the least important of them.

Parashat Miketz

"For God has made me fruitful in the land of my affliction." Bereshit/Genesis 41:52

Yosef names his second son "Ephraim," from "P'ri," – fruit. At the same time he is careful to mention, in the midst of the joy of naming his new-born son, that in general terms, Egypt was not a happy place for him. What lesson is the Torah trying to convey with this mixed message – that Yosef is fruitful, powerful, famous, and wealthy, yet at the same time these things do not bring him full joy and satisfaction? The message seems to be that the one thing that was missing in Yosef's life was his family.

Yitzhak Abravanel (15th century, Portugal) comments that since Yosef had to live in a foreign land for a long period of time, separated from his family in Canaan, he looked upon Egypt as "a land of affliction."

This contrast, between the satisfactions brought by fame, power and wealth, on the one hand, and unhappiness in one's personal and family life, on the other hand, is one that we see often in our own day. Whether it be politicians, Hollywood stars, or powerful corporate moguls, we read almost daily in the media of such famous people who have everything in life but one important component: a happy family life. This is the fly that spoils the ointment of a happy existence. It is difficult to feel totally content when the most important thing in one's life goes unfulfilled. Often common people who lack the fame and fortunate of "important" and "well-known" movers and shakers, feel a sense of jealousy that they have not achieved what famous people have.

The truth is that many ordinary people often lead happier lives, even though their name may not be spread out in the press or their photograph dramatized in the media. They have a satisfying marriage, loving children, good values, a sense of loyalty, commitment and normality that so often eludes the rich and famous. As Pirke Avot advises us, "Who is truly happy? One who is satisfied with her lot in life."

Parashat Vayigash

"For how can I go up to my father if the youth is not with me?" Bereshit/Genesis 44:34

Judah pleads with the "Egyptian viceroy" (Yosef) to bring Benjamin back to Eretz Yisrael, because, since Yaakov already thinks he lost Rachel's oldest son Yosef, he will die if he thinks Rachel's youngest son, Benjamin, is lost too. He pleads: "How can I go up to my father if the youth [Benjamin] is not with me?"

Rabbi Yaakov Yosef of Polnoye has a special twist in his interpretation of the pasuk. In his homiletical comment, he sees "father" as "Father," – namely, God. (Based on the verb – "**to go up** to my father"). Then Rabbi Yaakov Yosef interprets "youth" not as referring to Benjamin, but referring to Judah's youth, his younger days. In other ways, when I am ready to die and go up to my Father in Heaven, how can I go up without my youthful days which I wasted on unimportant tasks. I did not study enough Torah or perform enough mitzvot when I was young, so how can I face God, knowing the failures of my younger years? This, of course, applies to all of us.

Another Hasidic master, Rabbi Meir of Premishlan, has a slightly different slant on the pasuk. He takes Rabbi Yaakov Yosef's interpretation of "Father" as referring to God, but he sees "youth" not as his own youth, but the youth of his generation. In other words, when our time comes to face God above, at the end of our lives, we will have to answer the question: Why did we not give our youth a better foundation in Jewish learning and practice? How can we go up to God without our youth – without our youth being fully educated and deeply involved in the performance of mitzvot?

Rabbi Meir places a primary obligation of every Jew on passing on our heritage to the next generation. If we are derelict, and neglect the Jewish education of our young people, if we do not fund religious education to the proper level, if we do not give sufficient financial, emotional and spiritual incentives to Jewish educators and teachers, we will be held responsible for the lack of transmitting Jewish life to the next generation. If we do not make sure that our youth attend Jewish day schools, intensive Jewish summer camp programs, and trips to Israel, we will have to face our Creator and admit that in this important regard, we did not do an effective job.

Something important to reflect upon. It's never too late.

Parashat Vayehi

"Yaakov lived in the land of Egypt." Bereshit/ Genesis 47:28

There are two parshiyot that begin with the story of the death of great people, Hayay Sarah and Vayehi. Both use the word "the life of," even though they speak of death. As the Talmud teaches, "Even in death the righteous live on (Berakhot 18a)." In other words, even though Sarah and Yaakov die physically, their good deeds and their legacy still live.

I write during the week in which Prime Minister Ariel Sharon suffered his second recent stroke, the second one life-threatening (January 2006). Sharon may or may not survive, but experts say he will never return to his post. His political life is over. Yet whether he lives or not physically, his legacy will continue. His remarkable example of one who metamorphized himself from a warrior to a peace-maker is one of the amazing examples in modern times of people who were able to adjust their views according to new conditions. This is perhaps his greatest legacy, though surely not his only one. He will live forever in the annals of Israeli history as one of the great "fathers" of modern Israel, along with David Ben-Gurion and Yitzhak Rabin.

Rabbi Abraham Joshua Heschel died on the Sabbath (it is deemed a great mitzvah to die on Shabbat). In Heschel's case, whose name is forever linked with Shabbat because of his immortal book on that theme, *The Sabbath*, in which he writes of Jews sanctifying time rather than space, we have another example of one whose physical death did not end his spiritual life, his eternal legacy. His teachings, writings, and personal example of metamorphizing himself from a teacher and writer to a social activist (after writing his book on the prophets), will live on forever among all people, not only Jews.

This idea of the Talmud, that the righteous live on even after their death, does two things. It encourages us to live lives of righteousness, and it gives us comfort and assurance that even after physical death, our lives need not be consigned to oblivion.

Parashat Shemot

"A man from the house of Levi went and married a woman from the house of Levi." Shemot/Exodus 2:1

The Torah does not mention here the names of Amram and Yokheved. Rabbi Samson Raphael Hirsch explains that even though these two parents were great individuals, by naming them there might be an implication that Moshe was born a great hero because his parents were special people. This is not, he claims, what the Torah wants to teach. Rather the message is that any child can become a great person and reach high levels of spiritual achievement, if she makes the effort. Rambam holds a similar view when he wrote (Hilkhot Teshivah 5:1-2): "Do not think that God decreed on a child from conception that he will be either righteous or evil. That is not the case. Anyone can be as righteous as Moshe Rabbenu."

This kind of wholesome and affirming view of the nature of humans is found throughout the Tanakh and the rest of Jewish literature. Our tradition is positive and optimistic, encouraging people of all strands of economic and social background to rise to his greatest potential. It is not an accident, it seems to me, that the great humanistic psychologists of the 20th century, founders of the human potential movement, were Jews – people such as Abraham Maslow, Fritz Perls, and countless others. Their "new" idea was that God implanted within every one of us the ability to rise to unpredictable heights. Our ability, creativity, and intelligence, should never be limited by expectations due to our background. No matter where we came from, with the proper psychological, spiritual and intellectual upbringing – whether it be from parents or others – we can become righteous and influential people in society.

When we think of the great giants of all ages, most of the time they emerge from families whom one would least expect such greatness. The exceptions are families that produce many generations of outstanding people, such as the Rockefellers, the Kennedys, and other "dynasty" families. If one studies the background of the presidents of the United States, one mostly finds backgrounds of poverty and simplicity – such as that of Abraham Lincoln. The rise to greatness comes from the individual's faith in herself, determination and perseverance, and the thirst for knowledge and growth.

The names of the parents of Moshe Rabbenu are specifically and intentionally omitted in this pasuk to draw our attention to that fact that it was not his parentage or genes that made Moshe great, but his own personal qualities that he developed out of his life experience and his spiritual striving.

Parashat Va-era

"I (God) appeared to Avraham, to Yitzhak, and to Yaakov…." Shemot/Exodus 6:3

Rashi's comment on this verse is that God appeared to the Patriarchs. What does Rashi intend to add here? The verse mentions the three patriarchs, so it is obvious that that is what the pasuk means. How then does we understand Rashi's comment? The Hatam Sofer (Rabbi Moshe Schreiber, 1762-1839, Hungary) tries to solve our dilemma by translating the word "avot" (patriarchs) in a novel way. The Hebrew root *ava* also means "desire." Thus, says Rabbi Schreiber, that what Rashi is telling us is that the pasuk means this: God only appears to those who are "avot" – who have a desire for a relationship with God. This is the source of the special relationship between these three fathers of the Jewish People and their Maker – they all had a longing to connect with God.

There is a wonderful insight here. We all know people for whom God is an irrelevant idea. They may, or may not, believe in God, but surely God plays no part in their thinking, their behavior and their religious life. On the other hand, there are those whose lives are God-intoxicated. Every moment they long to please God, to speak to God, to listen to God, and to live lives compatible with the presence of God. And there are those in the middle, for whom God is an important presence, even though not their object of constant longing.

What is it about people that makes them one way or another? Is it nature, nurture, or some other factor? We cannot know, of course. But it does seem that some individuals are more sensitive to spiritual matters than others. Some are more "right-brained," – creative, non-linear, spiritual, poetic and focused on the non-material things in life. I believe that everyone can develop this quality. Some are more prone to be spiritual, but there is no one who cannot in one way or another search and work to develop a more spiritual orientation in their lives. I believe that it is a combination of nature and nurture. No matter what genes children have, their parents can do many things to direct the lives of their children in a spiritual way. Reading books, taking walks, appreciating nature, spending time in forests, beaches, in the countryside, talking about deeper questions, noticing the less obvious things in our environment, participating in social betterment, etc.

By reaching out to God, as the patriarchs (and matriarchs) did, we too can be more like these great ancestors of our people.

Parashat Bo

"So that you may tell your child and your child's child." Shemot/Exodus 10:2

God tells Moshe that God wants Pharaoh to realize that the Almighty is making a fool of the Egyptian King who thinks he can ignore God's desire to bring freedom to the Israelite nation. God's message to Moshe is that the power of God is ultimate, and it should be known to all future generations, to the children and children's children of the generation of the slaves. That way they will be aware of the power of God to bring redemption and justice to the world.

One of the questions the commentators ask about this pasuk is Why are the "children's children" mentioned, in addition to the children? It is conventional wisdom that Jewish tradition has a strong imperative to pass down our Heritage from generation to generation. Thus one might argue that mentioning grandchildren as well as children is to be expected.

One fascinating wrinkle comes from Rabbi Shlomo Ganzfried (author of the *Kitzur Shulhan Arukh,* Hungary 1804-1886) who claims that individuals are prepared to be very strict with themselves with regard to the observance of Judaism, but may be less forceful with others. Many people feel that it is fair to be more restrictive with yourself than with others. This kind of altruistic compassion for our children and others may seem to be an act of care and concern for them. However, in the long run, when we are lenient with our young people, we are not doing them favors. In the end it is not a favor to be lenient. Training oneself in self-discipline, while being less strict and demanding toward others, may seem to be an act of kindness, but is a strategic mistake. It takes strength to appear to be a harsh parental taskmaster, even when you know that in the long run your demands are in the best interest of those in your charge.

Thus, when God mentions children's children, as well as children, it is the strength of discipline and experience that speaks to the younger generation – advising them to be firm, structured and consistent. This is what the Talmud refers to as taking the long way that is the short way, rather than taking the short way that is really the long way.

"May you see your children's children" – Psalm 128:6 – may you see them studying and practicing Torah.

Parashat B'shalah

"Then Miriam the prophetess, Aaron's sister, took a timbrel in her hand, and all the women went out after her in dance with timbrels." Shemot/Exodus 15:20

Dr. Ellen Frankel, in her *The Five Books of Miriam* (p. 111), writes: "Ancient Mediterranean cultures have left compelling evidence in clay of a widespread women's performance tradition, usually involving the three arts of song, drum, and dance. Such a tradition continues to this day in this region. In ancient times, women hand drummers would go out to greet troops returning home after triumphant battles.

"...How unfortunate that today musical instruments have been almost completely eliminated from our prayer services and that among the most traditional Jews, the voice of women – *kol isha* – has been silenced in the presence of men because it allegedly stirs up lascivious thoughts in them. So what were the Israelite men thinking when they heard Miriam and the women singing? Have men and women changed so much since then?"

As a progressive Jew (meaning non-ultra-orthodox) I am in favor of full women's participation in synagogue and other ritual events. I also encourage musical instruments in the proper context (for example, monthly Friday night services). I believe that musical instruments have the potential to add a great deal to the spirit, enthusiasm and spontaneity of public worship. On the other hand, even that can become stale. And on Shabbat morning I find that people prefer to pray a cappella.

Standards change from generation to generation, and surely from 1200 B.C.E. to the 21st century. In my view this pasuk is a good jumping-off point to re-think the whole question of women's role in worship (though most non-Orthodox synagogues today are fully egalitarian), and more importantly, the role of musical instruments when they enhance (and do not stifle) enthusiastic participation. In large synagogues across North America the "Friday Night Alive" programs, inaugurated by people like Doug Cutler, are enjoying enormous success. More experimentation along these lines should be encouraged.

Parashat Yitro

"You shall seek out men from among the people, men of accomplishment, God-fearing people, trustworthy men who spurn ill-gotten gain." Shemot/Exodus 18:21

Several questions arise from this story. Moshe receives excellent advice from his father-in-law, Yitro (Jethro), about finding assistance through a multi-tiered system of judicial leadership. Why did not Moshe himself think of this? Is not Moshe wise enough to come up with such an idea? Since God approved of this system, why did not God present it to Moshe, without the intermediary of Yitro?

Rabbi Abraham J. Twerski, M.D. (*Twerski on Chumash*, pp.145-6) has interesting psychological and rabbinic insights – being both a psychiatrist and a rabbi – on this event. First Rabbi Twerski points out that God consults the angels in the creation of humankind. "Let us create Man…." Rashi interprets this to mean that God consulted the angels before creating humans. Of course it was not necessary for God to consult anyone, but God did so to teach an important lesson. That is that we can and should learn from everyone and anyone. For even God allowed Himself to be taught by angels – not out of necessity, but out of the desire to be a role model who consults with those of lesser stature.

It was surely possible for Moshe to design a judicial system, and for God to teach Moshe to do so. But God wanted us to realize that it is worthy of great ones to consult with those of lesser stature. It is only those of small ego (who act arrogantly, a sign of a shrunken ego, of feelings of inferiority) who refuse to listen to others, especially people of lower stature. A great person has no fear of listening to, and learning from, anyone. Moshe can learn from Yitro, even as God was willing to consult the angels.

The opportunity to listen to the advice of people who have fewer degrees, or lesser training or education than we, is an experience that occurs often in our lives. When we are secure enough to accept second opinions, to consult with other professionals, to let a simple person offer advice, we are evidencing strength of character and great wisdom. This is one of the important lessons of Moshe taking advice from Yitro.

Parashat Mishpatim

"If you buy a Hebrew servant…." Shemot/Exodus 21:2

Ancient biblical law demands that a Hebrew slave should serve his master only for six years. On the seventh (sabbatical) year he will go free. One commentator, the Avnei Nezer (Rabbi Avraham Bornstein, 1839-1910, of Sochaczev, Poland) raises the question why the Torah does not refer to the slave as an *Israelite* slave. Why a "Hebrew" slave? The word "Hebrew" comes from the Hebrew word "ever" – or "side." It is used in connection with Avraham in Bereshit/Genesis (14:13), upon which the rabbis say that Avram is called a Hebrew because the whole world was on one side and he was on the other. Morally, Avraham was willing to stand up against the whole world in order to defend his principles. What mattered to him was righteousness, not the will of the masses. So too in our pasuk. A Hebrew may be a servant/slave for a period of six years for certain economic restraints in his life, but ultimately he is a Hebrew, a free person, who stands up for his own truth. The mark of a Hebrew is that truth trumps numbers. A Hebrew is willing to fight for what he believes, and not be swayed by the majority. Hebrew and slave almost don't fit together in the same sentence. A Hebrew slave is, in a sense, an oxymoron. So slavery is limited to six years, because a Hebrew cannot remain enslaved to the will of another, except to that of God.

Parashat Terumah

"You shall make two Cherubim of gold." Shemot/ Exodus 25:18

In the case of other vessels of the Mishkan, the Torah does not command as specifically or as forcefully as in this pasuk, that the material should be of gold. The midrash (Mekhilta, Yitro 10) claims that in the case of other vessels, if gold is not available, then other material may be substituted, such as silver or copper. But in the case of the Cherubim, only gold can be used. Why the insistence of gold in this case? Rabbi Meir Shapiro (1888-1933, famous rav who inaugurated the daf yomi in Lubin, Poland) gives the following interpretation. Rashi had connected the Cherubim with an Aramaic word which means "children." It was assumed, from the middle ages on, that the Cherubin were child-faced angels. Prof. William Foxwell Albright, the greatest biblical archeologist and interpreter of the 20th century, showed that the actual shape of a Cherub was that of a winged sphinx (a sphinx has the body of a lion and the head of a human). Midrashically, the interpretation of the Cherub having a child's face has been widely accepted, even though technically not accurate. Thus, says Rabbi Shapiro, the Cherubim were on the top of the Aron (Ark) to emphasize the significance that the Jewish people ascribes to their youth, and the importance of attaching them to Torah (inside the Aron).

What Rabbi Shapiro is teaching is that in other realms of the worship complex, the Aron and all the Mishkan vessels, it is acceptable to use lower standards (silver and copper), but not in connection with Jewish education. There the highest standard must be employed – i.e., the gold standard. We must be as generous as we can in providing the very best Jewish education available for our children. We must not stint. We must not cut our budgets or allocate our funds to other areas, even if it means sacrifices in other realms of our relationship to God. There is nothing more important, or more worthy of generosity and munificence than providing the highest and most intensive level of Jewish education for our youth. As the Talmud states, "Talmud Torah k'neged kulam," "Study of Torah is equal to all the other mitzvot combined."

Parashat Tetzaveh

"You shall make sacral vestments for Aharon your brother for dignity and majesty." Shemot/Exodus 28:2

Why are there two reasons for the sacral vestments of the Kohen Gadol – "for dignity and majesty"? An interesting explanation is brought by the Ktav Sofer (Rabbi Avraham Sofer of Pressburg, 1815-1879, leader of non-Hasidic Hungarian Jewry). One is to remind the person wearing it that s/he is a special person in a special status, and that person must not violate the high expectations of the office the person holds. This applies to the company the person keeps, the language they use, the deeds they do, the values they live up to, and all other aspects of their being and doing. Others expect them to be a cut above the crowd, and they should know that and live by it.

The other reason is for others to recognize that this is a person whom one must respect and venerate. Of course, we respect a person for what they do, not for the office they hold. But the office or position itself (Kohen, government official, police person, rabbi, teacher, parent, etc.) deserves respect. Even if one has no respect for the person as an individual, one must have deference for their status. The garments remind us that the way we speak to them, the jokes we tell them, the willingness to follow their direction, the help we afford them, the privileges and restrictions they have, all are affected by the position they hold, in addition to other factors such as our affection (or lack thereof) for them, our feelings about who they are.

It occurs to me that these two reasons apply to the wearing of a kippah. It is my custom to wear my kippah at selected times – when I eat (for saying motzee & Birkat HaMazon), when I study holy books, and when I pray (in synagogue or elsewhere). I usually also wear it at interfaith clergy meetings, for symbolic purposes. I also wear when in Jerusalem (don't ask for too specific a reason – it's just the way I feel). I have struggled with the question of whether or not to wear it in other places. A Reform colleague of mine wears it all the time, but somehow I do not fear comfortable doing that (ironically). I was not raised that way, and that's probably the most important psychological reason – habit. If I ever decide to change my mind, the reasons above give me solid and ample justification for wearing it all the time.

Parashat Kee Tisa

"However, you must observe My Shabbatot…." Shemot/Exodus 31:13

Some commentators question the reason for Shabbat appearing in the plural ("Shabbatot") instead of the singular ("Shabbat"). The meaning would surely come out the same if were written: "However you must observe My Shabbat…." In other words, every week, you must observe My Shabbat. So why does the Torah use the plural?

The commentator known as the "Hafetz Hayim," – after his book title of that name about the prohibition of slander and gossip (his name was Rabbi Yisrael Meir Kagan HaKohen, Poland, d. 1933) – makes a very interesting point. How would it be if you went to synagogue and there was no minyan? How is it for a single person who has to make Shabbat at home alone – with no family, no neighbors, no friends, no guests, no Hevrah, just alone. It's really not the same kind of Shabbat. The point is that Shabbat is Shabbat because we share it with others. Though part of Shabbat is wonderful when we can sit alone with a book, or take a walk in the park by ourselves, many parts of Shabbat require company – family and/or friends. Such as Shabbat dinner, going to schul, having Kiddush, Shabbat lunch or Seudah Shlishit, etc. So, says the Hafetz Hayim, the Torah speaks of Shabbatot in the plural, to include the Shabbat of those around you. Not only your Shabbat, but the Shabbat of people you know, love and whose company you enjoy.

Thus, the Hafetz Hayim suggests that part of observing Shabbat is persuading others to observe Shabbat. Observe Shabbat by creating a Shabbat community. Then your Shabbat observance will be enhanced as will that of those around you. Be a missionary for Shabbat observance. Do things that will draw in people who might not ordinarily observe Shabbat. If you are a Shabbat observer, invite people to your home on Friday night and show them how beautiful the rituals, blessings, prayers, songs, food, and community joy is when friends and family celebrate together. Invite a friend to attend schul with you, or attend a Shabbat lecture or weekend seminar with you. Create a Shabbat Club that will help entice others to do things that are "shabbos-dik." In that way your Shabbat, and the Shabbat of those you know will increase in observance. You will, in fact, observe God's Shabbatot – yours and that of others.

What a wonderful idea the Hafetz Hayim has given us. "And if not now, when?...."

Parashat Vayakhel-Peduday

"These are the accountings of the Mishkan." Shemot/Exodus 38:21

With the ordination of women as rabbis, and the increase of female scholars of the Tanakh in Orthodox, Conservative, Reform and Reconstructionist streams, the Jewish world is not only empowering 50% of the Jewish population to take part in Jewish ritual life, we are also deriving enormous benefit from the fruit of the scholarship of the women who are now more deeply engaged in Torah study. One excellent example of this is a comment on Parshat Pekuday, written by Rabbi Elana Zaiman (*The Women's Torah Commentary*, ed. Rabbi Elyse Goldstein, Jewish Lights Publishing, pp. 179-182).

Rabbi Zaiman points out that the root of the Hebrew word "Pekuday" is used in the birth stories of two prominent biblical women, Sarah and Hannah (see Bereshit 21:1 and I Shmuel 2:21, where in both cases God takes "account" of the women following which they each give birth (Sarah gave birth to Yitzhak and Hannah gave birth to Shmuel). Says Rabbi Zaiman, "By reinterpreting the building of the Mishkan in light of the birthing process, our perception of the building of the Mishkan and of its place throughout Israel's history, is given a new meaning." She then points out 3 areas of new meaning: Labor, Identity, and Continuity. In the case of building the Mishkan and in the case of giving birth, there is Labor. That is self-explanatory. Identity: each woman has a new identity – not only of woman and wife, but now of mother. By bringing God from the top of Mt. Sinai to their own "neighborhood" on the ground, their relationship with God brings them a new identity, people with an intimate and involved relationship with their Maker.

Finally, Continuity. Sarah and Hannah's becoming parents links them with those before them and after them; they are now a link in the chain of Jewish continuity. In building the Mishkan, too, there is continuity – from the wilderness to Jerusalem (the Bet Mikdash). But a physical place to communicate with God was not sufficient, because both the Mishkan and the Bet Mikdash were lost physically (in different ways). The people had to have a dwelling place for God that would outlast anything physical. So the rabbis created the term "Shekhinah," based on the same Hebrew root as Mishkan. Rabbi Zaiman quotes the Talmud (Megillah 29a), "Every place to which Israel was exiled, the Shekhinah went with them." She writes, "Through the name Shekhinah, the rabbis enabled God's physical presence to exist in exile." Since today we have neither Sinai, nor the Mishkan, nor the Bet Mikdash, what remains of them is the Shekhinah – both a name and a place. Thus, "we can enable it [God's Presence] to dwell anywhere and everywhere."

Through this creative interpretation of the feminine name "Shekhinah" God becomes accessible to all of us at all times and in all places.

Parashat Vayikra

"You shall season every offering of grain that you bring with salt." Vayikra 2:13

We are familiar with the custom of sprinkling a drop of salt on the Hallah when we sit down to the Shabbat evening dinner (or at any meal for the more traditional). The table of the Jew is to resemble the altar in the ancient Temple. Each time we eat a meal we are re-enacting the sacrificial service of biblical times. First we wash, as the Kohen did, we recite the motzee prayer in thanksgiving for the bread we are about to eat, and just before putting the bread in our mouth we sprinkle some salt on the bread. In ancient times salt was an inexpensive and easily available preservative. It was used for meat offerings since meat spoils quickly. Probably to be consistent, it was also used for grain offerings.

An interesting midrashic (homiletic) interpretation is offered by a hasidic commentator, Rabbi Uziel ben Zvi Hirsch Meisels of Richival, Poland (1743–1785), who understood salt not only as a preservative, but as an ingredient that supplied a heightened sense of taste. How often do we throw some salt on our soup or entree, and many of us probably remember eating French Fries as a youngster, smothering them with piles of salt and ketchup? Thus, says Rabbi Uziel, when we make an offering, or recite a prayer, or practice a ritual, it must be sprinkled with the salt of feeling and emotion, without which the act can be bland and tasteless.

Too many of us go through the motions of performing rituals pro forma – in a mechanical way that lacks heart and passion. It is important to pause and think about a religious act before performing it. For this reason, most of our rituals prescribe a b'rakhah to be recited prior to the act. This gives us an opportunity to remember that we are doing what we are doing because God commands us to do it, and because we wish to perform this ritual (affixing a mezuzah, wearing a tallit, drinking wine, lighting the Shabbat candles) with intentionality and meaning. Just to run through the act because "it's the law," does not satisfy those who want their religion to be passionate and impactful. Doing a mitzvah with feeling, care and love is so much different than just mechanically acting out the deed with no concomitant fervor and enthusiasm.

Parashat Tzav

"Moshe said to the community: "This is what Adonai commanded to be done."

Vayikra/Leviticus 8:5

What is it that Adonai commanded to be done? This verse seems to hang alone, without clarity, without antecedent. The commentary known as "Y'khahayn Pe'er" understands the matter by referring to the previous pasuk, "Gather the entire assembly to the entrance of the Tent of Meeting." The comment of Rashi on that pasuk (8:4) is that even though there were millions of people in the desert (according to the Torah's count), they miraculously all gathered in the small space outside the Tent. They were able to gather because whenever there is love and unity, there is always enough room for everyone. As Pirke Avot teaches (5:5), one of the ten miracles in the ancient Temple was that even though there was a huge crowd, when they bowed down, there was enough room for everyone. This, then, is "what Adonai commanded to be done," that every Jew love one another and feel a sense of unity among the Jewish people. When that feeling is present, there will always be room for every Jew.

Jews are known for many things. Whenever I ask individuals in a group to name the one quality that makes them feel most proud to be Jewish, the attribute that is repeated most often is "a sense of family." "We care about each other, we reach out to Jews all over the world. When there is need felt by one Jew, there appears help from another Jew." This is so often the case that it is hard to imagine that a lack of unity does exist. And yet! So often in Jewish life there co-exists along with the sense of family, and unity, and mutual commitment in the abstract, a concomitant occurrence of disunity and divisiveness. Jews who have a different theology, or a different level of observance, or a different personal agenda, cause polarization and antagonism. In Israel and in America this happens far too often. Observant and secular Jews constantly clash. In synagogues in North America there are cliques that exclude others from the "inside" ruling faction. There is far too much bitterness and competitiveness among Jews within communal and institutional life. Organizations that fight anti-Semitism compete for dollars and for national attention.

It is high time for Jews to take seriously the admonitions of tradition that "every Jew is responsible for every other Jew," and "Love your neighbor as yourself!" The Jewish world would be far better off if these teachings were taken more seriously.

Parashat Shmini

"Moshe said to Aharon: Approach the altar." Vayikra/Leviticus 9:6

Two commentators, who lived some 700 years apart, combine their thoughts to bring us a very penetrating insight into this dramatic scene. Aharon is about to be consecrated as Kohen Gadol. This is a great moment in the life of the older brother of Moshe. To be the High Priest, the Kohen Gadol, the chief religious officer (C.R.O.) of the Jewish People, - and the first one ever – is a momentous opportunity. The fact that Moshe has to almost "push" Aharon to the altar for the sacred ceremony of consecration raises an interesting question in the mind of Rashi. Rashi's explanation is that Aharon retained a degree of shame about his role in the incident of the Golden Calf, and was reluctant to accept the great honor of being the first Kohen Gadol. "Who am I?" he must have thought, "to be Kohen Gadol, when I facilitated the construction of the Golden Calf, and thereby encouraged the people to lose their faith in God and in Moshe.?" Rashi says on this pasuk: Moshe told his brother: "For this you were chosen" – to be Kohen Gadol – "don't be reluctant Don't hesitate or think yourself unworthy."

A comment on this comment is offered by the Baal Shem Tov, the Founder of Hasidism (b. 1700, Ukraine), who gives a slightly different interpretation of Rashi's words, "For this you were chosen." "For this" does not refer, says the Baal Shem Tov, to the act of becoming Kohen Gadol, but it refers, rather, to Aharon's hesitation and sense of being unfit for the exalted religious position he was about to enter. In other words: Aharon, you were chosen to be Kohen Gadol precisely because of your humility and sense of being unworthy. "For this you were chosen, Aharon, for your humbleness and your unassuming nature, your awareness of your past mistakes."

It is important for all of us to recognize that we may not be completely deserving of all the privileges and honors that come to us in life. The most common reaction to being honored, or elevated to a position of importance or power, is to think more highly of ourselves, not to feel a sense of unworthiness. In many cases this is good, because when we work hard and receive recognition, it boosts our sense of self worth. On the other hand, it is also good to recall that we have a way to go in our spiritual growth, and that some of our past actions may mitigate our total worthiness for the position to which we are elevated.

As Moshe had to "push" Aharon to overcome his self doubts, those very self doubts were what may have made Aharon deserving of becoming Kohen Gadol.

Parashat Tazria-Metzora

"...and bathe his body in water and become pure." Vayikra/Leviticus 14:9

The Book of Vayikra is filled with passages dealing with purity and impurity, and rites of purification. The primary vehicle for ritual cleansing is water, an important symbol in religions generally and in Judaism particularly (mikveh, the laver in which the kohanim washed before sacrifices, levitical washing of the feet of the Kohen, netilat yadayim, mayim aharonim, etc.). Water has mystical properties – as does fire – which make it a useful symbolic rite for purification. It brings about both physical and spiritual cleansing. There is a return to the use of the mikveh in our day by women and men, not only following the woman's menstrual period, but to cleanse one's body and soul before Shabbat and holidays, before a wedding, for conversion, and other occasions.

Some of the unique and "magical" qualities of water are that it is transparent, that it is liquid and thus does not stick to any surface, that it seeks its own level, and has properties unlike most other entities. It brings refreshment, relaxation, bodily hydration through drinking, cleanliness, arousal, spiritual and physical stimulation, and many other positive features. The world, including our bodies, is made up mainly of water – so it is the indispensable elixir of life.

Rambam (Maimonides, Spain and Egypt, d. 1204), as a philosopher, physician and halakhist, understood all this when he wrote in his *Mishneh Torah (Hilkhot Mikva-ot* 11:12) that there is no logic to the laws of purity and impurity. The whole process of purification is a mystery wrapped in an enigma. Likewise, "tum'ah," impurity, is not grime or muck that can be washed away with water. Too often commentators, philosophers and rabbinic authorities attempt to create logical explanations for the processes of impurity and purification, when, at bottom, the whole matter is not given to rational understanding.

Is there any lesson that we can derive from these sections of the Torah dealing with purity and impurity? Rambam, ever the master teacher, claims that there is an important lesson to be gleaned from these verses. Often in Jewish tradition Torah is compared to water. Both are indispensable to life, and both give nourishment and refreshment. Thus, writes the Rambam, just as water purifies the body through immersion, so also one who wants to purify the soul must be totally immersed in the waters of Torah.

Parashat Aharay-Kedoshim

"You shall reprove your kinsman...." Vayikra/ Leviticus 19:17

Criticizing someone is one of the most difficult, and yet one of the most important things one can do. Why does the Torah make this a "mitzvah," a commandment? Simply because one's natural tendency would be to hold back criticism for fear of insulting or hurting a friend. On the other hand, many go around criticizing everything and everybody. This is not the kind of person whom the Torah is commanding. The Torah is speaking to one who would hold back, be reluctant to criticize. Even though the motive in not criticizing may be positive- to be sensitive to the feelings of another – the truth is that a good friend is one who criticizes.

The biblical Book of Proverbs says, "Admonish a wise person and that person will love you" (9:8). Clearly the position of the Tanakh is that criticism is a good thing. This is based on the assumption that something positive will emerge from the act of criticizing a friend. That positive result will be that the criticized person will take the suggestion seriously, make the change, and emerge a better person. If that happens, then the act of criticism will in effect be an act of caring, even of love.

Naturally, there are careful parameters which must be utilized when criticizing someone. Books have been written on this subject, but let me make a feeble attempt at summarizing some of the basic criteria for useful criticism.

First there needs to be trust between the parties, if not genuine affection. When we hear criticism from someone we don't trust or like, we will quickly become defensive, reject the charge, and in all likelihood nothing positive will emerge. On the other hand, if trust has been established, and the person being criticized realizes that it is done from a place of caring and concern, for her welfare, the person may initially be hurt or saddened, but eventually may accept the suggestion, make a change in her life, and a positive outcome will eventuate.

Other ways to insure that criticism will be constructive, and not a "put-down," are to say it at the right moment, in the right way, in the right circumstances, and about important things. If these and perhaps some other criteria are followed, the relationship will be strengthened, and both people will come out better for the act. This is the underlying assumption of the Torah and the Book of Proverbs.

For these reasons, Jewish tradition has taken this commandment seriously. Religious Jews who are focused on bettering their character are scrupulous in following this mitzvah. Rabbi Abraham J. Twerski (*Twerski on Chumash*, p. 236) tells the story of the great Gaon of Vilna (Elijah ben Shlomo Zalman, Lithuania, 1720-97), who went out of his way to seek criticism in order to fulfill this mitzvah in the Torah, and to improve his character. Realizing that no one would dare rebuke the great Vilna Gaon, he went to Rabbi Yaakov Krantz, the Maggid of Dubnow, to invite him to offer some criticism. The Maggid suggested that it is easy for one who sits in solitude and studies all day, and does not mix with people in the marketplace, to lead a sinless life. If he wants to be a real tzaddik, he should go and mingle more with the common folk. The Gaon humbly accepted the suggestion.

If the Gaon of Vilna can seek out criticism, it behooves the rest of us less grand souls, to accept it when it comes our way.

Parashat Emor

"When any man of the house of Israel or of the strangers in Israel presents a burnt offering…." Vayikra/ Leviticus 22:18

Humash Etz Hayim explains that in ancient times "non-Israelites also donated sacrificial offerings to the God of Israel. In the ancient Near East, it was customary to pay respect to the deity of the host country." Over a century before Etz Hayim was written, Rabbi Shimshon Raphael Hirsch, a pious Orthodox scholar in Frankfurt, Germany, pointed out that the beginning of Sefer Vayika (The Book of Leviticus) begins with a similar expression – "When any man brings an offering unto Adonai" (Leviticus 1:2). Hirsch writes that "This teaches us that every person – not just an Israelite – is permitted to bring sacrifices if one has a spiritual need to do so."

Rabbi Simcha Raz (*The Torah's Seventy Faces)* points out that one small Hebrew word, "ish" (man), in this pasuk expresses a great idea which Isaiah's prophecy uses an entire verse to express: "Even [foreigners] will I bring to My holy mountain, and make them joyful in My house of prayer. Their burnt offerings and their sacrifices shall be acceptable upon My altar. For My house shall be called a house of prayer for all peoples" (Isaiah 56:7).

The Torah and its commentaries expound a revolutionary idea. The Talmud itself says it this way: "The Hebrew word "ish" (a man) included non-Jews who made vows and freewill offerings like the People of Israel (Nazir 65a). It seems that from the days of the Tanakh, through the period of the Talmud, to modern times, the notion existed that the Bet Mikdash in Jerusalem would be open to all peoples for worship – not just to Jews.

Would this not solve the problem today of ownership and use of Har Ha-bayit – the Temple Mount. Moslems call it Haram al-Sharif (the Noble Sanctuary), and Jews call it the Temple Mount (Har Ha-bayit). Since the sixth century Jews have not been able to consider rebuilding their temple on the Temple Mount because the Dome of the Rock and the Mosque of Omar are located there. What if Jews, Moslems and Christians joined together to expand the present structures on the Mount to create an interfaith building in which peoples of all faiths could worship? This would be in line with the thinking of Jewish tradition from the days of the Torah to the present time. And it would not be a "reform" idea, but rather a traditional notion that has come down to us from the most traditional of Jewish sources.

A novel, yet ancient idea- and one with profound political and moral implications. Have these texts been hidden from us for some reason? Or are the present bearers of religious traditions too closed-minded to consider such an option?

Parashat Behar

"If your brother is in difficult times and comes to reside under your authority...strengthen him and let him live by your side." Vayikra/Leviticus 25:35

The subject of Tzedakah is never exhausted in Jewish deliberations. The theme of helping others, with money, food, moral support, job training, and other means, is a silver thread that runs through all of Jewish literature. There are many aspects of the theme of Tzedakah that can be elaborated upon in a discussion of this pasuk, but let us focus on one small part of the larger process of sharing our largesse with others. That aspect can be formulated in the form of a question: Is it acceptable in Jewish tradition to exert pressure upon someone to give Tzedakah? Should not Tzedakah come from the heart, and not from moral compulsion from the community? To ask the question another way: is it better that a person give as a result of pressure, or, lacking such pressure, not give at all? Granted that a willing heart is the highest moral state that should motivate one to give, what happens if a person would not otherwise give? Is it acceptable to exert such pressure so that the person be "forced" to give?

The conventional response from American Jews in the 21st century would most like be this: A gift should be from the heart, and a person has the right to determine the level of their own generosity. No one should have to suffer embarrassment or coercion of any kind to encourage them to give. This kind of "forced giving" was common in past generations, when community organizations would call out names of those present, and the sheer embarrassment of being perceived by others as a miser, or a tightwad, would be enough to make a person contribute. Today that approach is seen as odious and totally objectionable by our community.

A Talmudic story seems to go against the grain of the conventional wisdom of our day. And yet it must give us pause. If without pressure the poor would continue to suffer and not receive the customary Tzedakah that the Jewish community is noted for, then it seems to this writer that pressure is indeed in place. In short, better that Tzedakah be given because of moral force than not be given at all. This is not a popular view, but I think it is the Jewish view.

Rabbi Tarfon was a well-known scholar, and a very wealthy man––an unusual combination in those days. Rabbi Tarfon was not accustomed to share his wealth with the poor. Rabbi Akiva, his teacher, decided to teach him a lesson.

The two friends met one day and Akiva asked Tarfon if the latter would like him to take some of his money and invest it in some property that would yield plentiful profit? Of course, the greedy Tarfon agreed, and gave his colleague four hundred golden dinar. Rabbi Akiva took the money and immediately began to distribute it to indigent students. Some time passed and the two men met once again. Tarfon inquired as to the disposition of his large investment. Akiva took his friend by the arm and brought him to the Bet Midrash. There they saw a young child with a copy of the Book of Psalms in his hand.

As the youngster was studying the Book of Psalms, he came upon this verse (112:9): "The one who gives freely to the poor, his beneficence lasts forever." Said Rabbi Akiva to Rabbi Tarfon: This is the fruit of your investment! (That is, your investment has returned rich and long-lasting rewards). How did Rabbi Tarfon react? He turned to Rabbi Akiva and kissed him. He then said to him: You are my master and my teacher – my master in wisdom and my teacher in morals! Rabbi Tarfon then took some more money and gave it to Rabbi Akiva to "invest" it for him. (Kallah Rabati, II).

What do we learn from this story? That it is permissible to coerce, and even trick another to give Tzedakah. Perhaps, one can argue, that will work when the person is a scholar, and when the relationship is such that the individual is likely to understand his faults and change his ways. Maybe so. But there is implied in the story the notion that giving immediately out of pure willingness and generosity is not necessarily a prerequisite for the bestowing of Tzedakah. The need for poor students to receive what they require is a community standard, and if it requires some public pressure, it's not such a terrible thing. The end may indeed justify the means, especially when the end is so vital to the survival of the community.

In short, the value of Tzedakah is such a primary and essential virtue, that the path to reaching it may not always be as important as reaching the goal.

Parashat Bemidbar

"These are the descendants of Aharon and Moshe... Nadav, Avihu, Elazar and Itamar. Bemidbar/Numbers 3:1-2

There's something out of kilter here. The pasuk starts out telling us that we will now learn the names of the children of Aharon and Moshe. However, the names given are only those of Aharon. What happened to the children of Moshe? It may be that because very little is heard about Moshe's children, Gershom and Eliezer (Exodus 2:11-22; 18:3-4). Nothing seems to be known of them, other than that they had children of their own. Was Moshe one of those famous people who helped the whole world, except his own kids? Was he another shoemaker who let his children's shoes go without repair? Very possibly.

Rashi (11th century, Troyes, France) however, gives a different explanation as to the absence of the mention of the children of Moshe. He draws on the midrash that says that whoever teaches another person's children, it is as if they were one's own. In other words, Nadav, Avihu, Elazar and Itamar were also the children of Moshe, because he was their teacher. As such he treated them as his own children.

This is a beautiful thought (and, of course, it covers the parental omissions of Moshe). The important thought that teachers should draw from this is that one should treat one's students as if they were one's own children. This, of course, is no easy matter. Students in a typical classroom are known to be less than lovable at times. What is the secret of reaching a child's heart and soul? Part of the answer is the technology of modern classroom management, clever pedagogic techniques that will keep students who are otherwise tired and bored, alert and focused on the studies at hand.

But one would hope that there is more to it than that. I have known teachers who care so deeply for the children they teach that the bond between teacher and student is enough to create deep interest in the subject, as a result of their mutual affection. A child will pick up very quickly the unspoken message left by a teacher who is in the classroom merely for the paycheck. Or the teacher who is so frustrated and burned out after many years of dealing with unruly kids that they are there simply because they do not know any other way to make a living.

There is no substitute for a teacher who truly loves his students, and conveys that caring by focusing on the students and not just on the material to be taught. This is what has been called in the 1960s and 1970's "humanistic education." While conventional education focused on the three "R's" – reading, 'riting, and 'rithmetic, the newer education paid more attention to three other "R's" – relating, renewing and rejoicing. It is the spirit of the classroom, the enthusiasm of the teacher, the joy of the learning process, the excitement of discovery that are the hallmarks of successful education.

Parashat Naso

"If any man's wife has gone astray and broken faith with him…."

Bemidbar/Numbers 5:12

Our pasuk opens with two identical Hebrew words, "Ish, ish." This Hebrew idiom means "Any man." But repetitions are the delight of the commentator's muse. The biblical interpreter Rabbi Hayim J. Zuckermann (mid-20th century, Israel), in his collection *Otzar Hayim*, gives a novel explanation. The phrase "ish," a man, is repeated here because the Torah implies that there are really two men in this man; that is, two personalities in one person. This man, whose wife breaks faith with him, is one kind of man on the outside, away from home, and another kind of man on the inside, in his own home. He is the paradigm of duplicity. He is a moral fraud. He acts like a saint and a pious person at home, but when he leaves the precincts of his home and hearth, his behavior is far from acceptable.

This duplicitous behavior, says the Otzar Hayim, is the cause of his wife's unfaithfulness. She is confused and dismayed by his inconsistent actions, and "catches" his moral disease, as it were.

Family therapists tell us that the family is a system, wherein each member is connected to and influenced by every other member. When a dysfunctional family comes to see a therapist, there is usually one person who is the designated problem. That person carries and acts out the problem which in actuality is that of the whole family. In the case of the biblical unfaithful wife, she may be the one who is acting out, but the cause of her immoral behavior, in large part, is due to her husband's initiating the dysfunctional and perhaps immoral behavior.

In fact, the Torah even points in that direction, when in the second part of the verse it states that she has "broken faith with him." "With him," is interpreted by the Otzar Hayim as meaning that the sin is due to him – it is "in him" ("bo" in Hebrew can mean "with him" or "in him").

What kinds of behavior might cause a woman to be unfaithful? When a husband ignores his wife, does not praise or appreciate her, treats her like a servant instead of like a partner, does not show respect and affection to her privately and/or publicly, demeans her in front of their children, and so on. In more extreme cases, more severe moral indiscretions may be the cause of the breach in the relationship between the husband and the wife. But it need not be something illegal or grossly immoral. Simple benign neglect can cause a deep loneliness and depression in the soul of the wife, who is pushed into looking for self-esteem and affection elsewhere.

Blaming the wife for marital infidelity and indiscretion is an easy way to cover up a deeper problem, and avoid the root of the family pathology, which may not lie with the wife at all. By delving deeply into this issue, the Otzar Hayim exhibits a profound understanding of family and marital dynamics.

Parashat Be-ha-alotekha

"But now our throats are dry, there is nothing but this manna…."

Bemidbar/Numbers 11:6

Life for the newly-liberated Israelites in the Wilderness of Sinai was difficult. There was almost nothing to eat or drink. One did not know where the next meal would come from. Finally, God brought manna to the nation of Israel. One would expect a feeling of gratitude. A hungry, isolated person, cannot be choosy. What a blessing God bestowed upon them in a forlorn, empty, dry desert.

But the reaction of the Israelites was negative. They still maintained their slave mentality, of anxiety, depression, hopelessness. They could not adjust to a life in which nothing was certain, and even the assurance of food was unpredictable. So often during their forty-year trek through the dry, barren and hostile desert the people complained about their difficult life and rebelled against Moses for taking them out of their "secure" status of slavery..

And yet… how grateful they might have been had they realized that without the manna they might have starved to death. God provides them with the basics – food and water. It was not a fancy menu, but it would keep them alive until they reached the Promised Land where they could grow a more healthy choice of fruits, vegetables and grains – and even meat from cattle and sheep. The Torah calls them a "stiff-necked" people, constantly dissatisfied.

Rashi had little tolerance for this ungrateful attitude. He quotes God as saying, "Just look at what my children complain about – this wonderful manna!"

Rabbi Abraham J. Twerski (*Twerski on Chumash*, ArtScroll, pp. 299-300) expounds upon the teaching of Rabbi Avraham Pam, Rosh Yeshivah in the late 20th century of Yeshivah Torah va-Daat in Brooklyn, who said that God's words ring in his ears every day – "Look at what my children complain about." He gives several poignant examples, such as a husband who returns from a hard day's work and complains about the toys strewn all over the floor, and cannot find some important papers. He angrily yells at his wife, asking why the children's toys cannot be put away neatly. Rabbi Twerski is a practicing psychiatrist who deals with marital and family problems, and knows how many families go through terrible agony and expense to have a child. God would say, explains Rabbi Twerski, "Look at what my children complain about!"

Rabbi Twerski gives another example: a youngster returns home from school for dinner and finds a lovely dish of tuna salad and vegetables on the table. He complains: What? Tuna again? His single mother had just returned from a hard day's work and put together a meal which would be a great blessing to many hungry children around the world. God would say, explains Rabbi Twerski, "Look at what my children complain about!"

Another example: At the wedding of a loving young couple the four parents get into an argument about how to walk the bride and groom down the aisle. What should be a joyous and thrilling simcha turns out to be a day of bitter fighting and arguments. Says Rabbi Twerski, “But God bewails this foolish squabble and says, ‘Look at what my children complain about!’”

Finally Dr. Twerski tells us that the Talmud (Avodah Zarah 5a) teaches that the sharpest reprimand by Moshe against the Israelites was that they were ingrates. “Should we not hang our heads in shame that we so often fail to appreciate God’s kindness?”

Parashat Shelah-Lekha

"In this wilderness shall your carcasses drop." Bemidbar/Numbers 14:29

During the forty years of wandering in the Sinai Wilderness the Israelite people sinned many times in different places. Some of the major episodes of faithlessness were the events of the Golden Calf, grumbling about not having enough food to eat, and the Great Mutiny of Korah, cousin of Moshe. In each case, God forgave them. Why, then, with regard to the sin of the people in the story of the Twelve Spies and the subsequent demoralization of the people, did God not forgive them? Instead, their punishment was to die in the wilderness, and not have the great privilege of entering the Promised Land?

Rabbi Yisrael Elhanan Spektor of Kovno, Lithuania (1817-1896) [after whom the famous Orthodox Rabbinical School at Yeshiva University in New York is named] answers our question. He explains that a person can be forgiven for almost every sin if one is repentant, including sins against God and sins against other humans. For one sin, however, there is an exception. That is when one sins against one's own people. For that there is no atonement. Even complete remorse is not sufficient to bring atonement in such a case.

Throughout Jewish history is has often been the case that terrible damage has come to our people from within our own ranks. In the Amidah we find a special prayer, one of the 19 blessings, that says, "For slanderers let there be no hope…." It happened that members of our own people betrayed the Jewish nation to the ruling authorities. Sectarian groups would sometimes report their own brothers and sisters to the government for violating civil law in order to establish their own authority.

An oft-quoted passage in the prophet Isaiah (49:17) is interpreted homiletically to mean that "Those who ravaged and ruined you came from among your own." This verse is highlighted whenever a Jew does something to injure or damage one's own people. During the Middle Ages it happened more than once that a Jewish scholar with knowledge of Hebrew would join the ranks of Christian persecutors to prove that the Tanakh or the Talmud were filled with defamation of Christianity. In the famous disputation of Barcelona in 1263, the apostate Pablo Christiani proposed to King James I of Aragon that a formal public religious disputation should be held between him and Rabbi Moshe ben Nahman (Nahmanides). There are many other examples of such heinous behavior on the part of renegade Jews.

In our own day people like Noam Chomsky, the son of two famous Philadelphia Jewish educators, has turned against the State of Israel in vicious and vile diatribes and persists in vilifying Israel in ways worse than any anti-Semite could possibly do.

It is no wonder, then, that God punished the generation of the wilderness by letting them die before entering the Land, and that Rabbi Yitzhak Elhanan Spektor considers those who damage the name and welfare of their own people to be of the worst kind of sinners, who in God's eyes are never to be forgiven.

Parashat Korah

"Now Korah...rose up against Moshe...." Bemidbar/ Numbers 16:1-2

The name Korah in Jewish literature is associated with the first and most well-known rebellion in the Tanakh. If one did not read the Five Books of the Torah, and would imagine any story of a mass of people spending forty years together wandering in the desert, it is most natural that part of that story would contain episodes of disagreement. Even in normal circumstances, leaving aside the harsh conditions of the wilderness, the hunger, thirst, and other conditions that obtain in that kind of difficult terrain, one would assume that a group that spent forty years together going from one location to another, would be bound to have many disagreements among themselves.

Even on the micro level, such as life within a household of 4 or 5 people, there are certain to be disagreements, even altercations, among the inhabitants. This is part of life and is to be expected. The midrash states, with deep psychological wisdom, "Just as no two faces are identical, so no two opinions are likely to be the same (Midrash Rabbah Bemidbar, 21).

It thus behooves all humans to adjust to the fact of differences in points of view. In the early part of the twentieth century philosopher Horace Kallen coined the term "pluralism." Kallen's idea was that it is necessary in society for a wide variety of points of view to co-exist. Opposing viewpoints, differences of ideology, and conflicting approaches are to be expected in a democratic, civil society. The question is how do the members of a group deal with such differences.

Korah and his rebellious congregation are noted in Scripture for their cantankerous and self-serving behavior in putting forth their own beliefs and ideas. Jewish history brings another example, in the post-biblical, rabbinic period, of two opposing cultures that were able to co-exist in a civilized and mature fashion. These were the followers of Bet Hillel and of Bet Shamai.

The Talmud teaches: "Even though the followers of Bet Shamai and Bet Hillel differed in their halakhic decisions – namely, one group declared something permissible while the other pronounced it forbidden – nevertheless that did not prevent them from marrying their children to each other's families. This teaches us that affection and neighborliness abided among them, upholding the prophetic verse, "They loved (both) truth and peace" (Zechariah 8:19). (Talmud, Tractate Yevamot 14a).

Constant bickering and argumentation is a sign of human weakness and, in the phrase of psychologist Daniel Goelman, poor emotional intelligence. Emotional maturity and wisdom dictates that people learn to accept differences of opinion, sometimes agreeing to disagree, without a relationship disintegrating into childish and malevolent belligerence.

We read in the Midrash (Vayikra Rabbah 9:9): "Bar Kappara taught: Great is peace. If the angels, who have no jealousy, hatred, competition, quarreling, or bickering, nevertheless need shalom (wholesome relationships) – as it is said, 'God makes peace in the heavenly bodies,' - how much more so do human beings, who possess all the foibles and weakness that angels lack need God's special blessing of peace to reign in their midst."

The story of Korah is a lesson in tolerance, acceptance and open mindedness, and the dire consequences that can eventuate when these precious human qualities are absent.

Parshat Hukat

"This is the law that Adonai has commanded…. Bring a red cow without blemish in which there is no defect, on which no yoke has been placed." Bemidbar/ Numbers 19:2

The law of the red cow is one of the most perplexing and confusing in the entire Torah. To purify one who has become ritually impure (through contact with a dead person), a red cow must be slaughtered and its ashes become part of a mixture used to bring purification to the impure person. The paradox is that he who uses the ashes in the purification ceremony becomes impure, while the ceremony of using the ashes of the pure red cow make the impure person pure. This is the law that is always used as an example of rules that must be carried out even when we do not understand their meaning. It is a test of one's loyalty to God and God's Torah.

The Hasidic masters always find ways to make meaning when there seems to be an absence of meaning. Rabbi Yisrael of Kozhnitz came up with a brilliant twist in parsing this pasuk. He reads the phrase "in which there is no blemish, no defect," as referring to a person, not to the red cow. Then, the phrase, "which no yoke has been placed" refers to this same person who sees himself without blemish. In other words, says Reb Yisrael, if a person sees oneself with no defects or blemishes, as a perfect human specimen, and a completely pure Jew, it is clear that such a one has not accepted upon oneself "the yoke" – i.e., "ol malkhut Shamayim," – "the Yoke of the Rule of Heaven."

What an ingenious interpretation. By a clever shifting of words and their interpretation, and a modification of referents, Rabbi Yisrael makes a wonderful point. That is that only a person who has not accepted the obligations of the Torah could possibly think of oneself as perfect, without blemish or defect. If, then, such a person, proceeds to accept God's Torah and its requirements to behave righteously and clings to the observance of Jewish ritual and ethical law, that person will realize how many faults she/he has. When we know what our duties are, we can see how far we are from fulfilling all of them.

Reb Yisrael is making a plea for knowledge of and obedience to Torah, which, by doing so, will make us more aware of the things we need to improve on our path towards purity.

Parshat Pinhas

"God said to Moshe: "Tell Pinhas that I grant him My covenant of peace."

Bemidbar/Numbers 25:12

Many midrashic comments from Sages of all generations grow out of passages in the Torah when people are told things by this person or that person instead of another, from whom one would expect to hear it. In our pasuk the question arises in the mind of the teachers as to why God had to tell Moshe to tell Pinhas of his great reward of an eternal pact of friendship, instead of telling him Godself.

Perhaps, it is suggested, God is disappointed in Moshe for not being as zealous as Pinhas. By sending Moshe to be the messenger who would reward Pinhas, God is simultaneously rewarding Pinhas by receiving his honor from Moshe, and rebuking Moshe for not being as passionate as Pinhas.

The rabbinic leader, Rabbi Moshe Teitlebaum, (Hungary, 1759-1841, Founder of the Satmar Dynasty of Hasidism), in his commentary *Yismah Moshe*, asked why Moshe was not, indeed, as zealous as Pinhas. Defending Moshe, the teacher explains that the ardent behavior of Pinhas may have been the proper way to punish Zimri for his idolatry and immorality, but it might be considered extreme. There may have been a more reasoned and less zealous approach to bring the culprit to justice. Such behavior is known in the tradition as "Halakhah v-ayn morin ken," "This is an appropriate response, but not one that we should necessarily demand of others."

In other words, Moshe could have acted with an abundance of eagerness, but he may have appeared to be overly righteous for one with the dignity and humility of a community leader such as Moshe. Leave this kind of extreme obsessiveness to the more passionate and fanatic souls among us. Leaders like Moshe, who prefer to walk the middle path, may not be the right ones to demonstrate an excess of zeal.

There are many different personalities among leaders, and each must know her own personal style. Some are dramatic and demonstrative. Others are quiet and understated in their strength. This does not imply that they are less effective or sincere in their leadership. Moshe was obviously a strong leader, and often acted with power and zeal. Sometimes to an excess. But perhaps he learned from these experiences, like smashing the Two Tablets of the Law, or striking the rock, or killing the Egyptian, and in his later years decided to utilize a style that was more calm, subdued and confident.

Among the many lessons we learn from the story of Pinhas and his extreme zeal is that there is no one correct way for leaders to accomplish acts of importance. Each in her own style and personality. Pinhas had his, Moshe had his. Neither is the "right" way. The path each chose fit him at the moment. In the same way should we conduct ourselves. We need to follow our instincts, recognize our inner moods and take heed of the environmental factors that dictate one kind of behavior or another. As the Talmud says, each of looks different, and so each of us thinks differently and acts differently. And God made us all.

Parshat Matot/Mas-ei

"You shall stay outside the camp seven days, every one…who has slain a person or touched a corpse and purify himself…. You shall also purify every cloth, every article of skin, everything made of goats' hair, and every object of wood."

Bemidbar/Numbers 31:19-20

In the Torah's discussion in Bemidbar, chapter 31, of the war against Midian, we find rules not mentioned before, about the conduct of war. Specifically, the Torah demands that anyone who has come in contact with a dead person must become ritually purified. Not only the individuals (soldiers) but also any object they may have had on their person or carried with them.

The *Etz Hayim Torah and Commentary* explains that the reason is "not only because of corpse contamination but as a transition to the world of normal living."

There are several items of particular interest in this Torah law. First of all, the laws of contamination by contact with the dead may be traced to early experience of disease resulting from such contact. In addition, from a spiritual point of view, Judaism is a religion of life, and any contact with the dead – which represents cessation of growth and inability to learn, develop and mature – must be reckoned with by awareness of the contrast between the potential of life and absence of potential in death. The Torah's preference toward life is ever present ("Choose life!" – Deuteronomy 30:19), and once more emphasized in this law.

Second, the Torah recognizes that while sometimes war is inevitable, it always carries with it collateral damage, even to those fighting for justice and truth. No one carrying a weapon is free from some psychological, spiritual and emotional harm. As necessary as war may be in many cases, there is no such thing as a good, or clean, or perfect war. Killing any of God's children, even in cases of self-defense and preservation of national security, as evil as the enemy may be, is to be considered an act that is to be taken with the utmost seriousness, in which negative consequences even to the just are inevitable.

Thus, those who engage even in just wars must go through a process of purification and decompression. This allows the individual fighter an opportunity to transition to his/her normal state of moral cleanliness, to take the necessary time and thought to return to their previous non-belligerent psychological and spiritual status, and to consider the weighty process of fighting, conflict, battle, harm and killing other human beings.

It is to the credit of the Torah, written thousands of years ago, long before Geneva Conventions, Nuremburg trials, and other modern understandings of the ugly and painful ramifications of even a necessary war, that it took into account such high moral and spiritual procedures to isolate the evil of war from daily, wholesome and holy existence.

Parshat Devarim

"These are the words that Moshe addressed to all Israel on the other side of the Jordan.." Devarim/ Deuteronomy 1:1

Moshe stands at the end of his career, after forty years of wandering in the wilderness, and is about to summarize the journey and the teachings delivered during that journey, as a reminder to the people whom he birthed by bringing them out of Egyptian bondage. All he has to do is step over the Jordan River, and he will have fulfilled his life-long dream. But those few small steps elude him, as God denies him the privilege.

Rabbi Analia Bortz (*The Women's Torah Commentary*, ed. Rabbi Elyse Goldstein, pp. 331 ff.) notices that the Hebrew root a-v-r occurs several times in the introductory chapters to Sefer Devarim. After bringing several interpretations from various traditional commentators, she points out that Rabbi Yehoshua, in Midrash Tanhuma, connects the verb with the Hebrew root for pregnancy ("m'uberet"). Rabbi Bortz then says that Moshe realizes that being "m'ubar," pregnant, as spiritual mother of his people, is also "me'ever" – beyond. "Beyond" in two senses. First, beyond, or, on the other side of the Jordan River. Second, having given birth to the people, accompanying them to the Promised Land is beyond the capability of Moshe because of the Divine decree.

Thus Moshe looks to the future, and begins to teach the people, to remind them of all that they need to know after he is gone. Moshe was born, like all humans, in the amniotic sack, in water, was later rescued from the waters of the Nile, at a later point opened the water of the sea that made it possible for his children to escape bitter slavery, and now, as spiritual mother, teaches them so that a new birth can take place. In this way the people can find new life beyond the Jordan when he is gone, and their national life embarks on a new existence in Eretz Yisrael.

Moshe and the people struggled in the Wilderness of Sinai for forty years. Forty is the number representing fullness, completion. A pregnancy is also approximately forty weeks, and Moshe is about to 'reach his term."

At this painful moment of parting, from his people and from the world, Moshe suffers delivery pains. He must give his children roots and wings. The roots are the teachings he is about to review, and the wings are the symbol of the rebirth in a new place, with new opportunities. He is truly the mother of this people, about to fly off and be on their own.

The symbolism which Rabbi Bortz sees in these pages is touching, and real. It is doubtful that a male commentator would have seen the nuances and symbolism that she appreciates as a woman and a Jewish scholar. We are blessed with this novel interpretation, and with the birth of a new Judaism that enables our people to enter a new stage of rebirth with women like Rabbi Bortz who can bring us to a new Promised Land.

Parshat Va-et-hanan

"Therefore take heed to your souls…." Devarim/ Deuteronomy 4:15

Rabbi Joseph Caro (1488-1575 - Turkey & Safed), was a master of the Hebrew language and of Torah, in addition to his mastery of Jewish Law (he compiled the comprehensive Code of Jewish Law, the Shulkhan Arukh, and wrote a Torah commentary called *Or Tzaddikim – Light of the Righteous*). Such a punctilious expert, who paid attention to every detail of large bodies of Jewish literature and tradition, would likely notice the unusual grammatical form of the Hebrew in our pasuk. "Take heed to your souls" literally means "for your souls," not "to your souls."

Long before moderns discovered the so-called "mind-body" connection, Rabbi Caro saw that harming the soul also harms the body, and vice versa. Thus he reads our phrase to imply that when we care "for our souls," we also care for our bodies. Jewish tradition has long interpreted this pasuk as meaning that a human being has an obligation to pay close attention to the needs of the physical as well as of the spiritual. When we care for our souls, we also care for our bodies – i.e., take great care to watch out "for" your soul, and thus you will care for your body.

Students of medical history have long recognized that Jews have been predominant throughout the centuries in the science of medicine. The most well-known example of this phenomenon is Maimonides, who was both codifier of the law (cf. his *Mishneh Torah*, the major Code of Jewish Law that preceded the *Shulkhan Arukh*) and brilliant physician. He was the private doctor to the Sultan of Egypt (12th century, Cairo) as well as author of many important medical works extant today. It is no doubt this pasuk, and this Torah attitude that body and soul are one, that was a primary factor in the prominence of Jewish physicians from ancient times to our own day.

Jewish physicians and medical researchers have won Nobel Prizes in medicine and science in extraordinarily large numbers in proportion to the general population. A glance at the list of leading medical researchers at NIH and in the world's great hospitals, not to speak of those who discovered cures for many of the modern diseases of our time – such as Drs. Salk and Sabine who discovered the vaccines for polio - will show that Jewish physicians are still leading the pack.

During a recent war in the Middle East, Dr. Sanje Gupta, surgeon and medical reporter for CNN, visited the Rambam Hospital in Haifa, and called it a "world-class hospital." Israel today is known for its medical advances, including the world-renowned Hadassah Hospital (where Arab potentates stealthily enter during the middle of the night for treatment, from Jordan, Egypt, Saudia Arab and other Arab countries throughout the Middle East). The Teva Pharmaceutical company in Israel and the Weizmann Institute of Science in Rehovot, Israel, are also known throughout the world for their high standard of medical and scientific achievement.

One of the things that draws Jews and non-Jews to respect Judaism is the sense that the Jewish tradition values this world in all its physicality, even while highlighting and giving pride of place to matters of the spirit. There is an exquisite balance between body and soul, heaven and earth, physical and spiritual, in Judaism, that makes life real, logical, rational and recognizably lucid, balanced and wise.

Parshat Ekev

"You shall not bring an abomination into your home." Devarim/Deuteronomy 7:26

The Hebrew word "to-evah," (abomination) specifically refers to an idol. Of course the second of the Ten Commandments (Shemot/Exodus 20:3-6), already prohibits idolatry. Moshe repeats this prohibition probably for several reasons.

First because it is the most serious sin an Israelite can commit. The entire religion of Israel is based on ethical monotheism – the idea that one God created everything in our universe and thus all God's creatures are equal in the eyes of the Creator. To violate this command transgresses the essential ethical principle of the Covenant God made with Israel at Sinai, that every human being has been granted the divine right of justice, equality and freedom.

Second, because the Book of Devarim/Deuteronomy is a repetition and summation of the entire corpus of law that was given to the people in the Wilderness of Sinai, it is reviewed now as they are about to enter the Promised Land and have more opportunity to violate Torah laws in their own autonomous national life. In the desert it is not as easy to break many laws, but in an inhabited land of towns, farms and cities, where the people will interact with other tribes and ethic groups, it is more likely that one might violate a mitzvah of the Torah.

Third, once the people cross the Jordan River and enter Canaan (later Israel), they will come into more frequent contact with the idolatrous seven nations, the Perizites, Hittites, Amalekites, Hivites, Amorites, Jebusites, and Canaanites, and be influenced by them.

Yehezkel Kaufmann, preeminent twentieth century biblical scholar of the Hebrew University in Jerusalem emphasized (*The Religion of Israel*) that the Torah's obsession with uprooting idolatry among the nations of Canaan was based on the immoral cultic practices that accompanied idol worship. He refers to such things as fornication on the altar, which they believed would induce fructification of food from the soil. It is thus not too far a stretch to understand the comment of Reb Levi Yitzhak of Berditchev, who also sees the sin of idolatry as more than just the worship of idols.

Reb Levi notices that the word "to-evah," abomination, is also mentioned in another biblical text, Proverbs 16:5. There it is connected with a different moral sin: arrogance. "Every haughty person is an abomination to Adonai." While some may see Reb Levi's comment as midrashic, or homiletical, it does not seem to this writer to be too far from the original text. Bringing an idol into one's home is surely a violation of the Torah, because idolatry is immoral. Another example of idolatry, another abomination, is arrogance. We are not about to rate these sins as to their level of evil. An argument can be made that they are closed related, and equally dangerous to the soul, and to society.

In any case, Reb Levi makes this Torah law more relevant in its clarity and more connected to the modern reader, who is not likely to bring a statue or graven image into one's house for the purpose of worship. The implication in Reb Levi's comment is the important point that the Torah is a book of up-to-date ideas that help us live better lives – both in ancient times and in modern days – or, as the Hanukkah prayer states: in those days and in ours!

Parshat Re-eh

"See I set before you today a blessing and a curse." Devarim/Deuteronomy 11:26

One of the great philosophical errors prevalent in modern times is known as "moral relativism." Those who espouse this point of view articulate their point of view in terms something like the following: Everyone is entitled to her/his opinion. There is no right and wrong. It's all relative (they pretend to be students of Einstein!). Some are liberal, others are conservative, both are right. It is not fair to characterize a viewpoint as true or false. What is true to you may be false to me. I believe that the President is doing a good job, you think he is failing. We each have a right to our position."

There is room for gray in many matters, and it is true that two opposing opinions may sometimes be accurate. An Orthodox Jew may claim that it is necessary to wait six hours after eating a meat meal in order to partake of a milk dish. A Conservative Jew may argue that three hours is sufficient. A Reform Jew may argue that the whole system of Kashrut is unnecessary and outmoded (though today more and more Reform Jews are returning to Kashrut). In the area of ritual, as in politics, taste in style, and many other matters, there is no right and wrong. There is an old Hebrew saying, "B'ta'am va-rayah ayn le-hit-va-kay-ah." This rhyming jingle means: In matters of taste and smell, there can be no argument. In other words, there is no right and wrong. Each person is entitled to her/his own preference.

The confusion lies in the realm of morality. Here there is often no room for gray areas. Something is either right or wrong. It may be either good or bad. There is no in between. This is what the Torah means when it says "I set before you today a blessing and a curse." You must choose between A or B; there is no C, D, E, or F. For C, D, E and F are outside the parameters of the right and the good. It is as simple as this: A is good, B is bad. That's it!

The medieval biblical commentator, Rabbi Ovadiah Sforno (Bologna, Italy, 1475-1550) puts it this way: "Be cautious that you not be like others who have gray areas. The Torah warns: God presents to us a choice of a blessing or a curse. There is no gray area."

As my late teacher, Rabbi Sidney Greenberg, taught – when you go to a surgeon for a serious operation, you do not want someone who is relatively knowledgeable and skilled. When you need a lawyer to protect your rights, you do not engage someone who is in the gray area between well-trained and not-so-well trained. When someone is put in jail for life for committing a crime, you should not be satisfied to know that six members of the jury thought he is guilty and four thought he is innocent. To put it simply, in most areas of morality, we have two categories: right and wrong; truth and false, good and bad.

This fallacy of moral relativism often crops up in discussions on Israel and its place in the Middle East. Some claim that Israel is wrong when it uses its powerful military arm to strike back at its enemies. After all, the argument goes, what is a "militant" to one news network is a "terrorist" to another. One European country calls Israel an aggressor and another dubs her a sovereign nation defending its citizens – "which every country has a right to do."

The error people make here is that in moral issues such as Israel's right to exist, or murder of an innocent person, there is no room for differing opinions. That is not to say that everything the government of Israel decides is absolutely correct. I sometimes disagree with Israel (the disproportionate funding it gives to Israeli Arab towns in comparison with the abundance of allocations for Jewish communities in Israel, for example). I sometimes disagree with my own government (the inadequate attention to global warming and ecological dangers confronting us). But sometimes there simply is no room for gray. No one can say that "maybe Hitler was right, and maybe he was wrong – it all depends on your point of view." Hitler, like terrorist groups such as Hamas, the Al-Aksa Brigade, Hezbollah, Al Qaida, is evil. No two ways about it. No room for argument. No right and wrong. Evil – that's it!

So God says: I set before you today a blessing and a curse. Good or evil – take your choice!

Parshat Shoftim

"When the king is enthroned, he shall have a copy of the Torah.... Let him read it all his life, so that he may learn to revere Adonai his God...." Devarim/ Deuteronomy 17:18-19

The first remarkable thing we must note in these p'sukim is the notion that no one is above the Law, not even the King. Throughout ancient and medieval times the supreme Sovereign (King, Caesar, Czar, Dictator - whatever the title) was a mortal ruler who held the fate and destiny of his subjects in the clutches of his personal power. The decisions of life and death all of citizens of a country were subject to the whims of one powerful, and mostly ruthless individual.

Not so in Israel. Even the King had to be subject to the noble ethical standards of the Torah. The classic case that exemplifies this sacred principle is the parable of the poor man who had a sheep that was taken away from him by a rich man who owned many sheep. This parable was enunciated by the prophet Nathan to chastise King David, who had many wives, and took yet another one, Bathsheba, by sending her husband to the front lines of battle so he would be killed. "You are the man!" screamed Nathan to David

(II Samuel 11).

Any other king would have such a brazen prophet beheaded immediately. Yet, King David knew that the word of the prophet was the word of God, the moral law of the Torah, and he was ashamed. It was the King who was chastised, not the prophet. The subjugation of the king to the higher authority of the Torah is a hallmark of Israel's high standard of moral values in a world where passion and appetite, whim and caprice ruled the day. Truth and justice came second.

But we boast of the Torah's high moral standards from a historical perspective millennia later. Some of the later teachers, Talmudic sages, took for granted the ideas we now see as remarkable in the light of comparative governance in the ancient and medieval world. They were not satisfied to simply say that the Torah was morally ahead of its time. They looked for deeper and different interpretations.

One inspiring comment on this pasuk is that the leader of a people must use the Torah as his guide book. He should let Torah values infuse his life in every way. "In all your ways, know God" (Mishle/Proverbs 3:6). The Ruler must be so familiar with the words of the Torah that he himself becomes a Torah. As Rabbi Abraham Joshua Heschel once wrote, the best learning tool is not a text book, but a text teacher.

The Talmud is puzzled by people who foolishly rise up for a Sefer Torah (Makkot 22b) yet remain seated when a teacher of Torah enters. As one sage put it, the Sefer Torah is God's word in black and white on an animal skin. If it is proper and fitting to rise for an animal skin, how much more so should it be appropriate to stand up at the entrance to the room of a student of Torah who reflects the Torah's thought and action.

Writing a Torah thus implies to the sages of many generations that the contents of the Torah must be taken to heart, — practiced, learned and taught, observed, carried out and fulfilled!

Parshat Kee Teze

"When you see among the captivity a beautiful woman, and desire her, you may take her to yourself for a wife." Deuteronomy/Devarim 21:11

At first blush this special permission to marry a captured woman and make her your wife seems against the grain of our ethical instincts. How can a Code of Law whose moral standards are considered very high, especially considering the environment and historical period in which it was composed, permit such an act? Such permissiveness strikes the reader as a bending to tolerance that is opposed to what we think of as the general thrust of the Torah's exalted norms of behavior.

Rashi, in eleventh century Troyes, France, writes of this pasuk that its intent is to describe the "Yetzer haRa," "the evil inclination." Is, then, the Torah to defer to man's passion just because it is a time of war, when it is considered conventional for males to lust for the woman who are under their heel, who have no power to resist or refuse? Something is "rotten in the state of Denmark" if we take this pasuk at face value.

A wise solution to our conundrum comes from the great master Reb Menahem Mendel of Kotzk (1787-1819, Poland). Preeminent psychological mayven that he was, the Hasidic rebbe knew the heart and soul (and the body!) of mortal men. Is it not true, he must have thought to himself, that things which are forbidden to us are more appealing. Were Reb Menahem Mendel living in the modern age he would have been hired by the advertising firm that gave the name to the perfume dubbed "My Sin." What appeal that product has! To the careless, lustful warrior, grabbing whatever is beautiful and appealing is the norm – but ah, even more so when it is off limits. That which is beyond the pale of the permissible is always, in the heart of the hungry, all the more delicious.

The biblical Book of Proverbs recognized this principle when it taught that "stolen waters are sweet, and bread eaten in secret is delicious" (9:17). There is no doubt that part of the appeal of illicit sex and adulterous trysts, are all the more popular in modern society because forbidden fruit is all the more tasty to the common (in both senses of that word) person.

So, reasons Reb Menahem, if the Torah makes this passionate relationship legal – by permitting the soldier to marry a woman whom his eyes fancy – perhaps she will be less appealing. By removing the label of "sin" from this prized catch, the evil inclination will be less likely to ply its trade. Maybe the rough and tough fighter, knowing that this beautiful female can be his legal wife, will make her a bit less beautiful in his mind, and he will be less inclined to seize her for his own.

So maybe the Torah was not so off target after all. Often we need to read between the lines and see the Torah's motives through a deeper psychological lens to understand its highly sophisticated psychological depth and to understand its ultimate goal. A Hasidic master can often plumb the heart of the Torah more effectively because he knew the highways and byways of the human heart and soul as he knew the streets of Kotzk and Jerusalem. This is one of the many great strengths of the Hasidic movement – its unique blend of the human and the divine, heaven and earth, body and soul. For the Torah is not a book of the spirit alone, but of flesh and blood, of love, sex, food, prayer, study, revelation, and Halakhah – all mixed into one indivisible whole.

D'var Torah – Kee Tavo

"The Egyptians treated us in an evil way...." D'varim/Deuteronomy 26:6

Many commentators have imposed their own translation and explanation on this pasuk. Let us focus for now on the perspective of the late Rabbi Mordechai Gifter, distinguished head of the Telshe Yeshivah of Cleveland, Ohio. Rabbi Gifter saw in this passage the template of anti-Semitism. The first thing an enemy of the Jewish People tries to do is to vilify the Jewish nation. He thus translates the pasuk, "They made us look evil." That is, they maligned us, they slandered and besmirched the name "Jew" and "Israelite." By doing so it made it easier for them to move to the next step and bring harm to us. After all, what is wrong with injuring or destroying a group that is perceived in the eyes of the world as evil? In fact, the world may well applaud such behavior – ridding the universe of an iniquitous and malevolent group, a festering sore on the universal body politic.

This is the tactic that Hitler and the Nazi regime used in their program of defamation and destruction that led to the Shoah. They pictured the Jewish people as sub-human, *untermenschen.* Cartoons, legal restrictions, and other methods of maligning and harming the Jewish people were all part of the first step in their nefarious plot to bring about the genocide that they ultimately attempted.

In other words, the Egyptians were the first group in history to use this classic method of bringing harm to the Jewish People. Many others followed suit. Christian anti-Semitism followed in their footsteps many centuries later. The Jews were painted as deicides, Christ-killers, whose Scriptures had been superseded by a New Covenant, making them a people rejected by God. With this picture of the "evil" nation of Jews, it was much easier to bring about such horrible pogroms and horrendous massacres such as the Crusades and the massive Cmielnicki massacre of Jews in 1648 in Poland.

Rabbi Gifter's interpretation teaches an important lesson. Many would be willing to let pass a nasty canard directed toward a Jew, or the Jewish People, with the thought that "Sticks and stones may break my bones, but names can never hurt me." No saying has ever been more dangerous. Names and vilification can be the first step to genocide, and thus is hardly innocuous. Thus, what the Egyptians did to the ancient biblical Hebrews, by treating them in an evil way – or, smearing them with the evil reputation of a horrible group – was no small matter. It was the beginning of the infamous period of 400 years of slavery and near destruction. Beware the danger of words!

D'var Torah – Nitzavim-Vayelekh

"You will return to Adonai your God…you and your children."

Devarim/Deuteronomy 30:2

This pasuk is a good example of how the simple meaning of a passage can be dramatically changed by an imaginative commentator, who sees between and lines and beyond the lines. The obvious meaning – at least it seems thus to this reader – is to remind the reader/listener that not only are you commanded to do Teshuvah – repentance, (or however one translates this), but also, in addition, you are commanded to make sure that Teshuvah is something that is passed down from generation to generation. That it is a positive value for the Jewish People, for all generations. One should do Teshuvah, one should return to God at all times – and continually return after going astray. The assumption is that Torah norms are not our normal way of functioning. To be a good, menschlich person we will have to return to Godly ways with a recurring rhythm. Thus, the Torah teaches that we are to return to God, and we are to teach our children that returning to God is a regular, repetitive activity in the life of any good person.

Along comes Rabbi Yehoshua of Belz (19th century, Poland), who sees in the text more than the ordinary eye might perceive. The question in the mind of a commentator is always this: Why does the Torah add words when omitting them would bring the same meaning? Or: Why does the Torah add things that would seem obvious to the average reader, and thus unnecessary to include in the text? In our case, we can assume that the Torah might just as well have taught: You will return to Adonai your God. Period. Of course, anything that you do, your children, and, in fact, all Jews, should also do. What I teach you applies to you, your household, and to the entire community. So the question here is: Why does the Torah add the words "you and your children."

Reb Yehoshua postulates that the Torah has something very specific in mind, and is not wasting words (which it never does, being a divine document). What does it have in mind by adding "your children?" What the Torah is emphasizing here by adding these seemingly "extra" words is this: If you do not follow the Torah, neither will your children!

Here we have an entirely new perspective on the pasuk. We might have thought that the Torah is commanding us to return to God. The theme then would be that every Jew must do Teshuvah – i.e., must always be on a path of return, since sin is constantly "crouching at our door," and it will be required throughout our lives to be on a path of return, to return and return and return.

But – in addition – or, perhaps, instead of that idea, what the Torah is saying, argues Reb Yehoshua, is not (only) about Teshuvah, but about *education*. How does one assure that our children will become students and observers of Torah? How do we make certain that our children do not break the 4000-year old chain of Jewish tradition? Part of the answer, at least, is that we exercise extreme care, caution and commitment, to observe it ourselves. We must become fastidious role models for our young in keeping the Torah alive, respected, and familiar in all its details. An old educational adage states that the best way to pass down a system of values is in these three ways: Model, Model, Model!

Thus, through the eyes of a world-wise and seasoned teacher, educator and community leader, our pasuk takes on an entirely new color by telling us that we dare not assume that our children will follow in our footsteps unless we furnish for them, by example and deed, that the Torah is our Guidebook, our source of inspiration and moral teaching, and the lodestone of our lives.

D'var Torah – Ha-azinu

"You ignored the Rock Who gave birth to you, and forgot God Who brought you forth."

Devarim/Deuteronomy 32:18

In the final Song of Moshe, the great Leader chastises the people, as they are about to cross over the Jordan River and enter the Promised Land, for forgetting God. After all, says Moshe, God, the Rock, gave you birth, brought you into the world. God created the world, redeemed you from the wicked burden of slavery, gave you the Torah. God did all these things, as Creator, Redeemer and Revealer. And what do you do in response? You forget God, the Source of all Life and birth!

Rabbi Menahem Mendel of Kotzk, the great Hasidic master (Poland, 1787-1859), who rarely read a biblical text in its literal sense, has his own spin on this pasuk. It is not only, says Reb Menahem Mendel, that the people forgot God, but they forgot something else too. They forgot a gift that God gave them – the ability to forget!

In Jewish tradition we are constantly reminded to remember. Memory is the key to keeping the treasure of our past heritage in tact. We Jews are a people who remembers. "Zakhor, al tishkakh!" says the Torah. But there are times when forgetting is also important. The ability to forget is one of God's great gifts to us. The perverse people, says Moshe, forgot God and also forgot God's gift of the ability to forget.

Why is forgetting important? Anyone who is married does not want to remember every single thing she is angry about her spouse. Or in any relationship for that matter. We should not remember all the pains, hurts, insults, we received throughout our lives, or we would be very depressed and angry people. True, the historian Santayana said that "Those who forget history are condemned to repeat it." But I wonder if he meant that we should forget every single detail. Some of it we should flush out of our souls.

We should never forget the horrors perpetrated upon the Jewish People by the wicked Nazi regime. But neither should we constantly keep it in mind when thinking about our relationship with modern Germany. Ben Gurion gave us an excellent example by purchasing important weaponry from Germany soon after the Second World War. Had he not been able to put aside the terrible memories of the previous decade, he would not have been able to avail the newborn State of Israel with much needed armaments that helped Israel to survive. There are those who refuse to set foot on German soil, and we cannot blame them one iota. On the other hand, the concept of Teshuvah is a counter-balance in our tradition to the idea that we must forever hold those who harmed us guilty for a thousand generations. Even God forgives and forgets, as we learn in the famous Thirteen Divine Attributes.

The Torah commands us to forget the sheaves, and the corners of our field, for the poor. Had we not the ability to forget, we would lose some very valuable mitzvot of tzedakah and social welfare.

Reb Menahem Mendel fell upon an important truth when he recognized that forgetting is an important gift from God. Just as is remembering. Both together make great aids to our ability to grow as spiritual beings.

Rabbi Dov Peretz Elkins is one of America's leading rabbis, and is a prominent internationally-known speaker and author, winner of the National Jewish Book Award. Dr. Elkins is Rabbi Emeritus of The Jewish Center of Princeton, NJ. He co-authored *Chicken Soup for the Jewish Soul*, among his 35 books and hundreds of published articles. His most recent book is *Jewish Stories from Heaven and Earth* (Jewish Lights). He has spoken and led training workshops for synagogues, Federations, JCCs and other Jewish organizations in North America, Europe and Israel. His books have been read by thousands throughout the world. He was a member of the Committee on Jewish Law and Standards of the Rabbinical Assembly. He and his wife Maxine live in Princeton, NJ, and travel often to see their children and 9 grandchildren.

Dr. Elkins' web sites are **www.JewishGrowth.org**, **www.WisdomofJudaism.org**, and

www.Eco-Judaism.org. His email address is **DPE@JewishGrowth.org**.